FINANCIAL EMPOWERMENT

More Money for More Mission

by
Peter C. Brinckerhoff

FINANCIAL EMPOWERMENT

More Money for More Mission

An Essential Financial Guide
For Not-For-Profit Organizations

by
Peter C. Brinckerhoff

The **MISSION-BASED MANAGEMENT**™ Series

ALPINE GUILD, Inc.
Dillon, Colorado

An Alpine Guild Book

ISBN 0-931712-19-X

To obtain information about this book or other publications by Peter C. Brinckerhoff, contact Alpine Guild, Inc., P.O. Box 4846, Dillon, CO 80435.

Library of Congress Cataloging-in-Publication Data

Brinckerhoff, Peter C., 1952—
    Financial empowerment: more money for more mission / by Peter C. Brinckerhoff.
      p. cm.—(The mission-based management series)
    Includes bibliographical references and index.
    ISBN 0-9317712-19-X
    1. Nonprofit organizations—Finance. I. Title. II. Series: Brinckerhoff, Peter C., 1952-   Mission-based management series.
HG4027.65.B75   1996
658.15′9--dc20   96-11813
                                        CIP

<u>Dedication</u>

For my father:

Clarke Brinckerhoff

who told me over and over in junior high that I would need
my math when I grew up.....

Dad, you were right!

Acknowledgements

Rarely is a book written solely by the author, and this one is certainly no exception. As with any "expert", much of my expertise comes from studying and observing the successes and the difficulties of others. As a consultant, I am often in the enviable position of getting paid to do just that, and then to recommend improvements where I see the opportunity. But I try to remember the best and the worst of what I see, and those experiences are a large part of what fills these pages. Thus, there is a great deal of the hard work and sometimes harder lessons of my clients represented in this book. These are experiences that I know that they are happy to share, but nonetheless they should know that they are appreciated.

In addition, early drafts of the manuscript were reviewed by Clarke Brinckerhoff and D.D. Fischer. Both made excellent comments and observations that made the text more focused and effective. Janet Marr, my loyal and unendingly cheerful associate in Springfield also cast her talented editing eye on the text, improving it as she has all of my writings for the past 8 years. Janet also did the lion's share of the initial work on the Bibliography.

I also want to particularly thank my editor, Bob Follett. For both this book and for *Mission-Based Management*, Bob has provided invaluable insights, excellent suggestions, and frank and on-target reactions to my ideas and my writing. He has infinite patience, which is good, because I've used up every bit. I appreciate him tremendously, and feel fortunate to have a mentor who is also a good friend.

Finally, I need to thank my wife, Chris, and my children, Ben, Adam, and Caitlin. Living with someone who is writing a book is not easy, and they handled it with patience and love.

Peter Brinckerhoff

About the Author

Peter Brinckerhoff is a nationally-known expert at helping not-for-profits get more mission for their money. He has consulted with and trained thousands of not-for-profit staff and board members since forming his own consulting firm, Corporate Alternatives, inc., in 1982. He is the author of numerous articles on not-for-profit management, and has had pieces published in *NonProfit World*, *Advancing Philanthropy*, *Contributions*, *Strategic Governance*, and the *Journal of NonProfit and Voluntary Sector Marketing*. Peter is also the author of the award-winning book, *Mission-Based Management* which is also published by Alpine Guild.

Peter brings a wide array of experience to his writing, consulting and training. He has served as a board member, staff member, and Executive Director of a number of local, state, and national not-for-profits, and understands all three of these perspectives and their importance in the not-for-profit mix.

Peter received his Bachelor's degree from the University of Pennsylvania, and his Master's of Public Health from the Tulane University School of Public Health. He lives in Springfield, Illinois, with his wife and three children.

Table of Contents

15. Putting It All Together

A recap of the key ideas in the book with some suggestions to make the path to empowerment easier. How not to spend every dime you save. How to keep what you earn.

Appendices

Financial Empowerment Self-Assessment
Bibliography and Reading List
Commonly-Used Financial Ratios

Index

1. Introduction

OVERVIEW

This is *not* a book that will tell you how to get rich quick. It is not the "Real Estate for No Money Down" seminar that you can see almost every night on some cable channel. There is no alchemy, no gold from lead. There is little or nothing in this book that will bail you out if your organization is in a financial crisis this fiscal year or even next.

This *is* a book on how to help your not-for-profit organization do more and better mission through becoming and remaining *financially empowered*. If you put into practice the ideas and suggestions in the following chapters, your organization will, over time, have the financial strength to plan, to grow, to attract the best staff: to do the most mission possible.

It is not a short journey, nor an easy one. When I use the term financial *empowerment*, I intentionally eschew the term financial *stability*. Too many not-for-profits and their funders think that being able to pay this month's bills on time indicates adequate financial stability. That is not where I intend you to be. Becoming financially empowered means that you have the money to pursue your mission with flexibility and high quality of service.

Getting there will take a while for most readers. Not-for-profits in this country are, as an industry, woefully undercapitalized, underpaid, and over-scrutinized. Becoming financially empowered will require changes in habits, management styles, cash management, investment policies, and contracts with major funders; all in addition to a re-thinking of your organization by your board and staff.

Seeking financial empowerment is a long-term process. Retaining

1

financial empowerment requires constant discipline. Is it worth it? Absolutely. As a consultant to not-for-profits since 1982, I have seen many organizations that have acquired—and work hard to retain—the financial empowerment that they see as key to doing their mission. Not coincidentally, these organizations are also centers of service excellence in their discipline, whether it is in education, the arts, human services, health care, or religion.

From these organizations, and equally important, from the more common not-for-profits that are not financially empowered, I have gathered the lessons taught here. You can apply them in your organization if you have the patience and the desire.

A. WHO THIS BOOK IS WRITTEN FOR

I have written this book for the senior staff and board members of not-for-profits to assist them in strengthening and empowering their organizations. The lessons and ideas here apply to not-for-profits of all sizes and missions, from the largest university to the smallest human service agency. A mid-sized church, a small start-up homeless shelter, a century-old ballet, or a trade association will all benefit from the ideas and concepts contained in these pages.

All readers will benefit from the entire book, but there are some readers who have special roles in empowering your organization: the CEO and the Board of Directors. Therefore, I have written two chapters, 12 and 13 respectively, to address the unique roles and responsibilities these parties have in the empowerment quest.

B. THE BENEFITS OF READING THIS BOOK

Why should you take the time to read this book? For all of these reasons and more:

1. You will have a better understanding of the characteristics that financially empowered not- for-profit organizations share and how to help your organization acquire and retain these same characteristics.

2. You will understand how to work with your funders to obtain and retain more funds.

3. You will have a better understanding of pricing and how to re-think prices in an increasingly competitive environment.

4. You will understand why it is important for many not-for-profits to have some debt, how to seek that debt, and how to work with lenders in a manner that benefits your organization.

5. You will have a better understanding of the business development process and how it can be used in everything you do as an organization.

6. You will learn a budgeting process that not only saves money but motivates staff.

7. You will learn how to use your financial reports as a tool and resource for all staff.

There is, of course, much, much more in the following pages, including practical examples and tips in every chapter. If you invest your time with me through this book, I am sure that you will be amply rewarded for that investment.

In this introductory chapter, we will look at the reasons for you to make the effort that is required in your quest for empowerment. We'll review my three core philosophies for not-for-profits, and then take a look at the nine characteristics of sucessful not-for-profits. Finally, we'll go over the format for the rest of the book, so that you can get the most benefit out of the time you invest in reading.

I'm glad you have chosen to invest that time for your organization, because the investment will be repaid tenfold for you, your staff, and, most importantly, the people that you serve.

C. WHY IS IT IMPORTANT TO BE EMPOWERED?

I hope the fact that you are reading this book is an indication that you want more than just tenuous financial stability for your not-for-profit. Most not-for-profit managers have lived through times of financial stress in their organization that they would rather not repeat. Some never get away from fighting the financial fires that always seem to raise havoc with their plans and eat away at their time and energy.

Attaining financial empowerment is not a short journey. It is not a one-year goal in your work plan. It is not achieved without discipline, sacrifice, planning, and endurance. There is no one path. Rather, many aspects of your management style, financial policies, and operating rules may need to change.

With all that in mind, why, then, is it important to become and remain financially empowered? For a number of reasons.

First, by becoming and remaining financially empowered, you can do more mission, meet more needs, and be more responsive to the ever-changing needs of your community. And, you can do all of those things promptly, rather than wait for a new need in your community to be noticed in your state capitol, or in Washington, and then for a solution to be proposed, modified, funded, and implemented. By being financially empowered, you can develop your own solutions to new problems this week, this month, this year. Now, I don't suggest that your organization is going to become so wealthy that you will replace the need for all governmental funding: you won't. Nor do I expect that you will be able to pay for programs to meet all the currently unmet needs in your town: you won't. But you will be able to attack some of the issues facing you with your own money. And that in itself is a tremendously exciting and morale boosting experience.

Second, seeking and achieving financial empowerment makes you more competitive, in a number of areas. First, if you are financially stable, you can attract and retain the high-quality staff that you need to provide top-quality services. You also are more attractive to customers (whether they are government or others) who want to purchase services from an organization that is not going to fold up tomorrow. Having capital to work with is a very key competitive advantage. As government funding moves away from the traditional geographic monopolies toward competitive bidding, this is an essential edge.

Third, if your organization is financially empowered, senior staff are freer to manage rather than merely administer. At so many not-for-profits senior management spends so much time simply putting out financial fires that they don't have time for strategic planning, good needs assessment, or good marketing. Nor is there money to invest in continual staff training—an essential element of high-quality services. Thus, financial empowerment can and should translate into a better-run organization with more focus on its mission, and less on its survival.

D. THREE ESSENTIAL PHILOSOPHIES

There are three philosophies that have guided me as a not-for-profit staff member, executive director, and board member. I took them with me when I started training and consulting, and they show up throughout this book. You need to have some exposure to these core philosophies so that you can understand my perspective on you and your organization.

1. YOUR ORGANIZATION IS A MISSION-BASED <u>BUSINESS</u>.

You are in the mission business. Whether it be performing or fine arts, education, religion, or human services, make no mistake, you are in business. The mission, not profit, is and always should be your bottom line, but that does not give you license to disregard good business principals. I've lost track of how many times I have heard board members, staff members, or funders say, "We need to do this program. Let's start and we'll figure out where the money will come from as we go" or "We don't need a formal set of personnel policies, we're just a charity." This attitude—that we can be forgiven our sins because we are not-for-profit—is bad management, irresponsible stewardship, and will lead to certain disaster in today's more competitive, faster-paced world.

You can be businesslike and still do good mission. In fact, I will argue throughout this book that you *must* be businesslike to do any mission at all, because you have to get the most social and financial return from every resource you have.

The tools are available. The for-profit world has spent billions of dollars developing and testing them, and they are there for you to learn and apply. Many of the tools are in this book. Others are covered at length in my book, *Mission-Based Management*. But the key point here is that you need to act like a business, pay attention to the bottom line, put a high value on customer satisfaction and quality of services, hire and retain good staff, and do all the other things that successful businesses do so well. Just because you are tax-exempt is no excuse for sloppy management.

2. NO ONE GIVES YOU A DIME.

What this means is that *you earn all your money*, even the grants and donations. Think about the transaction that occurs when you get a grant. Is this charity? Of course not. You are expected to perform a service or services to certain standards for that money. You do something for it. You earn it. What about a donation? When you solicit for that donation, you tell the potential donor about your services and may even ask for funds for a particular cause. When you receive the money, you provide services with it, either directly or through a piece of equipment or building that you buy. Again, you earn the money. You don't get donations to keep, you get them to use to do mission.

This concept is critical when paired with the idea that you are a mission-based business. It means you are not a charity, that your driving force is and should remain your mission, but that you earn your way in your community. Remember, you have economic value above and beyond the social value you provide: you have a payroll and you buy equipment and supplies. In short, you add to the economic activity in the communities in which you operate. Make sure that your staff and board understand this. Just because you take donations doesn't make you a beggar; take pride in what you do and have done, economically as well as socially.

3. NOT-FOR-PROFIT DOES NOT MEAN NONPROFIT.

This is a biggie—if you don't buy this idea, your organization will never be able to achieve financial empowerment. There is a major and unfortunate misuse of the term nonprofit—it is often applied to tax-exempt entities, and it shouldn't be. A nonprofit is an entity (corporation, partnership, cooperative) *that loses money.* Pan American Airlines comes to mind, as does IBM for a few years in the early 1990s, Chrysler in the late 1970s, etc. There are many for-profits and not-for-profits that are also, unfortunately, nonprofits.

But the correct term for your organization is not-for-profit. Congress uses this term to designate a tax exemption for a corporation set up to pursue educational, social, or religious purposes "not-for-profit". Such entities are given tax exemption for activities related to their mission under section 501(c) of the IRS code. They are established and operate to do mission, not to make a profit. But—and this is the central point—nowhere in any state or Federal regulation or any state or Federal statute does it say that a not-for-profit *cannot* make a profit, or that it is illegal. In fact the IRS code says that "the profits of the corporation shall not inure to the benefit of staff, board..." showing that Congress and the IRS knew about and condoned potential profits for not-for-profits.

Look at it this way: Congress has given your organization a tax exemption. From what? From paying taxes on losses? No business pays taxes on losses. No, the exemption is from paying tax on mission-related activities *that turn a profit!* If you were never supposed to make money, you wouldn't need the tax exemption.

It's the funders, the states, the Federal government, the foundations, the United Ways that want you to believe that you cannot make money. Their motivation is obvious: that way they pay you less. But I know that not only is it okay to make a profit in your not-for-profit, it is *essential* to your financial empowerment that you do so and do so regularly. But before we get to that, just understand that you can be a not-for-profit and make a profit at the same time.

The applications of these three philosophies run throughout the book. We'll talk about starting new businesses (not being a nonprofit), about dealing with bankers (remembering you have economic value), about cash flow, and financial reporting (acting like a business) and dozens of other applications of the three central themes. I hope you like them. If not, this is going to be an especially long book.

E. THE CHARACTERISTICS OF A SUCCESSFUL NOT-FOR-PROFIT

There are nine central characteristics that are found in the successful not-for-profits that I have observed, worked with, and consulted for since 1982. A thorough discussion of these characteristics, and how to attain them, was first presented in *Mission-Based Management*. I believe it is important, however, to review them here, with each viewed through the "lens" of financial empowerment. While financial empowerment is, in fact, one of the characteristics, each of the other eight also apply to your efforts to empower your organization financially. And, if you wish to attain the characteristics other than financial empowerment, you will need to be empowered to do so.

Please understand that by singling out financial empowerment for closer inspection in this book it is not my intention to imply that financial stability is the most important characteristic: it is not. The pursuit of your mission is, always has been, and, I hope, always will be the most important characteristic. But the characteristics below cannot and should not be singled out or chosen from like choosing vegetables in the produce department at your grocery store. Rather, all of the characteristics come together to make a successful, dynamic, and sustainable not-for-profit. Think of them as parts of the whole, not as stand-alone components. So what are these overall characteristics of not-for-profit success? I've listed them below. Following each in italics are applications to the attainment of financial empowerment.

1. A VIABLE MISSION. Without a mission statement that is designed to inspire your board, staff, and community, what's the point? Further, you need a mission statement that outlines the vision of what you are and what you want to be, not what you were 20 years ago.

▶*The point of financial empowerment is to be able to do more mission, more consistently. If this is just an exercise in enrichment or peace of mind for your treasurer, forget it. But if your mission statement is the point, it is also a tool to use to attain your empowerment: organizations that chase an outdated or unrealistic mission are less likely to be able to motivate staff, less able to attract funds for endowment, less consistent in their funding over time.*

2. A BUSINESSLIKE BOARD OF DIRECTORS. The board is the most under-utilized resource that most not-for-profits possess. The board needs to attend to setting policy, being the link to the community, and being the ultimate steward of the not-for-profit for the community. They also need the array of skills, experience, and interests to complement and support those of the staff.

▶*To become financially empowered you will have to make sacrifices. You and your staff will have to come to certain realizations about saving, postponing gratification, and financial management. So will your board and, without good financial skills on that board, as well as board members who think of you as a mission-based business rather than as a charity, your task is much tougher.*

3. A STRONG, WELL-EDUCATED STAFF. You need to attract and retain good staff people. To do that you need to treat your direct service staff as the most important employees you have, and view management as a support function, not a command and control position. You need to invest in your staff with continuing education, bring them into the budgeting and planning process, and make them an integral part of the team.

▶*Financial empowerment takes knowledgeable staff: ones who are committed not only to the mission, but to the idea of financial empowerment. A financially empowered organization is, of course, more attractive to the top staff you want to attract and retain, but the journey from here to empowerment will need to be navigated by your staff—they must have the same desire in this area that you do, or you will have significant barriers to overcome.*

4. A TIGHT SET OF CONTROLS. Having good policies and procedures frees you to manage rather than administer. This is true for financial policies, but it also is essential in personnel, quality assurance, media, program, and disaster policies, as well as bylaws.

▶*Any experienced financial manager reading this book will already have good controls on cash, receivables, payables, check signatures, and the like. But do you have savings policies, investment policies, protocols for utilizing your reserves? You need them, and it is part of the empowerment process.*

5. A BIAS FOR MARKETING. You, your staff, and your board all have to understand that everything you all do every day is marketing for your organization. You need to understand who your markets are and what they want. You have to develop the skills to reconcile the conflicts that often arise between what your payer markets want and what your service markets want.

▶*What does marketing have to do with financial empowerment? More than you might think. You are going to have to sell the idea of empowerment to your staff and board. That means treating them like a market: what do they want? What will make them willing to put up with this new idea, this added discipline? Good marketing techniques will help you customize your empowerment plans to meet the wants that are unique to your organization. Additionally, good marketing means more income, more retained customers, more profits—all of which are essential to financial empowerment.*

6. A VISION FOR WHERE YOU ARE GOING. You need to plan, especially in a long-range strategic sense. Without a plan, the only way you get where you are going is by accident. What you do is too important to happen accidentally. In addition to being good business, the planning process itself offers a unique opportunity to build staff morale and to increase input and ownership from all of the people that your organization touches.

▶*To become financially empowered takes many months and years. To make sure that you get there, you will need an empowerment plan. The skills that you should have developed while writing your strategic plan will benefit you in determining how to become and remain empowered.*

7. FINANCIALLY EMPOWERED. No money, no mission. Inconsistent money, inconsistent mission. Inadequate money, inadequate mission. Unfortunately, most not-for-profits have gone through (or are now suffering through) inconsistent or inadequate funding. While not a guarantee of endless positive cash flow, achieving and maintaining financial empowerment is an essential component of doing good mission.

▶*The focus of this entire book is on financial empowerment, but you should never lose track of the fact that financial empowerment is just one of the nine characteristics of success. Without the others, your organization will fail. If you are rich, but have no mission; if you have a cash surplus but a poorly trained board or staff; if you have a profit this year, but no plan for the future—you will lose your ability to perform your mission. Again, no money, no mission; but money isn't everything.*

8. SOCIAL ENTREPRENEURS. If your organization is not willing to take risks to perform your mission, you can't make it over this essential threshold. Not-for-profits that are willing to try, to sometimes fail, but to always try again to do better mission in a new and innovative way, *do* make the grade.

▶*It's a whole lot easier to take risks if you have some financial breathing room. Financial empowerment allows you to take big-*

ger mission-based risks without the threat of losing the entire or-ganization. It allows you to know where your risks <u>really</u> are. You can make investments of time and money with the assurance that if you fail, you will not lose your ability to perform your mission completely.

9. RAPID RESPONSE TO CHANGING CIRCUMSTANCES.

Part of being an entrepreneur is taking advantage of opportunities as they surface, not two years later. Additionally, the world in which we live, work, and serve is changing at an increasing pace. Organizations that are doing the same thing that they were doing five years ago are at least five years out-of-date. But flexibility, in organizations, as in people, is easiest for the young, and more of an effort as we get older.

▶*Flexibility is great, but it is often expensive. Dropping one pro-gram, picking up two new ones, investing in staff training to keep up with new developments—all of these cost money. Having a fi-nancial plan is essential, as is having the cash and capability to invest it in the change. Financial empowerment gives you that capability.*

There they are, the nine characteristics that I continue to see in the best not-for-profit organizations in the nation. If your organization can develop these characteristics, and maintain them through hard work, you will prosper, and your ability to perform more and better mission will be enhanced. If you can't, you may find it tough to compete in the 21st century.

F. OVERVIEW OF THE BOOK

Before you go further, it is important that I give you an overview of how the book is set up, and some suggestions on how to get the most out of it. I feel that you are trusting me with an investment of your money and your time, and that I am obligated to help you get the most return for that investment. This overview will help.

1. THE FORMAT

Each chapter starts with an **OVERVIEW,** intended to give you a brief summary of what that chapter will contain. The body of the text comes next. Throughout this portion of each chapter, I try to give you as many illustrations and examples as I can, as well as ideas for immediate application in your organization. These illustrations and ideas are highlighted by the terms ● **FOR EXAMPLE** and ☞ **HANDS-ON** respectively. Look for them in nearly every chapter. After the text, near the end of the chapter, I include a **RECAP** which is a brief review of the most important concepts and points covered in the chapter.

2. THE CONTENT

The book has two kinds of chapters. The first two chapters are "context-setting", and the rest I call "working" chapters. There are two chapters (12 and 13) that are designed specifically for CEOs and for Board Members to help them interpret their roles in the financial empowerment quest.

Context-Setting Chapters

▶ *Chapter 1: Introduction*
This is the chapter you are currently reading and it gives you an idea of my philosophy, why empowerment is important, how financial empowerment relates to the other eight characteristics of successful not-for-profits, and how the book is organized.

▶ *Chapter 2: The Characteristics of Empowerment*
This chapter will show you, for the first time, the eight characteristics that I feel you must have as an organization to become financially empowered. I touch on each in summary and then the working chapters expand on them in detail. Also in this chapter is a strategy to share with your board and staff to begin your empowerment-seeking journey.

Working Chapters

▶ *Chapter 3: The Outcomes of Empowerment*
Is empowerment worth the effort? Once you have attained financial empowerment, what then? This chapter will show you how to marry your empowerment to your mission, the results (both positive and negative) of becoming empowered, some options for using your financial flexibility both in the short and long term.

▶ *Chapter 4: How Much Money Will You Need?*
This chapter will show you how to predict how much money you will need for growth, for capital improvements, and for new programs, and how to plan now to have adequate capital to pay for everything.

12

▶ *Chapter 5: Working with Traditional Funders*
You need your funders, even if you don't always get along. They are, after all, your best customers. This chapter will show you some innovative methods of working with your funders as you seek financial empowerment, how to meet their wants and needs and understand their perspective. This chapter also lists the benefits and limitations of traditional funders.

▶ *Chapter 6: New Sources of Funding: Business Development*
Many not-for-profits are developing new businesses. This chapter covers the business development process in some detail, including how to assess your willingness to take risk, and a way to look at what return on investment is needed.

▶ *Chapter 7: Communicating Your Numbers: Financial Reporting In and Out of the Organization*
One thing that most not-for-profits can do is generate financial statements. But do we get information to the people that need it in the format and at the level of specificity that they need? Hardly ever. This chapter will show you what numbers and analyses your staff, your board, and your banker should see, and how to generate them inexpensively.

▶ *Chapter 8: Financing Your Empowerment*
You will learn new techniques of seeking debt, cutting interest payments in half on big projects, and self-financing some of your needs. In this chapter we also will review how to work with lenders.

▶ *Chapter 9: Budgeting from the Bottom Up*
One way to get out of control in finance is to budget poorly or, worse, to get locked into a budget that is unrealistic and not flexible enough. In this chapter you will learn the secret of bottom-up budgeting and a method of risk/reward that *always* saves money. I'll also provide you with some budget reporting tools and templates that work best in reporting your budget status to your staff and board.

▶ *Chapter 10: Pricing for Empowerment*
Nearly all not-for-profit managers are taught to *avoid* accounting for all their costs in developing their reimbursement rates, grant applications, and fees for services. This chapter will, hopefully,

turn that training around. You will learn the four essential elements of pricing accurately, ways to price your services (for grants and fee-for-services) and your products. You will also learn the concept of breakeven and how to apply it in a service environment.

▶ *Chapter 11: Corporate Structures*
Corporate structures are highly technical, highly targeted tools. They are incredibly valuable for organizations that really need them, but most organizations—surprisingly—don't. I'll show you the benefits and drawbacks of four different types of corporate structuring, when to use them and when not to.

▶ *Chapter 12: Financial Empowerment for the CEO*
This chapter is intended particularly for CEOs as they examine the issues surrounding empowerment. What the CEO should do, what financial information the CEO should see, and the roles that they should have are all included.

▶ *Chapter 13: Financial Empowerment for Boards of Directors*
Boards are crucial in the empowerment quest. But they have a special set of roles and perspectives. This chapter addresses financial empowerment from the view of boards, and discusses their role, some actions that only they can take, and the information that they should see.

▶ *Chapter 14: Mobilizing for Empowerment*
By this time, you will have all the tools, and all the theory, but how do you actually get started? What specific things can you do? This chapter will give you the sequence of things to address and a long list of action steps to achieve the characteristics of empowerment. I conclude with a sample empowerment plan.

▶ *Chapter 15: Putting It All Together*
In this chapter I will sum up the key points of the book, show you some techniques that may help you avoid spending every dime you save the same day you save it and show how to get the most from your empowerment.

Although I know that some of these chapters have a higher interest for you than others, I hope that you will be able to read the chapters in order. They are designed to build on each other. You will get more out of them if you follow the sequence.

RECAP

In this chapter we have given you an overview of this book, and the background you need to understand my philosophy of not-for-profit management. First, we discussed the reasons why it is important that you become and remain financially empowered, the rationales as to why all the effort will be worth it. Then we reviewed the three key philosophies that guide my writing, consulting, and training: (1) that you are a mission-based *business*, (2) that no one gives your organization a dime, and (3) that it's essential to make money, a profit, in most (if not all) years. Next we went over the nine characteristics of success in not-for-profits, and showed how the issue of financial empowerment is woven through the other essential characteristics of good not-for-profits. Finally, we reviewed the format and layout of the book, to allow you to get the most from your time.

One other suggestion: don't be the only person in your organization to read this book. Rather, read it with your management team. If you read the book, and then descend on your people with a huge bunch of new ideas, forms, and ways of doing business, you will meet with resistance. However, if you include your management team in reading the book, and then discuss the chapters as you read them, you can decide which ideas are most important to adopt now and which can be deferred until later. You, your staff, and your organization will get more out of this, and achieve financial empowerment faster if you do your learning as a team. I believe in this so much that I have written a *Discussion Leader's Guide for Financial Empowerment* that helps you go through this process. It is available from the publisher, Alpine Guild.

You should be excited about the information that the following pages hold. I have provided applications and specific ideas as often as possible, so that you can begin to apply what you have learned immediately. Some sections may seem dry, but the mission rationale for all this should be evident, even in the most mundane areas. Because that's the point: more and better mission for the people you serve. Their needs and wants are growing. Let's get started on increasing your ability to provide services to them.

2. The Characteristics of Empowerment

OVERVIEW

Now that we have laid some of the groundwork necessary for you to begin seeking financial empowerment, we need to finish the job by doing two things: explaining what the characteristics of financial empowerment are for your organization, and then giving you a tool to self-diagnose your current financial empowerment status before you move on to the rest of the book.

This chapter will cover that and more. First, I'll define in detail the eight characteristics that I have found are consistently present in not-for-profit organizations that become and remain financially empowered. We'll go through each of them and look at what impact they have on overall financial security and on your ability to do more and better mission.

Second, I've provided a tool in the Appendix that you can use to take a look at your current financial status. I urge you to do this now, as a method of really becoming aware of what your situation is. You may find that you are in serious need in some areas where you thought you were okay. Conversely, you may also find that you are in pretty good shape in areas where you feared the worst. It is important to know where you stand as you read the remainder of the book so that you can pay particular attention to the areas where you have found deficiencies.

The last portion of the chapter covers some strategies for you to use as you lead the board and staff in seeking financial empowerment. Many organizations find that the discipline needed to develop financial strength provides a fertile feeding ground for conflict and dissension about priorities. I want you to be forewarned about some traditional problems and forearmed with some strategies and tactics that can diffuse the conflicts before they get out of hand.

By the time you finish this chapter, you will be ready to proceed into the meat of the book, and get the most out of your reading.

A. THE CHARACTERISTICS OF EMPOWERMENT

There are eight core characteristics of financial empowerment that we will discuss. I see these repeatedly in organizations with whom I have consulted. As with the characteristics of a successful not-for-profit that were discussed in Chapter 1, these characteristics do not stand alone. Rather, they work as a group, supporting and reinforcing each other to bring about financial stability and the utilization of resources needed for your organization to do its mission better and with a shorter response time.

The eight characteristics of not-for-profits that are financially empowered that we will examine are listed below. Note that I have put them into groups labeled *Measurable* (having quantified outcomes), *Management* (characteristics that require changes in management style and attitude), and *Mission* (outcomes that directly impact on your mission capability):

▶ **MEASURABLE**:
1. The organization has more revenue than expenses in <u>at least</u> 7 out of 10 years.

2. The organization has a cash operating reserve of <u>at least</u> 90 days.

3. The organization gets <u>at least</u> 5% of its total income from earnings on its endowment.

4. The organization has sources of revenue from non-traditional non-governmental sources: it has business income.

▶ **MANAGEMENT**:
5. The organization shares its financial information widely, and practices bottom-up budgeting.

6. The organization is appropriately leveraged.

▶ **MISSION**:
7. The organization supports its mission directly by establishing and using a rapid-response mission reserve.

8. The organization is financially flexible enough to accommodate changes in service delivery.

These characteristics, their achievement, and their retention will be the basis of all that follows in the remainder of this book. I do, however, want to take a moment to explain why I use the term "empowerment" rather than "stability" in relation to your financial situation. Stability is a great thing, and financial stability to me means not having to worry about making payroll every two weeks, not having to watch the mail for the check from your largest funder with a huge knot in your stomach, not having to break into a cold sweat whenever your banker calls. Financially stable organizations have solid balance sheets, good cash flow, adequate resources to meet this year's demands and next year's as well.

So do financially-empowered organizations. But organizations that are empowered have attributes beyond mere stability. They are financially positioned to take prudent risk on behalf of the people whom they serve, they have resources to apply now, this week, this month to meet service needs that arise in their community, they have diverse income sources that complement each other so that their dependence on traditional funders is steadily less and less.

These organizations are empowered financially to do more mission, in more places, with more creativity. As I said in the first chapter, the point of all this is good mission, not the accumulation of organizational wealth. But mere stability is not enough. In an environment that is increasingly competitive, with major changes in the way traditional services are funded, you need to be empowered. Nothing is stable, everything is in flux. Empowerment enables you and your organization to change as the world does without the stress that those less empowered will have. Don't settle for stability. Go for empowerment.

With that settled, let's now look at the eight characteristics of financial empowerment in much greater detail.

1. THE ORGANIZATION HAS MORE REVENUE THAN EXPENSES IN AT LEAST 7 OUT OF 10 YEARS.

Too many not-for-profits, and even more of their funders, still labor under the assumption that a not-for-profit cannot make a profit. I discussed this misunderstanding at some length in Chapter 1 (see "Three Essential Philosophies"), but it bears repeating: it is okay for your organization to make money. You won't lose your tax-exempt designation, nor will you go to jail.

In fact, my belief is that you must make money, you must have a profit, in at least 7 out of 10 years, if you are doing your job well. Only by making money can you become and remain financially empowered. Only by making money can you take reasonable risks on behalf of your clientele. Only by making money can you take on debt. Only by making money can you develop the stability to attract and retain large numbers of the excellent staff you need to remain competitive.

What do I mean by making money? How do I define profit? For the purposes of this book, I will define net profit as the difference between all of your revenue and all of your expenses. This means that I include your fundraising revenues and interest on your endowment as income, and your depreciation as an expense. By defining things this way, we'll be able to look at the whole financial picture of your organization. You will see if your "profit centers" make up for your "loss centers". You'll see whether or not you are adequately using the resource of your charitable tax-exempt status to bolster your income. You'll be able to see if your operating income is covering most (or all) of your costs, or if you are taking a loss on everything you do and making up the difference in spaghetti suppers.

After all is said and done, you need to make money, and making money is okay. But how much? What is an appropriate amount or percentage of profit? That depends. It depends on your funding streams, and how much they allow. It depends on how much growth you are experiencing now and how much you anticipate in the near future. It depends on how much debt you are carrying, and how soon you want to establish operating reserves. It depends on what your board and staff feel are equitable, as well as how much profit the market will allow you to make in the increasingly competitive arenas in which you operate. I know of not-for-profits that need to make 4% profit per year to stay even, and ones that can grind out an 8% margin in good years.

This brings up another issue. While I urge you to set up your budgeting and planning processes and guidelines to generate a profit in most years, I also want to acknowledge the fact that you have a dilemma to confront that your for-profit counterparts do not. It is this: you need to be concerned not only about your financial return but also about your social return in each year and on each investment.

● **FOR EXAMPLE:** An agency that works with the developmentally disabled was developing a business plan that initiated a janitorial service, with most of the employees being persons with disabilities who were graduates of the agency's training program. In developing the business plan, the agency discovered that if all of its employees were people with developmental disabilities, its productivity per person would be less and they would make less profit. If, however, they hired workers without disabilities, they would have less people with disabilities employed in the community, a key part of their mission. Which is a better return for the investment of time and money that would be required to start up the business? More jobs and less profit, or more profit and less jobs?

● **FOR EXAMPLE:** A museum in the Southwest was approached by a foundation that was interested in funding an interactive arts program that would mix underprivileged children with senior citizens. The Director was asked to develop a proposal and in doing so, estimated that the museum would have to invest $40,000 of its own in start-up costs and working capital to secure the two-year $310,000 project grant. While the project would break even over the two years, and the $40,000 would be fully recovered at the end of the project, the Director and her board had to decide whether or not it was the best use of the money, the investment that got the most *mission* return in addition to a *financial* return on their investment.

Thus, you need to be thinking of your investment decisions (and resource allocation is an investment) not just in terms of cost recovery. What will be the return on investment *in both financial and mission terms*? Your for-profit peers only need to think about financial return on investment; you have a dual, and sometimes conflicting, responsibility.

However, to become and remain financially empowered, you need to make money, at least seven years out of ten, and you need to make enough money in those years to support your growth, and put aside reserves for future needs. Which leads nicely to our second characteristic of a financially-empowered organization.

2. THE ORGANIZATION HAS A CASH OPERATING RESERVE OF AT LEAST 90 DAYS.

I know that there are a number of you reading this that are saying, "Are you nuts—90 days' reserve?" Interestingly enough, you are saying that for two widely disparate reasons. Most are reacting to the 90-day number from the perspective and experience of never having ten days operating cash on hand, much less 90. But there are other readers (and more than you might think) who would not dream of having less than nine months rather than 90 days operating capital on hand, and whose opinion is that anyone (including me) who would advocate for any less is irresponsible if not incompetent. So be it.

Let me expand on my point a bit. First, let me define reserves as cash, money market funds, or CDs due within 30 days, not stocks, bonds, receivables, or any other fixed asset. Second, please notice that I say "at least 90 days". Thus 90 days is a *minimum acceptable reserve*. For many organizations, the comfort level of three month's cash will not be adequate. Third, let me concede that while 90 days is an arbitrary number, having that amount of cash on hand would be a huge leap forward for thousands of not-for-profits in this country.

☞ **HANDS-ON:** To calculate your number of days' cash reserve, take your most recent monthly statement. Look at the "Assets" section, specifically the "Current Assets". Add up the cash, money market funds and any CDs you have coming due in the next 30 days. Take that sum and divide it by your total expenditures for the last 12 months. Take the resulting number and multiply it by 365. The product is your number of days of operating expenses that are represented by your cash reserve. Let's look at an example:

CASH ON HAND: $45,689
PREVIOUS 12 MONTHS' EXPENSES: $1,245,443

$1,245,443 ÷ 365 = 3,412.17 (average daily expenditure)

45,689 ÷ 3,412.17 = 13.39 days of cash on hand

Thus, this organization has just over 13 days of operating cash reserves.

You are probably asking, "Why 90 days?" As I noted above, it is an arbitrary figure that, based on my experience, is a reasonable target for you. But it may not be enough. You need to work with your board, your CPA, and your funders to establish the reserve level that is appropriate for your organization, your plans, and the regulations under which you work.

You may also be in the unfortunate situation where one or more of your key funders is telling you that having a 90-day reserve is illegal or unethical. While they may be incorrect, they probably do have the capability to punish you by withholding or reducing your payments. In that case, you may have to move some of this money to a separate corporation. We'll discuss this at more length in the chapter on "Working With Traditional Funders". If you have this problem, you will also run up against it in relation to your endowment, and we'll cover that next.

3. THE ORGANIZATION GETS AT LEAST 5% OF ITS TOTAL INCOME FROM EARNINGS ON ITS ENDOWMENT.

Again, many readers are saying, "Yeah, right. I need every dime I get just to keep operating. And now he wants me to raise an endowment!"

Partially true. I want you to have a source of income that continues to come in whether or not your government funding continues at its current rate. In fact, I want you to have several sources, of which income from an endowment is only one. But you will not just raise an endowment, you will save for one as well. I'll show you how.

By getting a "nest egg" and by setting a goal that results in at least 5% of your total income each year coming from that nest egg, you do a number of things. You establish your organization as one that will be around for the long term, improving your reputation with funders. You can attract and retain better staff. You lower the stress on your board and yourself. You have a source for internal loans, and for funding of new projects in extraordinary circumstances. And, by establishing an endowment in a safe place (usually in a related but uncontrolled 501(c)(3)), you signal to larger donors such as businesses that you are protecting their donation from your major funders.

☞ **HANDS-ON:** To calculate the amount needed in your endowment, do this. Take your total income for this year. Multiply it by 5% (.05). Take the product of that calculation and divide it by 8, then multiply that number by 100. What we have done is assume that your endowment is capable of generating 8% interest and/or dividends each year. If you disagree with that number, or if rates have drastically changed since this writing, plug in the correct interest rate instead of the 8. Again, let's look at a "for-instance."

ANNUAL BUDGETED INCOME: $2,450,000

$2,450,000 x .05 = $122,250

$122,250 ÷ 8 = $15,312.50

$15,312.50 x 100 = $1,531,250

Thus, in this example, the organization's goal should be for a minimum endowment of just over $1.53 million.

This is obviously not a one-year project. It takes time and commitment but guess what? So does nearly everything in this book. However, I do not want you to write off this idea if you are not an organization that was formed in 1900, or if you have only $500,000 annual budget instead of $500,000,000. An endowment is a reasonable goal for *all* not-for-profit organizations. Like the other reserves we will talk about, its achievement requires a new attitude, a change from "If we have it, spend it."

4. THE ORGANIZATION HAS SOURCES OF REVENUE FROM NON-TRADITIONAL NON-GOVERNMENTAL SOURCES: IT HAS BUSINESS INCOME.

More and more not-for-profit organizations are developing business income streams to supplement their traditional sources of revenue. In simple terms, this means that they have set up new businesses, or have income from other markets than they have had in the past. For example, a YMCA that serves clients mostly in the inner city might set up a health center in the suburbs to supplement its income; an organization that provides day care for seniors might expand into day care for seniors with Alzheimer's; a museum might expand its gift shop income by offering a catalog or by starting to sponsor tours to study art in Europe or ancient civilizations in the Middle East.

The list of these types of enterprises is long and growing every day as more and more not-for-profits realize the hard truth; there is no more Federal, state, or local money coming. Why? Because the combination of a Federal deficit that is beyond everyone's comprehension, and a population that wants its entitlements and tax breaks, but at the same time gets apoplectic at the faintest whisper of the word "tax", precludes more spending for social, educational, or arts programs beyond increases to compensate for inflation. There is no cavalry coming over the hill to pour new dollars into your mission, no matter how desperate the needs of your constituency, no matter how articulate or passionate your argument regarding why your organization should be the priority. The cavalry can't come. The horses have been sold for glue and the saddles have been hocked. There is no more money.

For some lucky readers, there will be exceptions to my doom and gloom forecast. If you work for an organization providing a service that is high visibility and in a "politically correct" arena you may have a *temporary* increase in funds while you bask in the klieg lights of public demand for more of what you do. But the funding increase is only temporary, and it always comes at the expense of some other social need, some other not-for-profit. Substance abuse programs basked in this glow in the mid 1980s, rural health centers in the mid 1980s, AIDs research in the late 1980s, crime prevention (and corrections) in the early 1990s. But the attention span of the public and the press is pitifully short, and next week (next month, next year), there will be some other fashionable program to fund, and yours will be cut back.

Let's examine the Federal deficit for just a moment. It really is too big to conceptualize as a whole, and we have all heard illustrations of how big the deficit is, how high a stack of $1,000 bills it takes to make a trillion, etc. We've also been told by pundits of all persuasions how such a debt is (alternately) hideous and no big deal, the biggest threat to democracy since Stalin and much ado about nothing. The debate is moot. The point is, there is no more money as long as voters say no more taxes.

I want to look at the deficit a different way, to demonstrate why no Federal official, no matter how caring or altruistic, can do much about increasing social spending. At this writing, the national debt is approximately *$5.1 trillion* and growing at around *$200 billion* per year with no end in sight. The average interest rate on the national debt is about 6.9% per year. At that rate the cost of the *interest* alone—not the debt service, but just the interest, is $39.4 million ***per hour***. In one of your eight-hour work days, we as a nation pay over $315 million in *interest* on our debt. Think of that in relation to your organization's budget. How many minutes does it take to equal your entire annual budget? Not many. You are not alone.

If the Feds and states are going dry as a resource, what about private giving, foundations, or even corporations—the other traditional sources of income? Most of you already know the answer. With state and Federal resources no longer a sure thing, and with demand for all types of services growing, the competition for private, corporate, and foundation funds has never been more fierce. As an aside, if you are financially empowered, you will be more competitive for many foundation or corporate grants, as these funders often want to give to organizations that are going to be around for awhile and who can concentrate on mission rather than on just keeping the doors open.

The message? If you have more needs in your community than you can handle now, if the demand for the services you provide is growing, you are on your own. If there are no more funds from foundations, corporations, individuals, or the government, where do you go? Depending on the need, you start new businesses, you borrow prudently (see # 6 below), and you use your fund balance when you absolutely must. But you have to step outside the traditional streams of funding to become empowered.

5. THE ORGANIZATION SHARES ITS FINANCIAL INFORMATION WIDELY, AND PRACTICES BOTTOM-UP BUDGETING.

One way that you can become a more empowered organization financially is already in your grasp. It's your financial information. If you are like too many organizations, both not-for-profit and for-profit, you under-utilize this resource. You can get more—much more—from your numbers. Financially-empowered organizations use their numbers as a tool. They give people the financial information that they need, in the format they need it, when they need it to do their jobs better. You can too. The tools are available and cheap. The information is, for the most part, probably already in your accounting system or software. What it takes is an attitude of "knowledge is power, so let's share it and empower people" rather than the more traditional "knowledge is power, so let's hoard it and retain the power." Think of it this way: you are leading your organization, its staff, and board, through the woods at night. If you have the only torch, and you keep it, you can see your way, and others will follow you, but they will stumble a lot and run into low-hanging branches. If, however, you share the fire, and use it to light a lot of torches, everyone can see better, there are less stumbles, less turned ankles and scraped knees. Share your numbers. In Chapter 7, I'll show you some tried and true methods for this.

Sharing your numbers is essential if you practice bottom-up budgeting, and financially-empowered organizations do just that. They develop a budgeting system that allows for input from the line staff and managers, and then hold them accountable for the implementation of the budget. Using a combination of risk and reward, these organizations increase their staff ownership, save money, and share responsibility. In Chapter 9 on Budgeting, I'll show you how to implement this idea in your organization with as few glitches as possible.

6. THE ORGANIZATION IS APPROPRIATELY LEVERAGED.

Far too many not-for-profits still operate with a "we never borrow" millstone around their necks. The rationale for this policy is understandable, but outdated and misguided. It goes something like this: we are a not-for-profit and we only get our funds appropriated (granted, donated) once a year, and our funding is never certain, so we can't take on the risk of a debt.

By now, you should know what my response will be: you are a not-for-profit business, and leveraging (borrowing to do something today that will earn you the money to pay the loan back tomorrow and still leave a profit) is a time-honored business technique. You cannot, however, borrow if you are going to lose money: loans are paid back from profits. Thus, you must have more income than expenses most, if not all, years (see #1 above) if you are to take on any debt.

Also, please note that I use the word *appropriately* to describe your leveraging. What this means is that you have enough debt, but not too much, and debt for the right things, for the right terms, at the right rates. I am not talking about borrowing for everything and anything for a long time for any rate at all. Prudent, appropriate debt can help you do more mission sooner. Imprudent, inappropriate debt is a fast track to bankruptcy.

These days there are many, many ways to borrow, and we'll review them in Chapter 8. You will see not only the numerous ways to borrow, and how to evaluate each one, but also how to assess what kind of loan, if any, is appropriate, and how to assess how much money you will need and when the need will arise.

7. THE ORGANIZATION SUPPORTS ITS MISSION DIRECTLY BY ESTABLISHING AND USING A RAPID-RESPONSE MISSION RESERVE.

As I have already said—I hope with adequate emphasis—the point of your organization becoming financially empowered is not to get rich. You and your staff and board go through all the sacrifices necessary so that you can do more mission, more efficiently, more effectively, *and sooner*. This is where the mission reserve comes in.

I have seen many ways to do this, but the point is to have a reserve of funds, or at least an accounting for funds that can be used according to some pre-set criteria for a mission-related need on a short-response basis. It may mean responding to a new problem, like HIV or crack babies, it may mean helping out in a natural disaster in your community, or it could mean providing extra services such as concerts or other cultural events when a large group of people is coming to town (for a national sporting event, for example). The issue here is having the money to meet the need sooner rather than later, to be able to be responsive rather than reactive, to have the resources to apply to needs as they arise.

This reserve, the ability to be responsive today, this week, this month, rather than to have to go begging for the money and waiting months or years for a response; this is the essence of financial empowerment. And when you and your board and staff have this power, the morale boost will be incredible. You can truly say that you are no longer a charity, that you are a mission-based business, one that controls a great part of its own destiny. And that morale boost, that adrenaline rush of financial freedom, is worth all the work.

I am not pretending that you will ever acquire enough funds to meet all the needs in your community: you won't. You will, in fact, find out just how tough it is to decide between competing needs in your community, something your funders and donors have known for years. But just because you can't do it all doesn't mean you shouldn't do something. You need a mission reserve. Later in the book, I'll show you how to budget for just such a resource.

8. THE ORGANIZATION IS FINANCIALLY FLEXIBLE ENOUGH TO ACCOMMODATE CHANGES IN SERVICE DELIVERY.

When we are young, we are flexible both physically and mentally. As we age we lose that flexibility, becoming both less able and less willing to change direction on short notice. Organizations are no different. When they are young, they are often lean and very flexible with not a lot of investment in doing things a certain way. As organizations mature, add staff, develop long-term patterns of activities, they become less able and, thus, less willing to change. An example of this might be your accounting software. When you only had one computer, and had a rudimentary program, you were more able to seriously consider changing software than you are today. If you were to change now, you would have to buy the software, retrain staff, and learn how to customize it to your needs. Thus software salespeople have to have a major leap in product benefits to even get your interest. You are less flexible, and less willing to listen to a proposal for a change.

The danger in mission-based businesses like yours is that if you are financially inflexible or worse, financially insolvent, you are in danger of being permanently stuck in old and outdated methods of service delivery. Change, in any form, is costly. And it is costly in the consideration, the implementation, and the follow-up. If you do not possess the resources to pay for change, you are more likely to stay rooted in the present rather than moving into the future.

● **FOR EXAMPLE:** Hospitals are excellent examples of organizations stuck with what I call the "edifice complex". In the past twenty or thirty years they have spent billions of dollars adding buildings full of beds, and additional billions on expensive high-tech equipment. These investments were based on assumptions about utilization: usually overly-optimistic projections presented by administrators assuring their boards that the beds or equipment would be used a great deal. Now we are fast entering the era of managed care, a method of insurance reimbursement that will reduce the need for medical surgical beds and much high cost diagnostic equipment. The hospital administrators and boards are in a quandary. Do they jump on the train of managed care, and get forced to eat huge losses on their beds and equipment, or do they try to buck the trend and find that they are left off the train completely? Their edifice complex restricts their flexibility. They have to use those buildings. Here the largest asset on their balance sheet becomes their biggest program liability.

● **FOR EXAMPLE:** Another example of inflexibility has to do with the largest expenditure you have, personnel. From the 1950s through the early 1980s people with developmental disabilities, usually those with mental retardation or severe autism, were often sent to state-run institutions, which developed into huge complexes of buildings with hundreds or even thousands of employees. In the late 1970s methods of service changed, so that people with disabilities were more likely to be served in their communities rather than in an institution. Yet, all over the country, nearly a quarter of a century later, the buildings are still there, the institution still operates, albeit with a smaller number of residents. Why? Because of the political cost of firing so many employees. Thus the pursuit of excellent mission is blocked by the barrier of having employees who cannot be fired.

On a more local level, if program trends change, or funding streams opt for a new direction, how easy is it for your organization to adapt and prosper? Are you weighed down by property you feel you must utilize no matter what? Do you have the cash to carry you if you disrupt your normal income streams to adopt a new program or policy change? Are your reserves tied up in long-term notes that cannot be touched for six months or more?

The answers to these questions will give you a clue as to whether you are currently financially flexible enough to adapt to change. If you are not, increasing your financial empowerment through suggestions I will make in the remainder of the book will certainly help. We will talk about debt, capital investment, appropriate leveraging, and the strategy of owning versus leasing, and employing versus subcontracting in today's rapidly changing environment. These are all keys to flexibility and bear examination.

The ability to be flexible in terms of buildings and/or employees will vary greatly depending on your organization. If you are a museum you need display space. The funding sources of various types of organizations may dictate that they must employ rather than contract. But whatever your restraints, you need to maximize your flexibility in terms of your ability to pursue your mission in a rapidly changing world.

With these eight key characteristics in place, you can be assured that your organization will be benefiting every day from its financial empowerment. As I have already said, the characteristics are not easy to attain, and they are even harder to maintain. But they are achievable if you, your board, and your staff have the courage, stamina, and foresight to attempt them.

B. SELF-DIAGNOSING YOUR EMPOWERMENT STATUS

At this point some readers may be thinking, "Based on the criteria for financial empowerment you have listed, my organization is fine. We're already empowered." Perhaps, perhaps not. Before going any further, I suggest that you apply the self-assessment tool that is found in the Appendix. Copy the pages and let your entire management team in on the discussion.[1] If your organization collects the financial information that it should, the assessment will be relatively easy to complete and score. If, however, you have to create some of the data from scratch, there is a message: you are not tracking some of the numbers that you should.

Once you have done this self-assessment you will see your strengths and weaknesses, and perhaps have things to focus on further. You will also know which parts of the remainder of the book you should pay the most attention to as you continue reading.

One last note on the self-assessment. No matter how it turns out, date it and keep it. Then, after you read the remainder of the book and apply the things that you need to, perform the self-assessment again once a year when you receive your audited statements. This will provide an excellent method of tracking your progress toward empowerment from a baseline established with this first self-assessment.

C. A BOARD/STAFF STRATEGY FOR SEEKING EMPOWERMENT

I have already noted that seeking and retaining financial empowerment is not a short or easy task. Certainly you, as a manager, cannot do the work alone. You are going to need help, and you are going to need support from some key groups of people. Who? Your staff, board, and funders. All of these groups must be along for the journey. Otherwise, you probably won't be successful in your quest.

But each of these groups have different perspectives on money, different outlooks on what your organization should do with the funds that you have. How can you appeal to all of them? How can you make them acquiesce to long-term financial commitments? How can you convince them that financial discipline today—and its concomitant costs—will benefit the people you serve tomorrow? To start, you examine their needs and wants, just like you would any other market or customer. As you do that, remember that I have characterized each group as a whole, not as a collection of individuals, and I have offered up what, in my experience as a consultant, I have seen from hundreds of such groups. Yours may be different, and certainly individuals within the staff or board will have different wants than the group as a whole. But I want you to start looking at

---

[1] The Self-Assessment tool is also found in the *Financial Empowerment Discussion Leader's Guide*. This 8½ x 11, 3-ring-binder format facilitates making copies for your use.

these groups from the perspective of <u>their</u> wants, not yours.

1. STAFF: Most staffs are concerned about two things: services to the people that you serve and compensation for themselves. Most staffs are not well-versed in how your income is earned, or in how it is spent, and many, if not most, feel that their organization has more money than it really does. Thus, if you ask them to defer expenses to save for the future, they will resist: We need the money for this service now, how about a 1% higher raise, etc.

2. BOARD: If your organization has been in serious financial trouble in the past, you may have a board that is either gun-shy about setting long-term goals ("We'll be lucky just to keep the doors open") or who have a habit of spending whatever you have as soon as you have it (which may be why you had the financial problems in the first place). Most board members also want to do as much service as possible, and are often lobbied by friends and neighbors who express their need for more and more services. Finally, if your board performs fundraising duties, and they should, they may be uncomfortable asking others for money if the organization already has "large" reserves.

3. FUNDERS: Funders—whether they be government, foundations, United Ways, or other groups—want you to provide the services that they pay for in a high-quality manner, and account for all of your costs. While more and more governments are going to a fee-for-service mode in funding (where you bid a price, provide the service, and then keep the excess or make up any shortfalls) some still operate under the outdated and damaging "use it or lose it" philosophy: "If I give you a grant and you don't spend it all, you have to give it back." Others, most notably United Ways, won't fund you if you have too much money; the term "too much" varying from town to town.

Note that the terms "large" or "too much" in relation to any financial reserves, are extremely subjective. You may feel that 120 days operating cash in the bank is barely enough, while your board or staff may feel that 60 days of reserves is obscene. Your funders may have regulations which prevent funding you if you have over $x or some percentage of income in cash.

Also remember that many staff and board members look at the money in dollars, not as a percentage of your income, and get riled up if they see a lot of zeros in the cash and securities column.

● **FOR EXAMPLE:** A client of ours in the Southwest started sharing its financial statements with its staff in an effort to increase ownership and involvement with all levels of the organization. However, they did not accompany the distribution of the Income and Expense

Statements and Balance Sheets with any training on what these reports meant or how to read or interpret them.

The predictable results? Some of the staff went ballistic when they saw that the organization had over $250,000 in cash. *"You have a quarter of a million dollars in cash and you turned down my $500 request for equipment?"* This is an understandable reaction, especially if no one puts the $250,000 in perspective; it was less than 27 days' operating expenses for the organization which had an annual budget of over $3.5 million. After the fact, the organization called us and we came in to do staff and board training, but some of the damage was a long time healing. Remember, $10,000 may not seem like a lot of money to you if you deal in budgets of millions, but to someone (board or staff) who makes $20,000 a year, it's a ton of money. Be sensitive to their perspective.

With this many different wants and points of view, where do you start? Here are some ideas that work, but you will have to adapt them to your own set of particulars. I would urge you to do them in the order offered because there is, as I hope you will see, a process of gaining commitment.

I also suggest that when you talk these issues through you don't mix groups; don't have staff and board in the same meetings, don't ask funders to sit in on board discussions of your financial plans, etc.

FIRST: Have your own goals in mind. As a manager, you need to set some goals down for yourself. These should be rough goals, ones that sketch the outline of where you think your organization should be in five years. How large a reserve is necessary? Can you have an endowment? Should you develop a mission reserve? Set your own goals before you go out to the rest of the organization. These goals will be modified by the board, the realities of funders, and by staff input, and that is fine. But you need to have at least some idea of what you want before you start.

SECOND: Talk about mission outcomes. Sit down with groups of staff and board (and later your funders) and talk mission, mission, mission. What are the needs today that are not being met due to lack of funds? What actions in the past could have produced more money today? What future needs do these people see that will require more financial resources? Only *after* you talk about mission should you start talking about money, and laying out the rough outlines of where you want to go.

THIRD: Talk about sacrifices. Talk frankly about the sacrifices that will be necessary to get from here to empowerment: deferred spending, the discipline of savings, the focus on mission *and* net revenue. Both staff and board will be concerned about unmet needs, and one answer is that your organization cannot do everything for everyone. One skill that I think is essential for management and board to learn is the difficult skill of saying "no" to a good idea, saying "sorry" to a real need. There are simply more needs than you will ever be able to meet. Good stewardship requires that you focus on the things you do best and strengthen your organization to do those things with excellence and constant improvement. To be able to do this, you need financial strength.

FOURTH: Set goals and talk about results. With a group of staff and board, set goals. You need to come to some internal agreement about what levels of net income, reserves, endowment, etc. can help you meet the long-term goals of your organization. It should be noted here that this is much, much easier to do if you already have a strategic plan. If you don't have a plan in place, make sure that you revise your financial goals when you do develop your organizational strategic plan.

Once you have specific goals in place, go back to your staff and board and talk about the goals in terms of positive mission outcomes. For example, if your goal is to develop an endowment that contributes 7% of your total organizational income per year from its interest and dividends, explain to staff that this translates into a regular, dependable $X per year that can be devoted to services. If you can, translate that into service units such as patron visits, student days, cases closed, etc. Point out clearly to both staff and board the mission outcomes of the attainment of your financial goals. Don't just assume that the money will speak for itself. It won't.

FIFTH: Share your goals with funders. You need your funders "on board"—or at least on notice—about your financial goals. Why? Because some funders will have concerns with the legality of your retaining funds, making money, putting aside reserves, and you need to get to them early and often with the rationale that financial empowerment means more mission, less dependence on their dollars, more ability to do good things in the community. The more you can make that case, the more funders will be willing to work with you to get to that goal, by working around any regulations that get in the way.

● **FOR EXAMPLE:** A number of years ago, an organization that provided substance abuse treatment services desperately wanted to buy and renovate the building that they were in. They came to me to ask for strategies on how to build up cash to pay for the building. At the time, all their costs, including their lease, were reimbursed dollar for dollar, allowing them no ability to develop any significant reserves. A little investigation, however, showed that they were paying less than half the going fair market rate for their space, and the lease was coming up for renewal.

The agency Executive Director and I went to see the State project officer and the Director of the department to explain the situation, and had them come tour the current building and see the deplorable conditions. We proposed setting up a second, arms-length not-for-profit corporation that would become, in effect, a lease intermediary. The second corporation would lease the building from the owner at the current rate of $3 per foot, but charge the not-for-profit the documented market rate of $7 per foot. This rate, because it was the market rate, was reimbursable from the state, and allowed the organization, over the following two and a half years, to accumulate enough cash to buy its property.

The point here from the state's perspective was that their contractor was only reimbursed costs. They knew about the plan, agreed with the need for a new building, but had no real ideas about how to get from the need to the solution until the not-for-profit suggested it. By involving the funder early, we got their strong support.

Not all of you will be that lucky. Some funders—be they government, foundations, or United Ways—are very, very rigid and unsympathetic about financial issues. But, by talking to them early, you put them on notice that you are not hiding anything, and you identify your points of resistance early, which is very helpful. Talk to your funders—not to get permission, but to let them know your mission goals, and how your financial goals are set up to support them.
(For more on funders, see Chapter 5.)

RECAP

In this chapter, we have discussed some of the key elements of financial empowerment and set the stage for the remainder of the book. To review, the eight characteristics of an organization that is financially empowered are:

1   *The organization has more revenue than expenses in <u>at least</u> 7 out of 10 years.*

2. *The organization has a cash operating reserve of <u>at least</u> 90 days.*

3. *The organization gets <u>at least</u> 5% of its total income from earnings on its endowment.*

4.   *The organization has sources of revenue from non-traditional non-governmental sources: it has business income.*

5. *The organization shares its financial information widely, and practices bottom-up budgeting.*

6. *The organization is appropriately leveraged.*

7. *The organization supports its mission directly by establishing and using a rapid-response mission reserve.*

8. *The organization is financially flexible enough to accommodate changes in service delivery.*

These eight, as I have said, are not easy to either achieve or maintain, but in the second part of the chapter we looked at a self-assessment tool (in the Appendix) to let you diagnose your organization's current state of empowerment. Assuming you took the time to administer that tool, you now know your organization's financial strengths and weaknesses, at least in terms of my eight characteristics.

Finally, we reviewed the best methods to get your staff, board, and funders on the bandwagon for financial empowerment; to make them understand the mission outcomes that you foresee from attaining your financial goals, and to look with clear eyes at the sacrifices that they will need to make to get there.

In the remaining chapters, we will examine individual issues in much greater detail. I urge you to read all the chapters, even those that cover areas where you feel your organization is in good shape or in which you consider yourself an expert. You may just pick up a nugget or two, and you will certainly reinforce good patterns of behavior. Besides that, the chapters reinforce one another, and the issues, strategies, and theories that are brought up in one part of the book are often referred to in others. Thus, if you read the entire book, the parts that you are most interested in will be clearer and more immediately useable.

You have already made a start toward financial empowerment. You know where you are if you have completed the self-assessment. You know where you need to go financially. You have some of the tools to get you there. The rest of the book will give you the specifics.

3. The Outcomes of Empowerment

OVERVIEW

When you finish reading this book, you will have the tools to improve your organization's financial status and start down the road toward becoming and remaining financially empowered. It's a long road, and a long book. Most of the subsequent chapters will focus on technical issues such as cash flow, debt, bankers, and boards, I want to use this chapter to focus you on the issue that should preempt all others in a not-for-profit: your mission. In this chapter, I want to motivate you to do the work necessary to become empowered.

You may remember that in the first chapter I cautioned you that the point of becoming financially empowered was not to get rich: it was to be able to do more and better mission. Throughout the book, you will be told over and over that the point is mission. Discussions on empowerment, business development, mission reserve, and flexibility all start and end with the question: are we doing the most mission by selecting this choice?

This chapter will show you how to take the crucial step in becoming a financially-empowered *mission-based* organization rather than just a financially stable entity. First, we will review results of becoming financially-empowered, and all the new flexibility that it brings as well as the concomitant pressures that ensue. Second, we'll review what your basic options are once you become empowered, and how to deal with each. I know that it may seem as though your empowerment is years away (as it may well be), but you need to start thinking now about how to position yourself, your board, and your staff to deal with these issues.

Finally, I will show you the long-term uses of empowerment that your organization may be able to utilize. As I have said many times before, empowerment takes a long time and a lot of work to achieve, and even more work to maintain. With that much of an investment, what are the long-term benefits? I'll show you what they could be, and you can decide which ones are right for your organization.

I hope that this chapter will not only provide you with new ideas, but, more importantly, give you the impetus to hang in there through all the work ahead.

A. THE RESULTS OF BECOMING FINANCIALLY EMPOWERED

In Chapter 1, I noted three reasons that it is important to become and remain financially empowered: doing more mission, becoming more competitive, and freeing senior staff to manage rather than to administer. Here, I want to expand on those thoughts, and provide you with some real-world examples.

1. DOING MORE MISSION

In *Mission-Based Management* I stressed that the single most important thing that should come about from becoming a mission-based organization would be that the organization could do *more mission with the limited resources* at hand. With an organization that is financially empowered, you will have *more resources to do more mission*. Think of how great it would be if your organization could do both: become mission-based *and* financially empowered.

But the crux of the issue, the rationale that you need to use with staff, funders, service recipients, and, even on some days, yourself, is that your empowerment is or will result in more mission. You must be able to draw a direct (and short) line between your actions and more mission capability and mission delivery. And here is where having and using the mission reserve that is a characteristic of empowerment is most valuable. While proper amounts of debt, appropriate uses of financial information, and even a sufficient cash reserve are nice, and will make you a healthier organization full of happier people who (logic tells you) will deliver better services, the causes and effects are not clear or immediate. The mission reserve is. If you are directly funding the provision of some service (no matter how small) with a mission reserve, a service that was not being provided (or a service that was being provided but not to certain people), you are doing more mission. Visibly. Demonstrably. And you can show that result to any naysayers that may be around.

● **FOR EXAMPLE:** An organization that I work with serves the developmentally disabled and uses their mission reserve to send adults with severe disabilities to summer camp each year. There is no state or Federal funding for this. It is very, very important to the campers and they look forward to it; they remember and talk about camp constantly. The senior management reminds staff all the time that there would be no camp without the mission reserve.

● **FOR EXAMPLE:** A museum funds campers as well, but a two-week summer day camp for inner city kids that exposes them to art of all kinds. This camp is funded solely from the mission reserve, and the year that there was no money in the reserve, there was no camp. The camp was very popular and there was a general outcry among the community, but the executive director did an excellent job of explaining how the museum used its "profits" to fund the camp and that attendance and donations had been down, and so had the funds used to pay for the camp. The community responded and the camp has run every year since. Missing the camp was an experience that the staff has worked long and hard not to repeat!

There is no limit to the kind of things that you can fund, but try to make them visible, identifiable, and appealing, like the idea of summer camp in the two examples above. What you should not do is use the mission reserve as a source of money to just do regular activities.

● **FOR EXAMPLE:** I was working with an organization that provided a wide variety of services to senior citizens. As they developed their empowerment plan and, more specifically, their mission reserve, the staff had decided how much to set aside each month, what percentage of unrestricted net, and had also worked out a method of distributing the funds including who would decide, when in the year, etc. Then they got to the issue of what kinds of things would be eligible. It was suggested that they make the things funded directly attributable to mission. They agreed and then ignored the agreement.

Some suggestions included: "We could fix all the vans up, because without the vans we can't do our transportation services." "We should re-landscape, because that will make our clients have a better impression when they come, and more will come and we'll do more mission." "We could replace the furnace, because everyone is cold and you can't do mission when people are cold."

I hope that you get the point here, that these people *did not* get the point. They were looking at any rationale, no matter how vague, to use up the money that would be available for any leftover project. Not the point. Doing *more* mission is the point. Make sure your people see it and that you reinforce it all the time.

2. BECOMING MORE COMPETITIVE

One of the most critical strategic benefits of becoming financially empowered is that it will give your organization the ability to be more competitive, and the not-for-profit sector is becoming increasingly market-based. If you empower, you have the funds (in an endowment, a cash reserve, or available debt) to take advantage of a competitive market opportunity when it arises. What is a "competitive market opportunity"? How about a Request for Proposal from the state government for a $500,000 per year new program, one that allows you to recover all your costs plus 3%, but doesn't start paying anything for 90 days after the first service is provided. Even if you have no costs before the starting day (a very unusual circumstance) you still will lend the state $125,000 interest free (the amount of receivables you will carry) for the life of program. Do you have deep enough pockets for this? Would you if you were financially empowered?

Another competitive advantage that empowerment offers is one of being attractive to contractors and funders because you are financially stable. They realize that you will be in business for a while, at least for as long as they need you, and that you will not be folding your tent and disappearing into the darkness of bankruptcy when they are depending on you. I am seeing this criteria more and more on RFPs: a statement of financial viability.

Finally, there is the trend toward more partnerships, mergers, and collaborations among not-for-profits. If you seek partners, look at merging, try to collaborate, it is always better to go into the negotiations with financial strength. Financially weak organizations unfortunately get taken to the cleaners in these negotiations all too often because they don't have the cash to back up their negotiating stance. Mergers, or at least merger offers, will almost certainly come your way in the next few years. Will you have the cash to be a "player?" If you are financially empowered, you will have the choice.

3. MANAGING VERSUS ADMINISTERING

If you have even spent a month where all you thought about was your organization's financial situation, where you woke up in the middle of the night with a great idea about how to save $75 (when your organization's annual budget is $4.5 million), if you are not sure that you can make payroll next Friday, then you know what the issue is here. If you are focused on day-to-day financial details because your finances are precarious, you simply can't be doing the job of a mission-based manager: you are spending all your time worrying about dollars, or even cents. As the CEO you must make sure that the organization survives, and so it is logical that you focus on the area of most need—money.

As your organization achieves financial empowerment you can break that cycle. If you are always focused on money, you can't be focused on other financially-related functions: planning, marketing, fundraising, public relations, reporting to the board, or even being a financial check and balance. Having some financial breathing room allows you to do what you should: step back and look at the big picture.

If you let it. If you like the way that you manage your organization now, it may be tough to make the change. But empowerment will at least offer you the opportunity that you haven't had in the past.

The results of empowerment should embolden you, your staff, and board to move ahead. Achieving and maintaining financial empowerment is a long process and one that is not without sacrifice. The benefits discussed above should help get you started.

B. OPTIONS FOR ACTION

To look at the issues related to empowerment more closely, let's examine some options that you will have for taking action once you are empowered and how those actions could affect you, your board, your staff, your funders, and the people that you serve.

For the purposes of discussion, let's assume that your organization is already empowered, that you now have a 120-day cash reserve, 6% of your income coming from your endowment, a reasonable debt load that you are comfortably servicing, and a 7.5% projected net revenue over expenses for this year which will translate into a $90,000 "surplus". Your long-term projections are for more of the same in the coming three years. You have diversified your income streams and are not as dependent as you were on one main source of revenue. You have even developed methods to keep what you earn.

Sounds pretty nice, yes? With a situation like that, what problems could you have, at least on the financial side? I'm not sure that I would call this a problem, but you do have some difficult choices, ones that you do not have if you are financially impoverished. But these choices, once made and acted on, will define your organization well into the future, will distinguish a mission-based organization from a simple not-for-profit, will affect staff morale and the quality of services your organization provides long after you are gone.

Let me suggest a set of choices that are in reality the extremes of the range of possibilities that you can consider. I am sure that every reader will come down somewhere in the middle, but I want you to consider the benefits and drawbacks of all of these "radical" solutions.

I will group the choices into two pairs, one pair dealing with cash, and one dealing with how you portray your organization's empowerment outside your doors. These pairs of options are:

For cash:

▶ *Build a large mission reserve*

▶ *Spend your mission reserve*

For public relations:

▶ **Hide your empowerment**

▶ **Flaunt your empowerment**

Let's look at each, its benefits and drawbacks, and my recommendations on how to deal with it.

1. BUILD A LARGE MISSION RESERVE vs. SPEND YOUR MISSION RESERVE

It is always easier to spend than to save, but some organizations get into the savings mode so well that they forget the point. Having <u>reasonable</u> reserves is the key. Is a $200,000 reserve enough, or one that equals 90 days of operations? How about an endowment of $4,000,000 or $40,000,000? And what about the mission reserve? Should we spend it as we get it, or let it grow to a certain size and then spend it all? What's better? Let's look at an example of saving too much:

● **FOR EXAMPLE:** A client organization of ours is a school for children with a sensory disability. Their annual budget is about $15,000,000 and they have an endowment of $61,000,000! What's the problem? The problem is that the classrooms are bare, there are few if any computers, the windows leak cold air in the winter and hot in the summer. The place looks beautiful from the outside and like an inner city school on the inside. "With all your money, why don't you fix this place up?" I asked the board. "We don't want to have too low a reserve," they said!

By now, you should be able to recite the benefits of having a mission reserve: it shows that you are doing more mission with your empowerment—that's the point. But there are also drawbacks of amassing a large reserve, most notably that it takes time and there needs to be a fairly short time between the sacrifice of setting the reserve aside and the applying of the reserve to the mission. I assume that you will be sharing financial information with staff and board, and they will know the size of the reserve, and how it is funded. How long will they wait before the pressure to spend this "cash hoard" gets too intense?

My suggestion is to develop some criteria for your reserve early, even before you start to accumulate the money. Determine a process for the allocation of the reserve. Will the decision be made by line staff, management, board members, or a combination? What will the criteria be for funding, for voting, for allocation? You are, in effect, setting up a mini, internal foundation and now you have to decide how to make funding decisions. Will you let anyone in the organization offer a use for the funds, or will only the committee members be able to do that? Will you allocate annually, or quarterly, or on an as-needed basis?

These are all your calls, but I suggest setting up the process early, so that people know the rules before the money starts to pile up. In fact, one of the best kickoffs to this kind of committee I've seen is to convene the group, work out the rules, and then pick your first item to fund—even before there is any money available. That then gives a target for the reserve to achieve, and holds off the people who want to spend it now.

2. HIDE YOUR EMPOWERMENT vs. FLAUNT YOUR EMPOWERMENT

Do you have a funder that may want you to spend your money before they give you theirs? Or what about small donors? Will they resent your 90-day reserve? How about staff? Would they want to see any cash in their paychecks rather than on your balance sheet?

On the other hand, what about funders who want you to be financially stable before they fund you, or staff who want to be assured that you will not be in receivership in two weeks, or excellent board candidates who are worried about coming on to the board of a sinking (or even heavily listing) ship?

These are the questions that will help you frame your answer to the question above. If you hide your empowerment—or at least don't flaunt it—you may appease staff, funders, and donors who subscribe to the old school of thinking that you can't do well doing good. But you lose the benefits of looking good to new school thinkers who see you as a mission-based business.

My recommendation: be proud of your empowerment. It's out there for anyone who sees your financials anyway. But don't ever just tell people how well off your organization is and how long it took you to get there. Remember to focus on the mission results: "We can do more mission, more often, more responsively than ever before and here are some examples." Tie your empowerment to your mission, and eventually even the naysayers will come around.

C. LONG-TERM USES OF EMPOWERMENT

As a mission-based manager, it is important for you to have a long-term strategic plan. In fact, the use of a vision, or strategic plan, is a key component of a successful not-for-profit, as I noted in the first chapter. In planning, you look at the environment you will be in and the resources you have and can acquire, and compile a vision of what you want to accomplish during the planning period—five years, for example. As your organization becomes more and more financially empowered, you will be able to use that empowerment as a resource for your strategic thinking and planning. Thus empowerment is not just for today, for this year, for next year. Rather, it becomes a way of life, and a means to a long-term end.

In a number of sections of this chapter, I have noted that your organization will be more competitive the more empowered it is. As you plan your market strategies, think through new geographic areas to serve, or new groups of people to help. Empowerment is the key: you have the venture capital to allow you to take more risks (prudent ones of course). And, as your markets change, you can be more responsive. For example, if a funder goes to a 90-day payment cycle from a 45-day cycle, you can accommodate them more easily than a financially strapped organization. If your service recipients are used to more personal attention, you can invest in that by adding more staff. You will able to be more competitive.

But, of course, financial empowerment does not by itself guarantee your beating the competition. It simply allows a lot more options for you. Your attitude toward competition, your organization's bias toward marketing, your staff and board's willingness to take risks and be flexible, your ability to price accurately; all of these bear heavily on your ability to compete.

Speaking of flexibility, empowerment offers more of that as well, if your attitude and demeanor go along. Having cash to apply to a changing situation offers more options to you as you try to accommodate an increasingly fast rate of change. For example, if a funder demands that you invest in new software to accommodate their reimbursement system, you can do it now and invest in training quickly, where another organization may have to apply for a grant for the software and never have the funds to adequately train staff.

This flexibility and competitiveness also shows up in being more entrepreneurial. Again, you can take more risks if you are not at financial ruin's door. You can invest in new ideas, try new business ventures, and do new services because you have the money. Long-term thinking can change from "Can we hold on to what we've got?" to "What are the new things that we should do?"—a major psychological shift. One of the characteristics of empowerment is to have business income, and business begets more business if you keep focused.

Within the limits of staying financially flexible, and not too tied to your property, financial empowerment also allows you to buy and or keep up your property and equipment. UPS, for example, cleans every vehicle from their 747's to their two-wheeled hand carts, every night. That's expensive, but it pays them back in longer use, lower maintenance costs, and a better image. But you have to have the cash to do the cleaning. Empowerment gives you those choices. You also have more choices on how to finance equipment or property purchases. Perhaps its best to have your endowment purchase a building and lease it to you, or simply to loan you the money at cost rather than at open market rates. Again, you have more options.

Finally, you can do what few not-for-profits do, and that is service-based research. What works, what doesn't, and how can we tell the difference. Trying new things is the only way we learn, and part of being entrepreneurial, being flexible, and being a competitor is trying new things. Many service firms in the for-profit sector spend 10 to 15% of their budget on research and development. How about you? No, I know you have never had the funds. But in a few years you may. What new things do you want to try?

Imagine the benefits in terms of marketing, fundraising, competitiveness, and visibility to say that you were the trend setter, the model, the group that discovered this new great way to do mission! Good stuff, and the option to do it is provided by your empowerment.

Note that good research calls for good researchers, so unless you have a couple of hotshot PhDs on staff you will probably want to collaborate with a university or think tank. If this is in your long-range plans, start those conversations now: most academic institutions make government look like greased lighting in terms of making decisions and moving ahead. Don't wait to call until you have the cash.

All of these are new ways to look at your long-term plans. Start those thought processes now, think big, and think empowered.

RECAP

In this chapter, I have shown you the most important link that you can make with the tools that this book will provide you: the link between your mission and your financial empowerment.

First, we reviewed the results of your organization's achieving financial empowerment and noted that there will be positive and potentially negative results from this effort. I then listed some options for how you deal with cash and your financial status that present themselves to you when your organization is financially empowered, listing the pros and cons of each choice.

In the last part of the chapter, I gave you some ideas about the long-term uses of empowerment, including ways to improve your funding diversity, expand your markets, fund your research, marketing, and planning efforts, and appeal to new groups that may have interest in a financially healthy organization.

As I noted at the beginning of the book and in this chapter, the point of financial empowerment is not to have your organization get rich. It is not simply to have an attractive balance sheet, or a happy finance committee of the board. Financial empowerment must be joined with your mission to make the circle complete: you started out with the mission, and you went off to attain financial empowerment. Once you have achieved it, you need to come back around the circle and join up with the mission again, supporting it as it has supported you in your quest for empowerment.

I hope that this chapter has provided the mission momentum that you need to move ahead. Starting in the next chapter, we will begin to work our way through the technical skills and tools that you will need to make the journey to empowerment.

4. How Much money Will You Need?

OVERVIEW

You want your organization to become and remain empowered. You have seen all the characteristics of empowerment and they look like they require a lot of money. But how much will you need and where will the money come from? Part of the answer to that question is contained in this chapter.

One of the key parts that is missing in the training of not-for-profit managers is the concept of working capital, and that will be the focus of the first part of this chapter. While it sounds dry and only of interest to CPA types, the lack of understanding of the working capital needs of your organization may be what caused you to run short of cash in the past, and will again if you don't pay attention to it. So, in this chapter, we'll look at the issue of how much money you will need to grow, to expand, to adjust to changes in the market, and look to the speed with which your funders pay you. I'll provide you with forms and formats to plan your working capital needs and your expenditures for capital equipment. I'll show you how growth eats up cash and how to predict how much you will need.

By the end of the chapter, you should have a good handle on what your financial needs are for growth and empowerment.

A. HOW MUCH CASH WILL YOU NEED?

How much cash will you need? The answer, of course, is: "It depends". It depends on a lot of things, including how fast your income grows, how fast your funders pay you, your mix of funders, how many capital improvements or purchases you need to make, and how much you need to start up any business ventures. Notice that in the list above I did not mention monthly or annual expenditures. I did not mention payroll, rent, or utilities. This is intentional, because too many managers focus only on budget and forget about cash flow.

Let me be emphatic: good budget development and monitoring is critical to financial empowerment. That is why we'll spend an entire chapter on it (Chapter 9). But here we are concerned about cash, and cash is the equivalent of blood to an organization; without it you die.

B. BUDGETING

The first part of knowing how much you will need is budgeting. You project your budget each year, and the budget is part science, part art, part guess, part good luck. It is a document usually built on the past, predicting the future, but with impact now. All sorts of policy decisions impact on and are impacted by your budget. Your budgeting process needs to tell you these things:

1. Is the organization going to grow or shrink next year? By how much? In which programs?

2. Is the organization going to change funders, adding or dropping any?

3. Are major capital investments in the offing for the next year?

4. What is the projected income and expenditure spread (the profit or loss) for each month and for the year?

Armed with this information from the budget, you can move ahead to calculate the working capital you will need to support the budget.

C. WORKING CAPITAL

Here is a term that is central to cash flow planning, and yet few business people and fewer mission-based managers really understand it. Let's start with an explanation of what working capital really is, then move to how it affects you and finish with ways that you can predict your needs. Let me underscore the importance of this by stating simply: if you don't understand working capital, you probably will bankrupt your organization, particularly if you are growing fast. I know most readers want their organizations to grow, so pay attention—this is really important.

Working capital is, at its core, the money you need to run your organization between the time you prepare and provide a product or service and the time you get paid. The amount of working capital your organization needs is a function of the volume of products or services you sell, the delay time between the provision and payment, and the amount of delay time between the initiation of the provision and the provision itself. Let's look at each of these contributing factors (volume of products or services, delay in payment, and delay in provision) in the following three examples.

● **FOR EXAMPLE:** An organization provides counseling services at $20 per hour, which is their actual cost of the counselor plus overhead. Today, one counselor provides 8 hours of service, billing $160. Tomorrow the counselor provides another $160 worth of services, and the next day and the next. If the services are being reimbursed under a Medicaid contract, it may be 120 days until the organization gets paid. In the interim, what pays the bills? The organization's working capital. Now imagine that there are 20 counselors, each providing $160 worth of services each day. The working capital needs just went up 20 times. That is an example of a *VOLUME* effect on the amount of working capital.

● **FOR EXAMPLE:** In the organization above, let's go back to the single counselor. Let's assume that the payment delay (the amount of time it takes the organization to bill, and then the payor to pay the bill after the service is rendered) is 120 days. Suddenly in an effort to balance the budget the governor declares that Medicaid bills won't be paid for 180 days. What just happened to the working capital needs of the organization? They went up 50%. On the other hand, what if the counselor starts seeing private pay patients for half of her day every day, and they pay at the time service is rendered. The delay in payment is now dramatically reduced as is the working capital need. This is an example of the *DELAY IN PAYMENT* effect on the amount of working capital your organization needs.

● **FOR EXAMPLE:** The organization starts a small gift shop to supplement its income. The starting inventory of goods costs $45,000. It is anticipated that the turnover of these goods will be 48 days. But then new goods will need to be purchased, and put on the shelf in anticipation of sale. If the organization were actually producing goods, it might need to keep a certain number in inventory to satisfy different demand cycles. In both cases, money has been spent in anticipation of a sale. Even if payment is immediate at the gift shop, or upon delivery of the product, there is still a working capital need. These are examples of the *DELAY IN PROVISION* effect on the amount of working capital.

The sum and substance of all these examples are two key principals that you need to understand: that growth costs money, and that cash is blood. The little-known truth is that more small businesses go out of business *making* money rather than losing it. Why? Because they run out of cash. The most prone to cash shortages are rapidly growing new businesses.

Thus, you need to celebrate your growth with the understanding that it costs cash, and the cost is early and permanent.

● **FOR EXAMPLE:** Assume that your organization was just awarded a $1,000,000 per year contract. The payor, your county commission, pays its bills 90 days late. Even if you have no true start-up costs, and can just start providing service on Day 1 (in other words, in the cheapest possible case), you have just loaned the county $250,000—in cash, real money. Your flexibility is reduced $250,000. Your interest earnings are down. Oh, and the loan is for the duration of the contract. If the contract goes for 10 years, you won't see the $250,000 for decade, or until the county speeds up its payments, which for most governments is about as likely as the *National Enquirer* passing up the chance to report an Elvis sighting.

The point of all this is that you need to be aware of the cash costs of growth. This does not mean that you shouldn't grow, nor does it mean that you shouldn't be pleased if your organization was awarded the $1,000,000 contract. What I want you to develop is the ability to see the cost of that contract in cash, not just in income and expense. Having a cash flow projection, done every two weeks and projecting out six months in advance, is your best protection against running up on the rocks. I'll show you how to develop and use a cash flow projection statement a bit later.

PREDICTING YOUR WORKING CAPITAL NEEDS

To accurately predict your working capital needs you need to know a number of things. These are:

1. *How much income will you get from each source?*

2. *How long is the delay between the provision of service and the receipt of cash from the funder? (a combination of delay of payment and delay of provision)?*

3. What are the changes(if any) in these numbers from previous years?

Let's look at an example of what I mean by all of this. In the table below, there is a working capital projection for the coming fiscal year. The organization in question has four existing programs and is establishing a fifth in the coming year. You can see that the three programs that are growing are going to increase their working capital needs, and the one program that is shrinking will reduce the overall working capital needs. One program (residential) has its days-to-payment increasing as well, further exacerbating the cash (working capital) needs. Finally, the new program is very cash intensive, with both start-up dollars and delay of payment dollars involved. The bottom line is that this agency needs to come up with $94,973 in cash next year just to stay in business and add the prevention program.

PROGRAMS	STARTUP COSTS	CURRENT BUDGET	NEXT YR BUDGET	Days Payable Currently	Days Payable Next Year	CASH NEED
RESIDENTIAL	0	440,000	480,000	95	100	10,959
DAY	0	327,500	410,000	56	56	12,658
OUTREACH	0	457,000	395,000	55	55	(9,342)
HOT LUNCH	0	110,000	115,000	45	45	616
PREVENTION (new)	45,000	0	197,000	0	65	80,082
			TOTAL NEW CASH NEEDED:			$94,973

D. CAPITAL INVESTMENTS

Capital investments are the expenditures that your organization makes on things such as buildings, building improvements, equipment, and vehicles. They will affect your cash needs in a big way. In most cases, these kinds of needs do not sneak up on you. You know if your vehicles are old and will soon need to be overhauled or replaced. You know that the roof on your buildings is 20 years old and leaks whenever the humidity gets over 50%. You can tell that you are rapidly running out of space for your program. While there are occasions that you can be legitimately surprised, they should be few and far between.

The result? You should be able to plan your capital needs two to three years in advance with about 90% accuracy. I know that prices will change in the interim, and so will your needs, somewhat. But just as with cash flow projections, the fact that your predictions won't be perfect is not an excuse for not trying to make them as good as possible. Thus part of good financial empowerment is to predict the shortfalls and fill them with one or more of the sources of financing that we talk about in the next section. Look at the sample chart below. It gives you an idea of the kind of thing that I am talking about, and the level of detail. While your organization's needs will be different in scope and size, having a handle on your big-ticket expenditures early helps prepare you to work better with your lenders, or with your finance committee to come up with the funds well in advance of the need, and not in a crisis atmosphere.

CAPITAL EXPENDITURE PLANNING SHEET			
YEAR	ITEM	PROJECTED COST	TOTAL FOR YEAR
FY 97	1. Two new vans 2. Eight computer upgrades 3. New carpet in work spaces 4. Rewire 1 group home	1. $44,000 2. $ 2,600 3. $ 6,900 4. $12,500	$66,000
FY 98	1. Purchase new office space 2. Leasehold improvement 3. New network hard drive 4. Purchase additional van	1. $115,000 2. $ 28,500 3. $ 11,700 4. $ 23,000	$178,200
FY 99	1. Purchase 2 group homes 2. Roof replacement on office 3. Rewire 2 group homes	1. $240,000 2. $ 65,000 3. $ 28,000	$333,000
FY 00	1. New parking lot paved 2. Drainage work at 2 group homes 3. Asbestos removal	1. $ 56,000 2. $ 14,500 3. $ 70,000	$140,500

As you can see from the table, the organization really will be in a cash need situation in the third year of the projection. Whether they start saving now, or start getting themselves in shape to borrow some of the money, is their choice and the choice of their lenders, but they need to take some action now to avoid a problem down the line. It should also be pointed out that some of the needs, such as parking lot repaving, roof work, computer equipment, and rewiring are difficult to borrow for. They will probably need to be financed in cash, from savings or reserves.

In any event the ability to look out and see what is needed and when will significantly improve your ability to become and remain empowered.

E. RESERVES

In Chapter 2, I reviewed the characteristics of empowerment, and two of them had to do with reserves. The first was an operating reserve, the cash and easily sold securities that equal at least 90 days of operating disbursements. The second was the mission reserve, those funds that you put away to be able to apply to mission-related needs in your community when there are no other funders who can respond quickly enough or in a manner consistent with your values.

You must decide as a matter of policy how many days operating reserve you need, and then, if you do not already have that amount available, set a deadline for getting there, and set a budget to accomplish your goal. The same is true for your mission reserve. Set a goal figure, set a deadline for it, and start putting some away every month. For example, if you want a $100,000 mission reserve within 5 years, you are going to have to come up with approximately $20,000 per year—or about $1,666 per month—month in and month out (minus a little interest) to get there.

The amount of reserves that you decide is prudent and the speed with which you need to get from your current status to the levels set in your goals will together dictate how much you need to plan for reserves.

F. PLANNING AIDS

Now that we have covered the big items in your estimation of how much money you will need, let's look at some planning tools that can help you. The forms below are general ones, and you can adapt them to your own particular needs, but they outline the key things you will need to do each year to make sure you don't run out of money.

PROGRAMS	STARTUP COSTS	CURRENT BUDGET	NEXT YR BUDGET	Days Payable Currently	Days Payable Next Year	CASH NEED
New Programs						
A						
B						
Growth						
A						
B						
			TOTAL NEW CASH NEEDED:			

Note that the working capital sheet includes locations for new programs as well as growth. The cash flow projection sheet will need to focus on receipts and disbursements, not income and expenses. Thus there is a line for debt service (the sum of interest and principal payments) in cash flow, instead of interest and depreciation line items that appear on an income and expense statement.

Cash Flow	Month 1	Month 2	Month 3	Month 4	Month 5	Month 6
Receipts						
Grants						
Contracts						
User fees						
Donations						
Loans Recieved						
Total Receipts						
Disbursements						
Salaries						
Fringe Benefits						
Rent						
Debt Service						
Other expenses						
Other expenses						
Other expenses						
Other expenses						
Other expenses						
Other expenses						
Other expenses						
Total Disbursements:						
Net Cash Flow						
Cash Balance						

RECAP

In this chapter we reviewed the key area of getting a handle on how much money you will really need, including the fact that growth costs money, sometimes a significant amount. We covered ways to predict your working capital needs, your needs for long- and short-term capital investments, and how to finance your reserves, both operational and mission.

I hope that you have a better understanding now as to why you may have run out of cash in the past and how to be better at predicting your cash needs in the future.

So much of what is in this chapter relates to other areas of the book, that I feel obligated to note other chapters and their subjects here for fear that you will feel that this is a self-contained subject. It's not. Obviously, not running out of money depends not only on working capital projections and cash flow, but also on good budgeting, which is the sole subject of Chapter 9. Sharing information internally is key to staying on budget and making good predictions about when heavy cash expenditures will pop up. Better ways to use your financial information are the basis for the material in Chapter 7.

Financial empowerment means knowing what your needs are to do good mission. Now you know the working capital and long-term capital needs you will face. But as I have said repeatedly, achieving and retaining financial empowerment for your organization also requires ongoing discipline. One of those disciplines is learning how to deal with your traditional funders in a different way. By doing so you can get more money from existing sources. That is the subject of our next chapter.

5. Working With Traditional Funders

OVERVIEW

I think it goes without saying that your organization does not have enough money to meet the mission needs in your community. It also is important to state that your current sources of funds—either from donations, foundations, government contracts, or grants, are insufficient in their volume or restrict your ability to retain funds. In short, you don't have enough money to meet all the needs of your service recipients.

Here's the bad news: you never will. But you need to find ways to bring in more money while at the same time spending less if you want to be more efficient in wringing the most mission out of every dollar. In this chapter we will start the process of increasing your income by dealing in new ways with your traditional funders.

In the first section of the chapter we will start with the funder's perspective on the issue of your organization becoming financially empowered. You need to have this perspective to better understand the challenges that you face as you move ahead.

Next, we'll review each of the traditional kinds of funders you have, and look at the best and worst parts of receiving money from each type.

After that, we'll focus on the best way to treat a funder: like a customer, instead of someone resembling a mortal enemy. I'll even show you ways that you may want to involve your funders *more* in your organization rather than less, and why this can be a good thing for everyone.

In the fourth section, we'll look at ways that you can be more knowledgeable about your funders' regulations and how this can work to your benefit. Knowledge is power, remember?

One key way to overcome resistance to your empowerment from your funders is to talk to them about your mission outcomes rather than just the size of your bank account. The next section will provide you some strategies for that, as well as detail a number of examples. By the end of the chapter you should have an excellent handle on how to deal with your funders to get the most from the relationship.

One cautionary note before we move into the meat of the chapter. Increasing income is not simply chasing dollars. As you saw in Chapter 4, growth costs money. Too many not-for-profits chase any and all funds available, and in the process lose their focus on the mission while at the same time doing major damage to their cash flow. What I hope to accomplish in this chapter is to show you some options, some new ways of thinking about your funders, some alternative sources of funds, so that you can make a *focused selection* of the kinds of funds you want to pursue. You need to seek your growth in a carefully planned manner, one that enhances your ability to pursue your mission. If you just go after anything green, you will squander your resources, lose your focus, and be unable to do anything well, including your existing services. Planned, focused growth is essential.

A. THE FUNDER'S PERSPECTIVE ON YOUR EMPOWERMENT

We all have different perspectives on issues, just like the proverbial blind men who each grabbed a part of an elephant and described what they thought the elephant looked like in widely varied terms. While you may think that financial empowerment is a great and glorious thing, your funder(s) may have a different point of view, and it is essential that you find out what their perspective is so that you can work to have them as enamored of your empowerment as you are.

First, let's look at what most funders really feel about you: *that you can't do well doing good.* This feeling, that your not-for-profit cannot and should not have any financial wherewithal, that because you help people you must be poor, is widespread and longstanding. It dates from the time when the church and church-related organizations did most of the charity work in this country. Whether they were nuns, priests, or members of the Salvation Army, the people involved had taken a vow of poverty. They lived an austere life of good works. They were wonderful people who did much needed work. But their lives, their living conditions, and their financial states became over time the norm against which all not-for-profits are judged today.

☞ **HANDS-ON:** If funders have this perspective how can you overcome it? Unfortunately, there is no short road to a solution. You have to impress on them that you earn your money, that by having some capital you can do things in your community on your own. You have to act like you can manage your money, and stop whining about every rate, every cost disallowance. You have to turn down funder's money in certain cases where you can't make the costs equate to the price. In short, you have to start acting as though the funder is the customer and you are the provider of service.

Second, many funders (although not as many as in the case of "not doing well doing good") feel that they know what's best for you; that they, in effect, own you. This feeling of superiority and a combination of vested interest or outright control is not unusual for someone who, in many cases, controls your destiny through their decision to fund or not to fund. When someone "plays God" in the sense of funding decisions, it's not a big leap to decide he or she can be God in other areas as well, such as having omnipotent wisdom. This perspective can really get in your way if the funder gets upset about issues not related to the services that they fund.

● **FOR EXAMPLE:** In 1991, I was asked to work with the Illinois Department of Mental Health and Developmental Disabilities (DMHDD) to review and rewrite their regulations regarding "arms-length transactions and related corporations." I knew, from working with organizations that DMHDD funded, that the regulations were really a problem. The rules called for DMHDD to review potential conflicts from *all* contracts, whether or not those contracts related to the services that DMHDD purchased, and required that no related corporation could contract with a grantee, even if the contract was not related to the services that DMHDD funded. We got the regulations changed, and the revised policies are now used by about 60 state agencies nationwide.

● **FOR EXAMPLE:** The Federal government funds the development and operation of rural health clinics as a way of improving the access to medical practitioners in rural communities. These clinics, known in the jargon as "330" and "331" clinics (relating to the parts of the enabling legislation that funds them), get part of their funds from the Feds, part from private pay patients, and the rest from medical insurers. Even though some clinics get only 10-15% of their income from the Federal government, every dollar they spend is reviewed and questioned; every piece of property, whether a building, vehicle, or stethoscope, is considered Federal property and cannot be sold or even disposed of without Federal approval.

It is these kinds of examples that set a precedent for others in government service to think of you and your organization as really an extension of their department or agency. We'll talk more about how to overcome this perspective in the section on "Knowing the Regulations of Your Funders".

B. TRADITIONAL FUNDERS AND THEIR LIMITATIONS

Not-for-profits get their funds from a multitude of sources: government, foundations, fundraising, United Way, volunteer services, in-kind donations, insurance reimbursement, user fees, etc. Each of these sources can be further divided. For example, fundraising has many components including direct mail, large donors, bequests, sponsorships, special events and direct solicitation. Government not only can be broken down into geographic representation: Federal, State, County, Municipality, District, but also by different departments and further by program within a specific department. For example a not-for-profit might earn funds from three different programs of their state welfare department or from four different programs of the U.S. Department of Housing and Urban Development.

What we will do in this section is look at just the major categories and generalize about each type of funding's advantages, disadvantages, and limitations. Then I will predict the biggest change that will occur for that funding source in the next ten years. This is fraught with the danger of over-simplification, but I think you will see the point that I am trying to make: that your traditional sources of funds have some real limitations in the way that they can work with you. While these limitations may be changing, you need to understand what you can and cannot do within certain funding types.

1. GOVERNMENT

Like all not-for-profits, your organization gets a substantial financial benefit from government: the exemption from taxes earned in pursuit of your mission; your 501(c)(3) classification. Beyond that, most non-church not-for-profits get some funding from one or more government agencies. In fact, and to no one's surprise, government is the largest customer of the not-for-profit industry. Some have even characterized the not-for-profit community as an extension of the government. For many readers, one or more government funding streams will make up over 75% of their total annual organizational income.

Thus, working with government is essential for most not-for-profits. Let's take a look at the advantages and disadvantages of government funding. Again, remember that I am forced to generalize. The government agency or agencies that you contract with may be significantly different than the description below.

▶ *Advantages*

The big advantage of government is that it is, well, big. It has lots of parts, and lots of money (at least relative to your budget). Additionally, it often has a legislative mandate or court order to do something requiring it to seek out services each year. Thus, once you get established as a service provider, a continuity of funding (despite what you read in the press) is pretty much assured, barring an impropriety on your part, a major political shift, or a truly seismic budget problem. The final advantage of government funding is that most of the rules of how to apply for funds are spelled out in regulations which are public information. Thus, if you are new to an area, you can find out about the ground rules fairly easily.

▶ *Disadvantages*

Those who pay the money call the tune. The most discordant part of that tune is the oversight that comes as part of the cost of government funding. While this is everyone's biggest gripe, you simply have to accept it as one of the costs of doing business. It is going to be with us for as long as the media are out looking for scandals. Notice, however, that I have used the term costs. This is intentional. When contracting with government, many not-for-profits ignore the non-productive time that goes into writing the reports, documenting services, filling in reimbursement forms. This is short-sighted and can lead to your doing work at a loss. There are many costs to government money; try to remember them all when you are developing a price or a bid.

The second disadvantage is the way that government often distributes its funds. While more and more agencies are moving toward true fee-for-service contracting, where you provide service x to population y for z dollars, this is not yet true for a majority of government contracting. Much of it is still in the form of grants with two big problems: matching requirements and "use it or lose it" stipulations (if you don't spend all the money we gave you we get it back; thus you have no incentive to save on expenses). More about these after our list of funders.

▶ *Limitations*

Government agencies usually have very little flexibility in awarding grants and contracts (despite the press to the contrary). They are forced to go by the regulations and the enabling legislation. Thus it is difficult for them to add a little here or reward you there—no matter how good your program is—unless there is a provision for such action in the regulations.

Secondly, almost all government agencies write one-year contracts, as a result of the annual budget cycle that the Federal government and most states use. Thus your long-term funding is never *really* long-term: it is subject to annual changes. This can also be a problem for some of your lenders.

Third, most government agencies are interested in what their legislatures tell them they are interested in, or in what they have paid for in previous years. Thus if they fund a pilot for an innovative new program, and it works, they may be very interested in expanding it. But the same innovative program, funded by local donations, may hold no interest for them in terms of expansion, no matter how successful it is. In short, innovation, new ideas, and risk taking are not government's strong suit.

▶ ▶ *Biggest Change in the Next Ten Years*

Movement to competition: true bidding for all services.

2. FOUNDATIONS

Private foundations come in all shapes and sizes, for all sorts of purposes and with funding for all kinds of not-for-profits. With the slowdown in the growth of government spending in the early 1980s, the competition for foundation spending became and remains intense. They are, however, still a major source of funds for many organizations and thus bear examination. I must emphasize that there are thousands of private foundations in the United States alone, and the reader is cautioned not to assume that my generalizations apply to all of them. Each foundation has its own application procedures, funding cycles, restrictions, and areas of interest.

Additionally, the ways that foundations fund things are changing. Traditional grants still are the most prevalent. However, loans and what are called Program Related Investments, or PRIs, are becoming increasingly popular with foundations. PRIs are a way of getting money to a not-for-profit and then getting it back once the new program gets underway and can stand on its own. This is a laudable trend, and you should investigate the availability of this kind of money with any foundation that you pursue.

▶ Advantages

If you can get a foundation interested in the same things you are, they can be very generous in getting you started in a new area of service or a new innovative method of delivering existing services. Thus, a foundation grant can give you the seed money to reduce your dependence on government funding. Additionally, foundations will often approve multi-year funding, usually based on certain outcome measures being achieved each year. Once you secure this kind of funding, it can often provide longer-term stability than with government funds.

▶Disadvantages

The first two disadvantages I have already noted: intense competition and a wide diversity of funding cycles, application procedures, and interest. Thus the administrative and fund-seeking costs of researching, applying for, and retaining a foundation grant may be very high. Next comes a fairly standard matching requirement, ranging from 10% to 40%. This means that your organization may have to come up with as much as $2 for every $3 the foundation invests with you; a steep price. The next disadvantage is the flip side of the advantage noted above: foundations are usually uninterested in funding ongoing operations and services. This means that you will probably have to be developing something new (and thus inherently risky) to attract foundation dollars.

▶Limitations

The key limitation of most foundation funding is one that I frankly like: if the foundation funds a new program or method of service delivery for your organization, you will have to show how you can support the new program on your own in a set period of time. In essence the foundation is forcing you to make the program stand on its own and not become a permanent subsidy. This condition is often tough to meet, but one that should enter your thinking with *all* new or expanded programs.

▶▶Biggest Change in the Next Ten Years

Continued movement to program related investments (PRIs rather than grants).

3. UNITED WAY

There are hundreds of United Ways in the United States. Their original purpose was to coordinate and consolidate the fundraising in a given community, thus reducing those costs for most agencies, and reducing the "pester factor" for the citizens of the community (people wouldn't be knocking on the door every day asking for money). In my view it hasn't worked out that way. Notwithstanding that, many readers get some funds, perhaps significant funds, from their local United Way. So let's examine this funding source.

▶ *Advantages*
United Way money in the past has been a fairly predictable and consistent source for those not-for-profits already "in the club"; those getting funds. It is also, depending on your local UW, a fairly cheap way of getting money. Finally, it is a real and significant link to the community, and in most communities it is an implicit endorsement of the quality of your programs to be able to say that you are a United Way Agency.

▶ *Disadvantages*
First, to accept United Way money you usually have to agree to not raise funds on your own during the United Way funding drive. In our community that fundraising effort now extends from July through January, effectively eliminating over half the year.
Second, an increasing number of United Ways want you to submit to a rigorous application procedure for your funding. This paperwork, and the associated appearances by board and staff in front of the United Way committees that hand out the funds, is expensive. So expensive that a number of our clients have calculated that the expense of application (in staff time alone) is more than their grant, and have dropped out. The third disadvantage is that of your organization's funding from United Way rising and falling with all others in the community: if donations to your United Way decline, as they have nationwide in the past few years, you will get less money, even if you are the most efficient and effective program in town.

▶ *Limitations*
Most United Way funding goes to social services of some kind, with the arts and educational services getting less. It also usually goes to "poorer" organizations, the ones that cannot make it on their own. Thus, if your organization becomes financially empowered, you may well lose your ability to attract United Way money.

▶ ▶ *Biggest Change in the Next Ten Years*
More competition for the donated dollar. More accountability required from grantees.

4. DONATIONS

Donations from individuals are still a major source of income for many not-for-profits, and that is as it should be. Your not-for-profit has a resource that you need to exploit: the tax deductibility of donations made to your organization. For some readers, these donations may come from mail order solicitation or from special events, or from the efforts of a full-time fundraiser. They may come from businesses, or from church congregations affiliated with your organization.

Whatever the source, there are a few core rules of fundraising. First, it costs more than you think, especially for the beginner. There is a tremendous amount of time, energy, and effort put into soliciting initial—as well as repeat—gifts. Thus, the money is not *free*. The secret is to set a limit on how much you are willing to spend to get certain types of money, and then work to stay within that amount. These costs will vary. They may be low in relation to total donations for direct mail, high for special events, and somewhere in the middle for larger donations.

Second, don't expect an immediate return on your investment. Put a different way, fundraising will not help you solve this year's budget deficit, particularly if you have not emphasized it in the past. Getting people to part with their money to support what you do is a long-term task.

Third, the less you can use donations to support current operations, the better. Too many organizations depend on all of their donations to balance their budget. Having donations support a particular service or program that loses money each year may be good strategy now. But if the donations dry up so does the program. Try to put donations into your foundation, and use the income from the foundation to run your organization, not the donations themselves. Then you'll have the gift that keeps on giving.

With those ideas in mind, let's look at the advantages and disadvantages of donations.

▶ *Advantages*
These are unrestricted funds (unless the donor targets them for specific uses). Thus you can set them aside, use them for the area of the organization that needs the most help, use them as matching funds for other grants, or start something new. Donations have real flexibility, and, as noted above, can form the basis of continued unrestricted

income from an endowment or foundation. Additionally, donations can build loyalty to your organization. People who donate actually invest in your organization and have a commitment to see you succeed. Thus the donor base links you to your community in a very real sense. Donors can be sources of expertise, volunteers, or even board and committee members.

▶ *Disadvantages*

Private fundraising is extremely sophisticated and competitive, and getting more so every day. Even medium-sized not-for-profits are hiring full-time staff or consultants to help with their fundraising programs. This means significant up-front cash commitments years in advance of any financial return. Second, having unrestricted funds can actually hurt you with some funders. For example, you may be forced to spend donations before you take money from some government or foundation programs.

▶ *Limitations*

Donations do not come in on their own. They are in essence, one-time acts of charity, and, to renew those acts, you have to stay close to the customer; the donor. Also, you have to live with and be expert on changes in the tax law regarding the deductibility of donations. Did you know, for example, that a $10 ticket to a fundraising supper is *not* worth $10 of deduction on the purchaser's tax returns? It's only worth $10 *minus the cost of the meal.* This is true even if the donor doesn't attend the meal. If you don't know the basics of tax law related to donations, you may make a donor very angry.

▶▶ *Biggest change in the Next Ten Years*

Continued increase in competition and sophistication of the pitch for donations.

5. USER FEES

Many organizations have user fees. They may be called tuition, or per diem rates, or admission charges, or ticket costs, but they are, at their core, costs borne by the end user for the services provided. In most cases, user fees do not cover all the costs of the service provided, and here's a hint: even if you think you are recovering all your costs in a particular user fee, you probably are not. The subject of pricing will be dealt with at length in Chapter 10. More and more organizations are charging the end user, so what are the advantages and disadvantages?

▶ *Advantages*

First, the cost (at least most of it) is borne by the user. And the user *values* the service more than if it is free. Thus the service is not subsidized, or at least not as much, as if it is "free". Oddly enough, charging a fee often increases usage rather than cuts it.

● **FOR EXAMPLE:** In our community we have a world class example of the architectural genius of Frank Lloyd Wright. The home, once a private residence, and now owned by our State Historical Preservation Society, was restored and opened for tours in the mid-1980s. A few years later, state budget cuts forced the staff to make a choice: close the house to tours, or begin charging a fee. There was great resistance to the fee among legislators and the staff, but the patrons who were surveyed said they thought a fee was fine, and that they had been surprised that there wasn't already an admission charge. Even with this knowledge of customer wants, the staff would only institute an "optional donation" for the first two years, all the while predicting a reduction in utilization of the home. During the first two years, tour usage went *up* faster than in any previous two-year period that the home had been open, and belatedly the fee was mandated.

Another advantage of the user fee is that it is unrestricted income that can be used to support other programs if needed. Thus a "hot" program or service can charge in such a way as to maximize the benefit to the organization.

▶ *Disadvantages*

User fees are often very unpopular with staff and boards, for all the wrong reasons, and that results in a certain internal political liability. "If we charge, certain people won't come, or won't be able to take advantage of our services." This is true, but in some cases, if you don't charge you won't be in business at all. No money, no mission. Often set fees deteriorate into the dreaded sliding scale, which no one really understands and is too often abused.

▶ *Limitations*

The market places very real restrictions on user fees; competition will keep them low, perhaps even below your cost of doing business.

▶ ▶ *Biggest Change in the Next Ten Years*

More, more, more user fees.

6. TYPES OF FUNDING TO AVOID (IF AT ALL POSSIBLE):

► *Abusive match*

Many funders, whether they are foundations, government, or the United Way, insist on the not-for-profit recipient of funds providing a "match" to be eligible for funding. The theory that supports match is that local not-for-profits need to show community support for the program that they are trying to fund, and that support is demonstrated in match. Nice theory.

In practice it doesn't quite work out that way. Some match is so ridiculously high (25 to 75%) that the funder allows for indirect match, or "soft" dollars. This means that agencies with large overheads can allocate part of their rent, utilities, and administrative and support staff costs to the project, avoiding having to allocate "real" dollars, which in turn precludes being able to show any real financial support from the community.

What match really does is cut the funder's costs to purchase services. And, since nearly all of these grants and contracts are based on reimbursing costs, it means that the not-for-profit is forced to do one of two things: provide the service significantly below cost or lie in their budget. Some agencies double or even triple up on their soft costs (allocating the same resource to more than one grant in hope of never getting caught), or go broke because they can't make ends meet when only 75% of their costs are being reimbursed.

Match is good theory, bad policy. Work with your funders to end it or at least reduce the percentage dramatically.

► *Use it or lose it*

This one isn't even good theory. "Use it or lose it" goes like this: the funder grants your organization $X for Y services. If you spend less than $X you have to give it back. If you should be efficient and effective, instead of keeping the difference between your budget and expenditures, you are penalized. Thus the incentive for effectiveness is gone. This policy has been *de rigueur* for decades within governments and I suppose they assumed that what was good for them is good for you. It's not.

Work with your funders to move toward fee-for-service contracts so that if you provide Y services for less than $X, you get to keep the difference. If you spend more than $X, you are on your own!

► *Undue oversight*

Some funders are convinced that because they provide *10%* of your income, they have the right to look at *all* your transactions, review *all* your associations and alliances, should have access to *all* your contracts, etc. This is ridiculous and dangerous to let continue. Work with your funders to separate out those expenses that are related to their funds, and limit their oversight to what is appropriate.

C. TREATING YOUR FUNDERS LIKE CUSTOMERS

Let's start by doing a little self-examination. Take a piece of paper and write a list in descending order (largest to smallest) of your major funders. Don't look at your audit or your most recent financial statement first. If you are a senior manager or board member you should know this without looking it up. If you don't know your key funders by heart, you need to focus more on developing reports that are digestible and on sharing your numbers. We'll cover that at length in Chapter 7.

But back to your list of funders. It may look like this one:
1. Federal Government (name the agency)
2. State Department of XYZ
3. United Way
4. Donations
5. User fees

Or, it may more closely resemble this one:
1. Local Donations
2. User Fees
3. Foundations
4. United Way

Or this one:
1. Insurance Reimbursement
2. County Revenue Sharing
3. Fundraising Events
4. User fees

Your organization is unique and will have its own list, but I want you to examine your list and consider your reactions when you write down these funders. When you think of the Federal government, or the state, or the county, or the United Way, or your primary funding foundation, what do you think of—a valued customer or a pain in the derriere? If you are like most not-for-profit managers, it's the pain in the whatever. In my consulting and training with not-for-profits across the country I've observed one of the real curiosities of the not-for-profit culture (and one of the industry's greatest barriers in an increasingly competitive environment):

not-for-profits are the one industry that views their biggest customers as *the enemy*. Think about it and think about it honestly. If you are like many, if not most, of the staff at the organizations I consult with, you have joined a state or national association, and at the meetings that association holds, you spend a fair amount of time "dumping" on your largest common funder, probably a government agency.

Trust me. While you are in some hotel conference room with your peers griping about how your biggest customer (state, Feds, county) doesn't understand you, is ridiculously rigorous in their oversight, wants more and more for less and less, and doesn't really care about the people you serve, there are people in the next conference room from IBM or AT&T or one of 100,000 smaller companies. And, they are spending *their* time figuring out how to meet their major customer's every want.

That's different, you say. Those are *for-profits*. Their customers are reasonable businesses, not the government. They see things the same way. Their customers understand them.

I disagree. First, you are a not-for-profit business, as we've already seen. Second, if you will remember the characteristics of success, one is a bias toward marketing, where you view funders, service recipients, staff, and board as key markets. So you need to think of your funders as markets, as customers of something you have to offer.

Does a customer (the government, United Way, or foundation) really have to understand you, the seller of services? No. It would be nice, but they are really just your *customer*, not your therapist. Do they want too much oversight? Absolutely, but that goes with the territory when you work with government. The common "knowledge" that government has too much fat and makes terrible spending decisions nearly mandates that most government agencies be able to document every dollar spent in case someone ever asks. Usually no one does, but you still have to do the paperwork just in case. Is it fair that your government is trying to get you to do more for less? Frankly, as a taxpayer, I applaud such efforts toward more efficiency, and in the business world people are always trying to get more for less. You should too. I hope, for example, that you already try to buy some of your organization's supplies (food, office equipment, copier paper, etc.) on sale or at the cheapest possible location. That's good stewardship, isn't it? Same for your customers. They are trying to get the most for the taxpayers' dollars.

I know that it is not this simple and that, often, government as a customer is the "customer from Hell". But you have to accept the fact that as long as they pay a lion's share of the funds to your organization, they are your biggest customer, and you need to do the best you can to meet their wants.

Put another way, how long has it been since you went to the contact person at your major funder and asked this question: How can we make your job easier? If you are like most readers the answer is a somewhat outraged, "NEVER!" And you may tag that answer with a "Like it would really make a difference."

It does. Asking people what they want, and trying to give it to them is the central premise of marketing. People buy what they want, not what they need. (Just look at the success of *Toys R Us* and compare that to an examination of how much of what they sell children really *need*.) Finding out what your customers want is your job—they will not tell you unless you ask. You have to develop and maintain a culture of asking: asking all of your customers—your markets—what they want. This is true for your funder markets as well as for your service markets (the different people you serve) and your internal markets (your staff and board).

But, you say, trying to do a marketing pitch on a government (or a United Way, or a foundation) won't work; they are a big bureaucracy. Their decisions are dictated by funding formulas and regulations. You can't just sell to them.

Well, yes and no. First, more and more governments are moving to a more and more competitive model, where they are going to truly bid services, as opposed to just automatically granting funds. You will have to compete every year or two for their business. Second, even with governments where there is not a full competitive model in place, decisions are still affected by the way that they think of you. You can impact on that by asking, and by responding even to little things.

● **FOR EXAMPLE:** An organization that provides housing for homeless persons had been receiving state funds for four years. As part of a marketing exercise that I suggested, the Executive Director went down to the head of the state homeless shelter program and asked another key question that marketers ask: tell me what your biggest problem is these days. The state official answered that the Feds (the original source of the money for the shelters) had recently changed their reporting requirements and that her staff was spending an inordinate amount of time transposing reports from agencies that they funded to meet the Fed's needs.

Upon returning to his agency, the Executive Director met with staff and tried to see if their reporting could be put in a form to ease the state's problems. They found a cost-effective solution and proposed it to the state agency official. Not only was the state grateful, it *paid* the agency to show other grantees how to make the same reporting change.

Here, the simple act of asking uncovered a concern of the funder/referrer that the agency had never heard before. Also, remember the old adage that nine out of ten customers never complain: they just repeat their complaint to ten other potential customers. This is true for you too. And the problem raised here was easy (and cheap) to resolve and yet had a major impact on the perception of the funder about the not-for-profit.

Ask! Respond! More importantly, think of your *funders,* all of them, as important *customers.* They are not perfect customers, but perfect customers are few and far between. Resolve yourself to ascertain and meet their wants, and spend less time and energy griping about their shortcomings.

One other reality check here. I am profoundly aware that your mission—the service that you provide—is the reason you exist. I am also aware that the wants of the people that you serve are often in conflict with the wants of the people that fund you. As I said earlier, that is one of the core challenges of being a mission-based manager. Asking and responding to one market group (the funders) cannot mean failing to ask and respond to the other market groups (service recipients, boards and staff). It does mean that you need to strike a balance, though. And only by asking can you find out what all of these people want. You may be surprised how easy it is to give it to them.

FUNDERS ARE CUSTOMERS

How can you treat your funders more like customers? There are a great number of ways, some that you may already be doing, some that may be easy to start, and some that may require a deep breath before you begin, because they require a new way of thinking. But let me emphasize here that treating your funders like a market is essential to attaining and maintaining your financial empowerment for two reasons:

First: It will bring you more money. People who feel that they are being treated well, asked for their opinion, and whose wants are being met and problems solved, are happier campers. This is as true for funders as it is for the rest of us. Do these things and they will think more highly of your organization. And then, when it is time to decide who gets the sweep-up funds, receives the pilot project funds, or gets an extension of their deadline for their grant application, who do you think is going to get the perk? The organization that has consistently tried to meet the wants of the funder.

Second: If the funders feel well-treated they are more likely to listen to you about why you should retain your profits. And they may even go along! For some funders, just getting them to listen to the idea that you should be allowed to retain what you don't spend is a steep, steep climb. If you have been treating the funder like a market then you have been developing and improving the channels of communication. You have been talking to more people than just your assigned contact. You have been around their offices, and not just to ask for more money. Thus, you have more likelihood of at least getting a hearing.

Those are the benefits. Now let's look at what the process of treating a funder like a market entails. There are, as always, a number of things to do, and you need to do them consistently over time to have them be effective.

1. Find out what the funder really wants. This means asking and going beyond asking the simple question: "What do you want?" What *you* want to find out is what are the *outcomes* that the funder wants. A great deal of funder time is spent dictating the process by which your organization must achieve the outcome that the funder wants, and in the regulatory smoke that rises from all this activity, the original point, the outcome, is often lost. Go talk to your funder about what they want. Often, particularly with government funders, the wants change with the political winds, so you have to make contact with people regularly.

The other side of this coin is to find out the absolute no-nos, the things that cause a funder to look at you negatively for years to come. What is their pet peeve? Find out and avoid it.

● **FOR EXAMPLE:** A friend of mine was appointed the Deputy Director of a state welfare agency, and after he had been on the job a few weeks, we had lunch and talked about his new job, the agency, and the culture. As an aside, he mentioned the irony of the fact that the government moved so slowly and rarely met their deadlines, but that the Agency staff—as a funder of a not-for-profit social services provider—"went ballistic" whenever a form, application, or reimbursement voucher was even a day late. Since nearly 10 of my clients at that time received funds from the Agency, I asked my friend to elaborate, and he told me about the anger and frustration that erupted when things came in after deadline.

Over the next two years, I was able to advise over 40 organizations about this particular "want." "Never be late, even for an unreasonable deadline," I told them. Here, as is so often the case, the customer was not always right, but the customer is always the customer.

Talk to your funders. Go to different people in the organization (if that will not get you in trouble), explore their problems, their wants, their issues. Don't spend their time and yours just asking for more money. Find out about their deeply-rooted issues and you will benefit much more over a longer period of time.

2. Involve your funder in your strategic planning. In my consulting with not-for-profits on strategic planning, I always recommend that the draft plan be widely distributed for comment among staff, board, clientele, referral sources, key members of the community, and— you guessed it—funders. This is just another way to do them the honor of asking their opinion. Send them the draft plan and ask for comments. Tell them, as you do all the people that you send the draft plan to, "We encourage your comments and suggestions, and our Planning Committee will consider all of your ideas carefully." In other words, no guarantees that you will do everything, or even anything, they suggest. But the inclusion of the funder is critical. I've lost count of the number of plans that I have been involved with where the funder came back with a critical piece of unknown information about a key trend, or endorsed a particular goal that had been controversial and at risk of being dropped. Ask your funders their ideas. You may be surprised what they say!

3. Send your funder positive information about your organization all the time. One of the key elements of good, consistent marketing is to keep your name in front of your customers, your markets. Part of this you will do when you spend time with them, as was discussed in #1. The other part is handled through the mail. Send the funder copies of newsletters, accreditation awards, honors, news stories that laud your services or one of your staff. Keep your name and logo on their desk in a positive light. Why? Two reasons. First, you want the instant association that they make with your name to be positive, and that takes regular reinforcement. Second, you cannot expect any market to ever make the association between their needs and your organization's capabilities. It's not their job. It's yours.

I could take up the rest of the book just telling you occasions when I was in a customer's office (particularly a government customer) or had just sent them a letter when they "thought of me" and offered me a contract to solve their problem. Did I just happen to be in the right place at the right time? Not at all. The right time happens every day. The right place to be is in front of them (in person or by mail). Then, when they have a need, want, or opportunity, and they are flailing around trying to find a solution, their eyes fall on you, or on your mailings and good things happen. Make sure they happen to you. Stay visible.

4. When there are problems or changes, let the funder know first. This is the flip side, the dark side, of keeping in front of your customers. When bad stuff happens, or if there are major changes in your organization, the funder needs to know and know soon, along with the assessment of your ability to continue to do your mission, or at least that part of the mission that the funder pays for.

● **FOR EXAMPLE:** A city museum got hit with a one-two punch. They ran a display of what some people called "tasteless" photographs in keeping with their mission to provide their community a wide variety of art. A board member, who was also a major contributor, resigned from the board and went to the newspaper complaining about publicly subsidized obscenity. Four days later, the museum's audit came back with a recommendation to the Board and Executive Director to go to the State's Attorney and pursue charges against the Financial Manager for embezzlement (which they did). Not a good week, by anyone's definition.

What the Executive Director did was masterful, in my opinion. First, she called her banker and her three main funders: a foundation, the United Way, and the National Endowment for the Arts to assure them that all major programs were intact, that services would still be provided, and that damage control was underway. Next, she wrote to the parents of a fee-for-service arts camp that was in session at the time, assuring them that their children would not be in the gallery where the photo display was housed. Third, she sent notes to all the people who provided donations to the organization, not only apologizing for the financial impropriety and detailing the steps taken to both prosecute the embezzler and recover the funds, but also noting that additional controls were in place to assure that donations provided services, not slush funding for staff.

In this example, the Executive Director could have stonewalled, or answered questions from people as they called, but she got ahead of the curve and her actions minimized what could have been tremendous damage to the museum.

Let your funders know your news, good or bad, *before* they read it in the paper. They will appreciate the "inside" information and you can offer assurances before they form any negative impressions.

5. *Meet the funder's deadlines every time.* Remember my story about the state welfare agency. Consider your funder, too. Is your funder often late? Ever hear the truism that people criticize most what they dislike in themselves? Think about it. And keep in mind that everyone values their time, thinks that they are overworked and underpaid, and tends to procrastinate. Summing all that up: be on time. For meetings, for scheduled phone calls, with letters of applications, with program audits. Be on time. It will continue to build that goodwill so essential to good customer relations.

D. KNOWING THE REGULATIONS OF YOUR FUNDER

Your funders usually operate under very strict guidelines. These may be a statute, an ordinance, a policy, a rule, or a regulation. The funder may be a unit of government, in which case it is buried in paper and red tape. It may be a foundation or a United Way. It may even be a corporate giving fund. In almost every case but a private donor, there is some constraint on what funds can be used for, how they are applied for, restrictions on association with corporate "cousins" like the ones I mentioned earlier about DMHDD and their excessive oversight.

But the key for you as a manager is to know these rules cold—and to keep up with the changes. Is this fun? Not unless you get your jollies late at night reading the Federal Register. But is it necessary? Absolutely. Why? Because on one very important level, the rules, regulations, policies, and statutes spell out for you the wants and constraints of your funders. You must meet these wants and stay within the constraints if you are to be a successful seller to them.

Most people complain about the restrictions of the rules. But from one perspective, they are a very easy way to gauge a market's wants and most of your for-profit peers don't have those wants spelled out in black and white for everyone to see. Remember, all of this bureaucratic information (with the exception of a corporate giving committee) is in the public domain and available for you to read and remember.

I know this is not very exciting, but it is an important component of good marketing to your funders. Do it.

E. EXPLAINING THE MISSION OUTCOME OF YOUR PLANS

Throughout this book I have repeatedly reminded you that the point of financial empowerment is not to have your organization get rich: it is to be able to do more mission, sooner, better, and more flexibly. If that is the case for you, and you have focused your organization on its mission and on how your empowerment enables you to do more mission, then you are ready for this part of keeping what you earn. If you are not focused on the mission, go and figure out why and how your empowerment helps your mission and then come back.

One of the most important ways to help keep what you earn is to work with funders to not take away what you earn. One of the best ways to do that is to make the case that you will be able to do more mission, more effectively, and more efficiently. To ride on the national wave of increasing conservatism and skepticism about government, you are privatizing the delivery of services, but you cannot do it well unless you have some financial flexibility. The more you tie your financial well-being to mission outcome that is cheaper in the long run for the funder, the more attention they will pay.

● **FOR EXAMPLE:** In Chapter 2 I described a client of ours who provided alcohol and substance abuse crisis treatment in a dilapidated, leased building. The organization wanted to do more mission and serve a higher income (and thus higher-paying) clientele, but there was no way that those people would come to the site for services, not because of its location or neighborhood, but because of its appearance and condition. Additionally, there were numerous life safety violations that were the responsibility of the tenant, not the landlord. The funder wanted these fixed as soon as possible, but was providing no money to help the organization come into compliance.

We explored the possibility of purchasing the building and renovating it, but the state funder would not pay for ownership costs (depreciation or interest on a mortgage). Rather, the regulations allowed for the reimbursement of rental costs up to the fair market value for a given community. We tried another tactic: the organization's lease was only at 1/2 the fair market rate for similar space across the street, and we could document that difference.

We went to the state and said: *"We want to do more mission, and we have a way to do it within your regulations. We cannot simply charge you the fair market rent, since the audit will show that that was not our actual cost, and actual cost is your limit on reimbursement. But what if we transferred our lease to a not-for-profit subsidiary that paid the rent to the landlord and then that subsidiary sub-leased the building to us for fair market rent? The subsidiary would keep the difference and when enough funds were built up we would do the renovations and fix the life safety issues. It meets your wants and the regulations you work under. We can serve more people in a safer environment."*

The state funder took one look, asked about ten simple questions, and said, "Fine." They were even willing to put it in writing. Why? Because we made a mission outcome the focus rather than just having a nice building. We also knew their regulations and used this information to overcome barriers before they arose.

The more clearly you can paint a picture for your funder regarding the mission impact, the mission outcome, the mission production that flows from your empowerment, the more quickly they will tend to agree. I wish that I could tell you that every single funder will care as much about your mission as they do about their regulations or about political issues. I can't. But I can tell you from repeated experience that many, many funders do care and care deeply about your mission and the people that you serve.

F. GETTING MORE FROM YOUR VENDORS

The previous pages of this chapter have focused on working with traditional funders, such as government, foundations, donors, etc. But there is one more group that you can work with who can provide you real cash, cash you can use: your vendors.

A vendor is a person or an organization that sells you either services or products. They include your landlord, your office supply company, your food supplier, your furnace repair people. You probably have 50 to 60 vendors, perhaps more. Look at your payables list, not just at the category, but at the recipients of the checks your organization writes.

How can vendors fund you? In a number of significant ways, and they may be ones that you haven't considered. First, by letting you pay *after* the delivery of goods or services, most vendors reduce your cash needs by reducing your working capital needs. If you buy $5,000 worth of supplies, and you don't have to pay for thirty days, you just got a thirty-day loan. My point? Make sure that you know all your vendors' allowable days payable and use every single one of those days. Your accounting software will certainly accommodate the input of a target date to cut checks for each vendor to maximize this benefit. For large accounts (where you buy a lot from a vendor and thus are a valued customer) talk with the vendor about picking up 10 to 15 more days in the allowable payables. This can mean significant money over the course of a year. For example, if you spend $60,000 a year (in 12 $5,000 amounts) with a vendor who currently allows you 30 days to pay, he or she is essentially loaning you $5,000 for as long as you do business with them. If the interest you get in your money market account is 7%, this means you earn $350 per year on this loan. If you can talk the vendor into extending your days payable to 45, the loan just increased to $7,500, the potential earnings went up to $525.

We've already had a discussion in Chapter 4 on working capital, and we'll discuss budgeting at length in Chapter 9, but suffice it to say that this is pretty safe borrowing. You put nothing up as collateral, and you know you will pay it off in, say, 45 days. It's really amazing how many vendors, particularly in very competitive arenas such as office supplies, food vending, office equipment, etc., are willing to extend your payables a little. Don't try to get them extended to 270 days from 30. You'll get laughed out of their office. But do go to the owner or at least the manager to negotiate this, and start with your biggest purchases, where you'll get the most good for the effort.

The second vendor benefit is an extension of the first: vendor-based credit. While your payables are really a loan, sometimes a vendor (particularly for a large sale of equipment, furniture, or other expensive items) will offer credit in the form of a payment schedule to stretch out payments. Buyer beware: the interest rates are often 20% per year or more. But there is a negotiating ploy that you can use. If the vendor is offering you credit for a year on a $20,000 purchase, ask for a one-year loan where you make small payments each month and a large payout in month 12. The loan should be at no interest if you make all the payments as well as the final balloon, but will bear the high rate if you don't pay on time. These loans are very common in the equipment and furniture industry lately and, if you can meet the payments, they are essentially free money for one or even two years. Again, buyer beware and read all the print on the loan documents, no matter how small.

The third vendor benefit is a marketing edge. If vendors are told a little more about what your organization does and the kinds of people you serve, they may well refer people to you. Remember, they have a vested interest in your success: if you are financially healthy, you will buy more things from them. If you have a newsletter, put your vendors on the mailing list. If you have an open house, invite them. The more they feel part of the team and the more they have faith in your operations, the more they will risk on your behalf.

☞ **HANDS ON:** The reverse is also true. When you have financial shortfalls, tell your vendors early. The worst thing you can do from a vendor's point of view is simply not pay your bill. If you are having a cash flow problem, first develop a plan for how you are going to overcome it. If that plan includes stretching out current payables, figure out who gets what when. Then call all your major vendors and explain the problem, how long you expect it to last and what you need to do with their account. Follow up this call in writing, and then keep to your plan. Don't tell a vendor you will pay him or her in 75 days and then pay them in 120 or 270. Let them know all the news at once, and give them the worst case. You can always make them happy by paying early. What a vendor wants to know is (a) that he or she *will* be paid eventually and (b) *when* they will get their money. So tell them, and tell them early. It will do much to cement the team nature of your relationship.

RECAP

In this chapter we have looked at funding sources in a number of new ways. We saw that by treating your major sources of funding as valued customers, by asking them what they want and trying to give it to them, we can get more revenue out of them. We reviewed the traditional sources of funding—government, foundations, United Way, donations, and user fees—and listed their advantages, disadvantages, and limitations, and then looked at my predictions for the biggest changes you can expect from these funding streams in the next ten years. We looked at ways to market to those funders, and examined ways to implement a customer focus.

Remember too, that knowledge is power. If you know the rules and regulations of your funders, you will have more power in the relationship with them, and can meet their needs and wants at the same time.

You now have tools to start expanding your income streams, the first part of becoming financially empowered. As I said at the beginning of the chapter, you will never have enough money to do all the things that you feel are needed in your community. But more money is advantageous, *if* your search for it is focused, and *if* you seek the money that you can afford.

6. New Sources of Funding: Business Development

OVERVIEW

One of the characteristics of financial empowerment is having outside sources of income: having a business. Throughout the nation, business activity in not-for-profits is on the upswing, and dramatically so. Why?

There are several reasons. First, the decrease in public support for many programs has necessitated looking for new dollars. This is true nearly across the board in not-for-profits, whether they be arts, education, human services, legal aid, environmental protection, or even trade associations. Second, this tightening of public purse strings has led to increased competition for foundation grants, and individual and corporate donations. What's left is earned income. Thus business development.

This chapter will take you through the key parts of business development, in the hope that you can reduce your risk (as all business is risky) and do more mission. I'll first run you through some risk assessment strategies. Then we'll talk through the steps of the business planning process, focusing on the three steps that people forget. Next, I'll provide you with the contents of a feasibility study and a business plan. Finally, we'll review how much return on investment you should expect and I'll show you that you really should be looking at two returns, not just one!

By the end of the chapter, you should have the tools you need to begin the business planning process with confidence that the product or service that you eventually produce will have a positive effect on your mission and your mission capability. Additionally, you will have the beginnings of a skill that you can use throughout your organization.

A. UNDERSTANDING RISK

First, all business is risky; that's the idea: Risk = Potential Reward. There is no sure thing. If there was, everyone would be doing it, and then the competition would be so intense that it wouldn't be a sure thing anymore! Different levels of risk appeal to different people—some of us like to gamble, some don't. Some rock climb with a rope, some without. Some people never fly in an airplane, some fly planes that they build themselves.

It is also true that risk is with us all the time. That's why we have insurance. But we get in our cars, or on the train in the morning to go to work, despite the risk, because we accept a certain level of risk without thinking.

The point here is that the perception of risk is relative: high risk to one person is a walk in the park to another. When you think about this in terms of your organization, you need to talk to your staff and board about two things. First, that business is *always* risky, and second, that you need to come to a consensus on how much risk is acceptable for your organization.

In the first chapter I told you that one of the characteristics of a mission-based organization is being a social entrepreneur; taking reasonable risk on behalf of the people that you serve. I firmly believe that in the increasingly competitive environment in which you will operate, the risk-taking organizations, the ones that are flexible, innovative, and adaptable, will be the ones who survive and prosper.

Risk is OK, and going through the business development process is intended to reduce risk to an acceptable level. What is acceptable level for you? I can't tell you that, but you do need to discuss it with your staff and board early and often, so that you can all be in agreement about what risk is acceptable and what is over the line.

With that in mind, let's turn to the steps of the planning process.

B. THE PROCESS OF BUSINESS DEVELOPMENT

Let's start with a few examples of what I mean when I refer to business development.

● **FOR EXAMPLE:** A small Midwest not-for-profit is in a community that has an annual craft and food festival in the spring. Tens of thousands of tourists come for the festival each year from the surrounding counties and states, and it occurred to the Executive Director of this not-for-profit that a catalog of foods and crafts, sent in the fall to those who had attended each year, might be a great sales success. After careful market testing and selection of only the best products, the exec set up the catalog. He subcontracted out the mailings, the order fulfillment, and, of course, the product manufacturing. In fact, all his organization did was handle the money. His initial investment: $4,000 for a test printing and mailing. His annual (pre-tax) **profits** each year now? $96,000.

● **FOR EXAMPLE:** An organization that provided residential care for abused teenagers on the West Coast was looking for new sources of revenue. In meeting with them, I asked them what it was they did, what was the essence of their service? Their answer: we are great with difficult teenagers. My immediate thought was: every parent of a child between 13 and 19 thinks that their child is "difficult". The result? The organization developed a two-hour presentation given at hotel conference rooms entitled "Dealing with Difficult Teens: a Parents' Workshop". This session—which goes into how to work with, confront, discipline, and encourage teenagers—was developed from materials already in-house and was designed to be presented by any one of a number of staff. The test session was held in a room set for 50 people: 430 showed up, each willing to pay $15 for the session. The revenues per year now: $205,000.

The issue of business development for not-for-profits is complex enough to fill an entire book, of which there are several listed in the *Resource* section at the end of this book. I also discussed this topic in *Mission-Based Management*. Here, I want to go over just the highlights with you.

I regularly hear from clients words such as "we had a for-profit business so I can't understand how it lost money." Just because you go into business doesn't mean that you are going to make any money, much less a lot of money. What you *can* do is have unrestricted funds, funds that you can reinvest in the business or in other activities of your not-for-profit. And, since you probably don't have the deep pockets to invest in something totally new, your organization will probably be like the thousands that I have advised on the business planning process: you will do more of what you do now, but for a different market, just like the presentation on teens in the example above.

There is an additional issue that I want to focus on here. In all of my work with not-for-profit organizations that are developing businesses, the *vast* majority (95 to 98%) develop a business that builds on one or more of their "core competencies"; businesses that grow out of what they already know. Doing more of what you already know—but for different people or in a different place—has a number of benefits. First, you capitalize on a skill or skills in place, and don't have to go learn something new, or necessarily hire someone new. Second, the work will be a more comfortable fit with your organizational culture, lowering resistance to the new venture among board and staff. Third, in most cases, if you build on a core competency, you will wind up doing a business that is related to your mission, and thus one that is not subject to the Unrelated Business Income tax.

In the examples above, the catalog department was new, unrelated, and a real risk. The development of the session on teenagers was simpler, related to the mission, and less risk.

Businesses throughout the world are focusing on identifying and building on their core competencies. Mission-based businesses like yours should do the same.

There is a sequence of steps that you need to attend to if you are going to develop a business plan. Why do a business plan? Because by doing one you will reduce your risk, focus on your markets, really know your costs, and be speaking the language of business all at the same time. Remember that I said that business is inherently risky. While even the best business plan will not eliminate risk, it will, if properly done, get the risk down to the "prudent" level.

Back to the sequence that you need to go through. Pay attention to the order: it is essential. Too many organizations start at the fourth step, the selection of the product or service. You need to start at the beginning.

1. ESTABLISH (REESTABLISH) YOUR MISSION.

As with any new activity, plan, or program, you need to check it with your mission statement. Why are you doing this? How will it support the mission? Talk this through with your senior staff and board.

2. ESTABLISH THE "RISK LEVEL" OF YOUR ORGANIZATION.

Once you have reviewed your mission statement, discuss with your board and senior staff your organization's willingness to take on risk. How much income do you need from this venture, how much social outcome? Each of us has a different willingness to take risks; so do organizations. You want to make sure that staff and board are on the same level of willingness to take risk on behalf of the people you serve. And you want to know *before* you start.

3. ESTABLISH USES OF PROFIT.

Of all the steps that people miss, this is the most important. You simply must specify what you want to do with the money you will earn. If you do, people will be able to rally around the extra work (and risk) involved in the business development process. If you don't, they won't be able to focus on the outcome—they will just wonder why they have all the extra work.

For example, will money earned from the venture be used for a new program, to pay for poorer citizens to use your facilities, to establish a 90-day reserve, or to pay a staff raise? What it will be used for must be spelled out in detail. Name the program that will be subsidized by the profit, and list the amount you need per year and by when to accomplish your social goal. Then when you finish your business plan, you can look back and see if your business meets your goals for social outcome.

4. IDEA GENERATION.

Only after you have done numbers 1, 2, and 3 should you seriously consider what it is that you and your organization can do to earn extra income and provide new services. Your staff and board will have hundreds of ideas about what you could and should do. You will be surprised at how much they have probably thought about this issue over the years. Get a facilitator and have a brainstorming session, and let the ideas flow.

5. FEASIBILITY STUDY.

There are two steps to establishing feasibility: draft and final. In the draft stage you write a total of three to five pages, reviewing the potential business, its markets in general, and what kind of services are being provided in this market. In the final feasibility study, you go into much greater detail about the market you want to serve, a definition of the service you want to provide, why the market wants this service, how you will provide it, the barriers to success and how you will overcome them, and preliminary financials.

The feasibility study phase should emphasize "Can we do this?", "Do we have (or can we get) the resources to accomplish this?", and "Does it meet our social outcome goals?" If you do your homework and complete the feasibility study, the majority of the work in your business plan will be done.

Do not, however, automatically proceed to the next stage without considering the key question: "Is this business feasible?" In some cases it will not be, and then your choice is to rework the idea or wait for conditions to improve. For example, if you are considering a re-cycling business, you might have to wait until the market for re-cycled goods rebounds to a certain level. Or, if you are in a highly leveraged business (buying, renovating, and reselling low-income housing for example), you perhaps could not afford to start the business if mortgage interest rates were high.

Remember my maxim of "prudent risk". The idea of a feasibility study is twofold: to focus you on what the business is, and to see if it is feasible. Some businesses will not be feasible and that's OK!

6. MARKETING PLAN.

The marketing plan portion of a business plan is crucial. In this section you will find out what the markets want and how to get it to them. You will have to overcome the marketing disability that most not-for-profits have: the idea that "we are the professionals and know what people **need**. Thus, it is a waste of time to ask people what they **want**." This is a fast method of business suicide. Ask people what they *want*, and give it to them if possible. It works.

7. BUSINESS PLAN.

Over half of all new businesses fail within the first two years of operation and over 90% fail within the first ten years. A major reason for these failures is lack of planning. If you have a well-written business plan that takes into account all the variables involved in starting a new business and is based on reality, you can move your venture on the road to success.

8. IMPLEMENTATION.

Once the plan is written, reviewed, and adopted, the final step—and certainly not the easiest—is to set up and run the business. Obviously, only through implementation of the plan can you hope to achieve the social outcomes you desire, as well as the new income streams that are so important to your financial empowerment.

Remember, the most successful entrepreneurs fail the first few times before they hit it big. I DON'T want you to be like them. I want you to develop a sound business plan based on good research and valid marketing—and succeed, in a big way, the first time out. With a solid business plan, you should only be taking prudent risks, not the "leap off the cliff" that so many small business people refer to.

Additionally, business planning skills can be transferred to other things that you do. When your funder comes up with a new program, you will be able to better evaluate the real costs to your organization of starting up and marketing the program. When you consider expanding to a new location, you can put together a business plan that takes into account the differences in costs and market wants at the new site. If you are thinking about a piece of equipment, a vehicle, or a building, you can better evaluate all your costs and benefits using the business planning process.

C. THE CONTENTS OF A FEASIBILITY STUDY

After you have decided on a business product or service to investigate you will develop a preliminary and final feasibility study. The outline below shows the sections of the feasibility study and some questions you should answer in the study itself.

INTRODUCTION
Statement on the business
▶ What type of business is the organization planning to run?
▶ Who will operate it?
▶ How will it benefit clients and the organization?
▶ Why does it "fit" your group?
▶ What are the characteristics of successful businesses of this type?
▶ Will it operate within your present not-for-profit's corporate umbrella or will you spin off the business venture into a separate corporation?

Information on industry
▶ What is happening in the industry? *National and state associations representing this type of business should be able to provide information about the industry.*
▶ Are there trends within the industry that you can tap?
▶ Will these trends continue or are they short-lived?
▶ How will you handle your business if demand drops off because the trend dies?
▶ What makes your business venture different from the competition?
▶ What is your special angle?

Information on competitors
▶ Who is the competition?
▶ Where are they located?
▶ How will you compete?
▶ Is there enough of a market to support you and the competition?
▶ How does your price compare with your competitors' prices?

▶ Can you price competitively and still make money?

▶ If your price is higher, how will you justify that to customers and still get their business?

Start-up capital

▶ How much capital do you need?

▶ Where will you get it?

▶ Do you have any other possible sources for capital?

Basics on pricing

▶ How will you arrive at the price you charge?

MARKET INFORMATION

Potential markets

▶ What is the market(s) for this business? Who is it? How large is it?

▶ How will you reach the customers within this market(s)?

▶ What is your marketing plan?

▶ What is your sales strategy?

Market research

▶ Have you asked potential customers to find out what they want from a business of this type?

▶ What makes a successful business of this type? Is it quality, dependability, innovation, or price?

▶ What are your survey results?

▶ What are some of the positive and negative things going on in the macroenvironment that could affect your business operation?

Need and demand

▶ Is there a need for your product or service? How do you know?

▶ Do potential customers want this product or service?

▶ If so, how do you know? What is your estimate of the demand?

Hurdles and pitfalls

▶ What problems could arise in the operation of this business venture and how will you overcome them?

▶ Are there some problems that cannot be resolved?

ASSUMPTIONS ABOUT THE SIZE OF THE BUSINESS

Growth and size

▶ How large an operation will this be in terms of items like revenues, expenditures, and staffing?

▶ If growth comes too soon, can you handle it?
▶ Can you handle any growth?
▶ What will you do if your estimates of growth are not accurate?
▶ Is a business that earns a small profit—or no profit at all—worth operating?

START-UP COSTS
Capital requirements
▶ What are your capital requirements?
▶ What are your other initial requirements? Will you require things like licenses, telephones, office supplies, insurance, and advertising costs?
▶ How long will you have to operate before you begin to generate income?
▶ Have you estimated monthly operating expenses for this long a period and included this much cash in your start-up costs to cover these expenses? *For instance, if it will take you four months to generate income, you should include four months of operating expenses in your start-up costs.*

PRO FORMA FINANCIALS
▶ What are your break-even numbers per month and per year?
▶ How long will it take you to reach your break-even numbers? (It always takes longer and costs more than you think.)
▶ Can you afford to lose money for that long a period of time?

DISCUSSION OF FEASIBILITY
▶ Is this business feasible for your organization?
▶ Does it meet your mission and goals?
▶ Is the risk acceptable?
▶ Will it raise wages, increase employment, and/or increase revenue to your organization?
▶ Is it worth the hassles?
▶ Can you compete with the competition?
▶ Is the market growing or shrinking and how will this affect your organization?
▶ Can you maintain quality?
▶ Will you alienate potential customers if growth occurs too quickly?
▶ Will it be possible for you to maintain quality control if rapid growth occurs?
▶ Is there some other activity that would be more beneficial to your agency and less expensive and/or time consuming?

D. THE CONTENTS OF A BUSINESS PLAN

If the study shows that your idea is feasible, then you proceed to a business plan.

A business plan consists of several parts. The most important components are:

1. A cover page identifying the business plan as the property of your organization. This cover page includes your name, address, and telephone number and the month and the year that the plan is written or revised. One paragraph states in simple terms who the business plan belongs to and the limitations on its distribution.

2. A table of contents.

3. A summary of the plan with a brief paragraph about your organization; a four-line description of the product or service; a four-line description of the market; a brief paragraph on production and one on distribution, if needed; and a short paragraph on the financing requirements.

4. A description of your organization and its business with the following subheadings:
- The organization.
- The product or service.
- The target consumer.
- The consumer's need for the product or service.
- The sales strategy.

5. A description of the market for your product or service, including information on the competition and cost/price comparisons between competitors and your organization.

6. A marketing plan that includes information on:
- the markets.
- customers.
- competitors.
- the macroenvironment.
- demography.
- economy.
- technology.
- government.
- culture.

- how each of these areas affects the marketing and selling of your product or service.
- evaluation of potential pitfalls.

7. A financial plan with sources and applications of cash and capital and:
- an equipment list.
- a balance sheet.
- break-even analysis.
- cash flow estimates by month for the first year, by the quarter for the second and third years; projected income and expenses for the first three years; and notes of explanation for each of the estimates.

Other reports and statements to include in this section are:
- historical financial reports for your organization, such as balance sheets for the past three years and income statements for the past three years.
- a current audit report.
- an annual report if one is available.

8. An appendix with:
- management resumes.
- your organizational brochure and newsletter.
- other pertinent material about your organization and its work.
- letters of endorsement.
- copies of signed contracts for business.

E. HOW MUCH "RETURN ON INVESTMENT" DO YOU NEED?

Although we have briefly looked at the issue of business plan development, the central question remains: If you develop a business, what is the acceptable level of return on your investment? How much should you earn? The answer is: "It depends."

The reason it depends is that, as a not-for-profit manager, you have a much tougher job than your for-profit peers. You should be considering not only the *financial* return on your investments, but also the *social* return. And, unfortunately, there is no fixed scale, no set percentage to refer to. It's more calculus than arithmetic. Let's look at a couple of examples to show you what I mean:

● **FOR EXAMPLE:** You are a senior citizens center that has the opportunity to establish a second center in a senior citizens' high-rise in a community that you haven't served to your satisfaction in the past. You also have the opportunity to establish a day care center for Alzheimer's patients. Which do you do?

First, as I said above, you go to your mission. Which of these choices better serves your mission? For the purposes of this example, let's assume that they both serve your mission well and thus you need to go forward to the next step. In doing this you would need to look at the financial return: the investment (start-up costs), the profitability (or lack of profit) from the new service, and when that profit will occur. Then, unlike your for-profit peers, you need to look at the social return—how many people you serve.

OPTION 1: EXPAND TO NEW FACILITY	
Your Investment (Start-up costs, including working capital and other costs)	$80,000
Total Revenue per Year	$290,000
Net Revenue over Expenses Per Year	$0
Return on Investment (Financial)	**0.0%**
Persons served: (45 people for 300 days per year)	13,500 person days per year

OPTION 2: ALZHEIMER'S DAY CARE	
Your Investment (Start-up costs, including working capital and other costs)	$120,000
Total Revenue per Year	$400,000
Net Revenue over Expenses Per Year	$ 6,000
Return on Investment (Financial)	**5.0%**
Persons served: (35 people for 200 days per year)	7,000 person days per year

Which do you do? While the financial return on investment is clearly better in Option 2, what about the social impact on your investment? Where do you get more mission for the money? Is there a clear "winner"?

First, as I said above, you go to your mission. Which of these choices better serves your mission?

Second, you need to look at your strategic plan and the other needs in your organization. Does the organization need the $6000 per year for other programs? Which is a more serious need in the community: expanded traditional senior center programs or the needs of families with Alzheimer's relatives living in their homes? Look to these documents and priorities for guidance.

There are other "social returns" to consider as well. First is the publicity return: will the organization get more good publicity (perhaps translating into more volunteers or donations) from one than the other? Will expanding into a new community (or a new service) make the organization eligible for funds from a brand-new funding source?

Another return to consider is the morale issue. Some staff love change and new challenges, some fear anything new. For some organizations a new service such as an Alzheimer's center would be a wonderful, energizing adventure. For others, the only thing that they want to contemplate is more of the same, and even expansion to a new community might be a stretch. But for those staff who are looking for new challenges, and even for career advancement, the choice of Option 1 over Option 2 could be significant. Thus, you should consider your "staff return" as well in making these choices.

There are no clear, easy formulas for social return. But I want you to think in terms of what you are getting for your investment, and to list the outcomes and benefits of your various choices. Look at each option that faces you as an investment decision that will affect your community and the people you serve.

Remember, you want *the most mission for the money*. You don't just want *any* money for *anything*. Understanding the returns for your investments and analyzing your options will help you, your staff, and your board make better decisions.

RECAP

In this chapter you have seen how to go through the business planning process. Remember, we talked about risk and how the planning process is designed to reduce that risk. But you need to talk to board and staff members now about how much risk is acceptable. As we went through the steps of the planning process, you saw that "Idea Generation" is actually *fourth*, not *first*. You and your planning team need to review your mission, assess your willingness to take risk, and decide on the mission uses of your profits *before* you figure out what you want to do. Start at the beginning.

I showed you the items to include in your feasibility study and business plan, and then we talked at some length about the fact that you are stuck with two criteria in evaluating your business: Return on Investment in both financial *and* social terms. This is a tough combination to evaluate, and it means that you have a tougher job than your for-profit peers.

Business development skills are essential to becoming a mission-based manager. You need to use the techniques described here to improve your evaluation of all "ventures", whether they be expansion of existing programs, acceptance of a grant, or new funding from a government agency. The more you apply the tools described above, the more you and your organization will benefit.

7. Communicating Your Numbers: Financial Reporting

OVERVIEW

A fundamental part of being a mission-based manager is getting the most out of all your resources. Imagine having a resource that is essentially free, one that is refreshed every thirty days, and that can revitalize your organization, promote teamwork, reduce costs, and increase staff ownership in your organization. It's right there in front of you—it's called your financial information.

If your organization is like most others (for-profit or not-for-profit) you probably keep the distribution of your financial statements extremely limited: senior staff and board. It is unlikely that you print both an overall income and expense statement as well as statements for each operational area. Your line staff don't know any more about your financial condition than what they read in your annual report (if they bother to read it at all) or the rumors that they hear around the office.

Sound familiar? If so, you are in a position to dramatically improve your utilization of an important resource, and this chapter will tell you how. Financially-empowered organizations know how to wring the most use out of their financials, and the first thing we'll discuss is how to use the financial reports as a management tool. Then we'll talk at some length about which numbers are important and which are not. There are more numbers to review than you have time for, so you need to know how to recognize the important ones and focus on them.

Next, we'll look at non-financial indicators—numbers that you can use to manage, but that don't come from your budget. After that, we'll go into who should see which numbers, including board members and different staff groups.

Finally, we'll look at an example of how one agency took its financials and did what they were supposed to: provided everyone with the information that they needed when they needed it in the format that they wanted. We'll review a group of reports that may surprise you with their simplicity and usefulness.

By the end of the chapter, you should have gotten a whole new perspective on financial reports and how to use them in new, more productive ways.

A. THE USES OF FINANCIAL REPORTS AS A MANAGEMENT TOOL

I know that you already use your financial reports in managing. You have a monthly income and expense statement and balance sheet. The senior management and board get that statement and review it in depth against the budget, assuring that each expenditure line item is not too much over budget and that each income line is not too much under expectations. For every line item that is over (or under) you take prompt action.

Does this sound like your organization? Then you are not managing with your financial reports. You are administering details. Let's look at what I want you to do as opposed to what you may already be doing.

1. BUDGET MANAGEMENT—NOT ADMINISTRATION

a. The Budget Template

Adopting and properly using a budget template goes the farthest of any single action in moving you from administering to managing. It lets you quickly see which lines are seriously out of whack, and then deal with only the important ones on a monthly or year-to-date basis. You need to adopt a percentage below which the board, or even the senior management, does not bother to get involved.

You also need to produce these statements by each budget area in the organization. You need income and expense statements each month versus budget for each area of your business. Only in this way can the budgets be monitored.

Many readers may already have budget reports that have columns for each program showing the income and expense of that program. But do the displays compare those numbers to budget? And, do they compare the monthly numbers to the year-to-date, or just give some useless data such as percentage of budget expended or amount of budgeted expenses remaining? Here is an example of a budget template.

LINE ITEM	MONTHLY ACTUAL	MONTHLY BUDGET	MONTHLY VARIANCE	% OF BUDGET	YTD ACTUAL	YTD BUDGET	YTD VARIANCE	% OF BUDGET
INCOME								
State Program	55,400	53,000	2,400	4.5%	310,045	321,000	(10,955)	-3.4%
Medicaid	65,443	61,000	4,443	7.3%	422,449	415,000	7,449	1.8%
United Way	5,000	10,000	(5,000)	-50.0%	30,000	60,000	(30,000)	-50.0%
Fees	18,440	19,500	(1,060)	-5.4%	114,598	124,600	(10,002)	-8.0%
Donations	250	500	(250)	-50.0%	10,500	3,000	7,500	250.0
TOTAL INCOME	144,533	144,000	533	0.4%	887,592	(887,592)	(36,008)	4.1%
EXPENSES								
Salaries	105,800	107,900	(2,100)	-1.9%	623,980	602,300	21,680	3.6%
Fringes	9,522	9,711	(189)	-1.9%	56,158	54,207	1,951	3.6%
Occupancy	2,500	2,500	0	0.0%	15,000	15,000	0	0.0%
Insurance	8,000	8,000	0	0.0%	8,000	8,000	0	0.0%
Utilities	1,244	1,200	44	3.7%	7,698	7,400	298	4.0%
Telephone	867	900	(33)	-3.7%	4,680	5,400	(720)	-13.3%
Depreciation	6,588	6,588	0	0.0%	39,528	39,528	0	0.0%
Supplies	2,240	2,500	(260)	-10.4%	12,679	15,000	(2,321)	-15.5%
Travel	1,243	1,500	(257)	-17.1%	11,340	9,000	2,340	26.0%
TOTAL EXPENSE	138,004	140,799	(2,795)	-2.0%	779,063	755,835	23,228	3.1%
NET	*6,529*	*3,201*	*3,328*		*108,529*	*(1,643,427)*	*(59,236)*	

b. Bottom-up Budgeting

In Chapter 9, we will discuss the benefits and methodology of bottom-up budgeting, so I will not take the time to do all of that here. What needs to be said here is that to make bottom-up budgeting work, the people who need information need to have it in hand, when they need it, in the format that is most useful to them.

c. Board Oversight

You want the board to have good oversight capabilities. You want them to have their fingers on the financial pulse, to actually have a good idea of what your organization's financial situation is, not just to stare dumbly at a pile of printouts each month. But you don't want to have the board signing every check, or approving each purchase order. The budget template, along with the discipline of a percentage below which they will not interfere, will do that. Additionally, different board members need different displays of information depending on their jobs on the board. More on that in a few pages. Also note that Chapter 13 discusses the board role in financial empowerment at length.

d. Senior Management Oversight

To a great degree (and an increasing degree in the financially-empowered organization) senior management is doing oversight and support rather than hands-on administering of the finances. You should be giving up initial budget development to line staff. You have policies in effect for savings, debt, and the like. You have a budget template that allows you to focus on important problems quickly. Still, different managers need to see different numbers, and we'll talk about that in Chapter 9.

B. TRAINING YOUR STAFF IN THE NUMBERS

You cannot give staff numbers without training them in what they mean, how they are generated, and what they should be used for. If you don't, you are asking for trouble.

If you agree that the sharing of information with your staff is important, develop a long-term training program for your people. Start with where your income sources are and what impacts that income. Talk about budgeting and why you can't spend money you don't have. Talk about savings, the mission reserve, the cash reserves, and why they are essential. Review cash flow and your times of cash shortfalls. Talk about income and expense together and what net revenues are used for in your organization. Talk about your debt structure, why you have debt, and what the value of leverage is. Discuss the balance sheet and show the staff what assets and liabilities are, how they balance, and even relate them to ratios. Talk about your ability to retain net income, or your problems with funders who want it back.

Many organizations relate these sessions to staff's personal budgets, showing them how they have income and expenses, assets and liabilities, and then move on to the organization's information. This helps staff understand and gives them a spinoff benefit: better understanding of their own finances.

This is obviously not a one-afternoon seminar. The best way is a series of one-hour sessions, with a little information each time. It's easy to overwhelm people with numbers, jargon, and strange financial reports. It is also easy to underestimate your staff's ability and enthusiasm for learning this information. Don't sell them short.

Also, get an outsider to help with the development of this information and even to provide the initial theory. He or she will have more authority and impact than senior management. Talk to someone who teaches introductory finance or personal budgeting at your Community College. They are already a teacher and may have a curriculum developed.

But don't scrimp on this training.

C. WHAT YOU SHOULD SEE—THE NUMBERS THAT MEAN SOMETHING

There are more numbers in your organization than you can see, much less remember or manage. Additionally, you have responsibilities beyond just looking at financial or even non-financial numbers. You need to be with staff, report to boards, be in the community networking, raise money, and market to funders. All of these demand time that will not be there if you are poring over your financial printouts.

So what should you see? What numbers are important? Which are meaningful and which aren't? Let's look at my suggestions for each major reporting area.

1. CASH

Cash is so important that if you only looked at one report, it should be your cash flow projection. Without cash your organization dies, now. And an amazing number of senior staff don't ever really know their cash situation or the projections.

■ *What's Important*

The essential management tool for cash is the cash flow projection, best done for six months in advance. Where will your cash come from and when, and where will it go and when? This display needs to be updated every month, or whenever you find out about a major receipt or disbursement change. An electronic spreadsheet is a great (and really the only efficient) way to keep this available and flexible.

■ *What's Not*

A report of your cash balance today, or this week, seen every week. I have seen dozens of organizations who have this report and tell me that they are managing their cash flow. They are not. Having only this report and not the cash flow projections noted above is like looking down at your feet with blinders on. You can't see anything but your feet and the ground that they are standing on. Now take a step. Are you at the edge of a cliff, the shore of a lake, near quicksand, or on solid, flat ground? You don't know without the ability to look ahead. That ability is your cash flow projection. It will give you the ability to see trouble coming and deal with it.

2. INCOME AND EXPENSE STATEMENTS

These statements tell you what you have taken in and spent for the previous month, quarter, or fiscal year. Note that this is already history, and if you don't get your monthly statements until the end of the following months, you are way behind the curve in their usefulness as a management tool.

■ *What's Important*
First, the information has to be pretty recent: invest in the software, or the training to allow you to get your monthly statements within 5 or 6 working days after the end of the month. If your financial people tell you they can't, talk with your CPA about how to design your systems so that they can.

Second, these numbers are only useful in context, not alone. How do the expenses relate to the budget for the month and for the year-to-date? What about the income lines? Better or worse?

Use the template I have shown you on page 93. Set limits for interfering. But see the income and expense sheets for the organization and for each program area within it, each month.

■ *What's Not*
Information that shows you the percentage of budget spent, the amount of budget remaining, the percentage of the fiscal year left, etc. These numbers are superfluous, and don't merit being on your reports. Get them off.

3. BALANCE SHEETS

Balance sheets are organizational snapshots—what your organization looked like financially the day the balance sheet was done, usually at the end of the month. They are reports that allow you to analyze *condition*, as opposed to the income and expense statement, which allows you to analyze *activity*.

■ *What's Important*
Develop ratios that put the balance sheet into context. Talk about these with your CPA, banker, and treasurer. The ratios allow you to analyze the numbers more quickly.

On the balance sheet itself, compare the numbers with those for the previous month, and the same month in the previous year. Look at payables and receivables. Is one growing faster than the other? Why? Look at unearned income. You may have cash you haven't earned. That's why it's a liability. How much cash on hand do you have? Is it at least invested in a money market fund or, better yet, a higher-yielding CD? (This is one use of a cash flow statement—when you don't need cash now, you can earn something with it.)

■ *What's Not*

Hardly anything on the balance sheet is unimportant. But you do need to learn how to read them efficiently, and to know what you are looking for. Talk to your CPA.

One last word of caution. Because this book is written for all not-for-profit managers, I must generalize to some degree. That means that there may be financial indicators that are crucial to your operations that I have not covered. Talk to your Finance Committee, your CPA, your banker, and your peers about the numbers you should see. If they give you a different set of numbers than I have, fine; go with them. The essential piece of information is that the numbers you need to see are less than you have assumed, and that you can develop them in such a way as to be able to review them efficiently and effectively.

D. NON-FINANCIAL INDICATORS FOR YOUR NOT-FOR-PROFIT

Now you know what financial indicators are important, but what about other numbers that affect your operation? Many CEOs and managers of for-profits and not-for-profits see a select number of non-financial indicators each day, week, or month. This helps them keep a handle on where the organization is going, without having to grill people every day. It also shows problems and lets the management check out the situation and offer help.

What do I mean by a non-financial indicator? Let's look at some examples:

Occupancy: How many clients/students/children do you have in relation to capacity: 60%, 79%?

Billable hours per staff person: How much of a counselor's time is billable?

Grievances per month: How many staff filed grievances?

Staff turnover per quarter: What percentage of staff left the organization?

New clients/customers: How many new individuals did you serve?

Donations per parishioner: What was the average donation of people attending your place of worship?

Revenue versus non-revenue patients: What percentage of your patients were paying versus non-paying?

Backlogs: What key items are behind? Responses to new customers? Billings to funders? Evaluations of staff?

Obviously, your indicators will not be these. They will be the ones that are important to you and your staff. Talk to your people and develop a sheet of indicators that you can see. Try to keep it to 10 to 12 total. That will focus you on the most important. And remember that your management team will need their own report of the indicators that are important to them. Ask and respond!

The important thing to remember about non-financial indicators, whatever yours may be, is that they should be *current* and *in context. Current* means just that; not out-of-date. Old numbers are not useful as management tools. Each indicator will be different in its ability to be generated daily, weekly, or monthly. For example, occupancy data should be available every day. Earnings per staff person is a once-a-month figure, as would be billable hours per staff person.

Context means comparing the number to either a benchmark, a goal, or a previous month's or year's number. Indicators taken out of context are meaningless; have something to compare them to.

E. WHO SHOULD SEE WHAT

Put simply, different people in your organization need different information. Give it to them. Remember, if knowledge is power, and we share the knowledge, we all get powerful together. Ask people what they want, when they want it, and be flexible enough to give it to them. If they need a report format changed to add a number or two, fine (if it can be done without a complete overhaul). If they need an additional management report, fine, give it to them.

This is a good time to talk about software. Many management reports that your people will want can only be generated easily by putting information into a database that is linked to a report generator. There are a number of excellent products on the market. Having your management data in a database allows you to go in and analyze things in different formats as conditions change. The database should also link to your financial software. With software and hardware becoming a commodity and no longer a luxury, these resources are too inexpensive not to have.

In Chapter 12, I will show you what the CEO needs to see and, in Chapter 13, I will discuss what the board needs to see in some detail. Additionally, in the next segment I'll show you an actual example of how to differentiate data for the main groups in your organization. But let me just note here some other groups and what they should see.

Staff: Staff should see the organizational income and expense sheet and balance sheet each month. They should see the income and expense sheet for their area of work. They should see non-financial indicators such as productivity, occupancy, etc., that you and they have decided are important. It is always helpful to attach a written discussion to these reports (for board, staff, and management!).

Management: Management should see the income and expense for the organization and for their area of responsibility and the organizational cash flow. They should also see the non-financial indicators for the organization and any that have been designed specifically for their area. For example, a residential manager may have had a target occupancy, or a maintenance supervisor a target for the number of vehicle days out of service.

Your Banker: Your banker should get your organizational income and expense statement, non-financial indicators, and cash flow projection each month.

One important note: *your financial information is confidential.* It needs to stay inside the organization with the exception of your banker and CPA, who are bound by ethical and legal constraints to keep your information closely held. But you still need to state explicitly and repeatedly to staff and board that the numbers that they see are not to be discussed or distributed outside of the organization. Period.

F. AN EXAMPLE OF DIFFERENT WAYS TO LOOK AT THE SAME NUMBERS

Now that you know my ideas on why and how to use your financial information, let's look at an example. All of the displays below are for the same organization and express the financial situation in Cash and Income & Expense on the same date. They are, however, targeted to different audiences, who have expressed different needs. In addition, I have included an Executive Director's Data Sheet, showing an example of what that person might want.

Executive Director's Income and Expense Sheet

Summary	Income	0.4%
	Expense	-2.0%

LINE ITEM	MONTHLY ACTUAL	MONTHLY BUDGET	MONTHLY VARIANCE	% OF BUDGET	YTD ACTUAL	YTD BUDGET	YTD VARIANCE	% OF BUDGET
INCOME								
State Program	55,400	53,000	2,400	4.5%	310,045	321,000	(10,955)	-3.4%
Medicaid	65,443	61,000	4,443	7.3%	422,449	415,000	7,449	1.8%
United Way	5,000	10,000	(5,000)	-50.0%	30,000	60,000	(30,000)	-50.0%
Fees	18,440	19,500	(1,060)	-5.4%	114,598	124,600	(10,002)	-8.0%
Donations	250	500	(250)	-50.0%	10,500	3,000	7,500	250.0
TOTAL INCOME	144,533	144,000	533	0.4%	887,592	(887,592)	(36,008)	4.1%
EXPENSES								
Salaries	105,800	107,900	(2,100)	-1.9%	623,980	602,300	21,680	3.6%
Fringes	9,522	9,711	(189)	-1.9%	56,158	54,207	1,951	3.6%
Occupancy	2,500	2,500	0	0.0%	15,000	15,000	0	0.0%
Insurance	8,000	8,000	0	0.0%	8,000	8,000	0	0.0%
Utilities	1,244	1,200	44	3.7%	7,698	7,400	298	4.0%
Telephone	867	900	(33)	-3.7%	4,680	5,400	(720)	-13.3%
Depreciation	6,588	6,588	0	0.0%	39,528	39,528	0	0.0%
Supplies	2,240	2,500	(260)	-10.4%	12,679	15,000	(2,321)	-15.5%
Travel	1,243	1,500	(257)	-17.1%	11,340	9,000	2,340	26.0%
TOTAL EXPENSE	138,004	140,799	(2,795)	-2.0%	779,063	755,835	23,228	3.1%
NET	6,529	3,201	3,328		108,529	(1,643,427)	(59,236)	

Cash Flow Summary

	Month 1	Month 2	Month 3	Month 4	Month 5	Month 6
Total Receipts:	144,000	144,150	149,400	134,080	120,575	265,625
Total Disbursements:	133,271	132,831	134,861	180,541	133,371	216,611
Net Cash Flow:	10,729	11,319	14,539	(46,461)	(12,796)	49,014
Ending Cash Balance	23,075	34,394	48,933	2,472	(10,324)	38,690

Cash Flow Detail for Executive Director

	Month 1	Month 2	Month 3	Month 4	Month 5	Month 6
Receipts						
State Program	53,000	53,000	53,000	53,000	53,000	53,000
Medicaid	61,000	61,000	61,000	0	0	183,000
United Way	10,000	10,000	10,000	10,000	10,000	10,000
Fees	19,500	19,500	24,500	18,500	17,450	19,500
Debt Received	0	0	0	40,000	40,000	0
Donations	500	650	900	12,580	125	125
Total Receipts:	144,000	144,150	149,400	134,080	120,575	265,625
Disbursements						
Salaries	107,900	107,900	107,900	107,900	107,900	107,900
Fringes	9,711	9,711	9,711	9,711	9,711	9,711
Occupancy	2,500	2,500	2,500	2,500	2,500	2,500
Insurance	0	0	0	48,000	0	0
Utilities	1,200	800	850	950	1,450	1,650
Telephone	900	900	900	900	900	900
Debt Service Paid	7,960	7,960	7,960	7,960	7,960	88,000
Supplies	2,500	2,500	2,500	2,500	2,500	2,500
Travel	600	560	2,540	120	450	3,450
Total Disbursemnts:	133,271	132,831	134,861	180,541	133,371	216,611
Net Cash Flow:	10,729	11,319	14,539	(46,461)	(12,796)	49,014
Ending Cash Balance	23,075	34,394	48,933	2,472	(10,324)	38,690

Board Financial Summary

INCOME AND EXPENSE

LINE ITEM	MONTHLY ACTUAL	MONTHLY BUDGET	MONTHLY VARIANCE	% OF BUDGET	YTD ACTUAL	YTD BUDGET	YTD VARIANCE	% OF BUDGT
TOTAL INCOME	144,533	144,000	533	0.4%	887,592	(887,592)	(36,008)	4.1%
TOTAL EXPENSE	138,004	140,799	(2,795)	-2.0%	779,063	755,835	23,228	3.1%
NET	6,529	3,201	3,328		108,529	(1,643,427)	(59,236)	

Cash Flow Summary

	Month 1	Month 2	Month 3	Month 4	Month 5	Month 6
Total Receipts:	144,000	144,150	149,400	134,080	120,575	265,625
Ttl. Disbursemnts:	133,271	132,831	134,861	180,541	133,371	216,611
Net Cash Flow:	10,729	11,319	14,539	(46,461)	(12,796)	49,014
Ending Cash Bal.	23,075	34,394	48,933	2,472	(10,324)	38,690

	Current Month	Last Month	Last Year	Budget or Goal
Revenue	600	142,456	132,677	560
Occupancy (Unit 1)	87.0%	88.0%	90.0%	95.0%
Number of Hours Billable (outpatient)	2,435	2,490	2,680	2,750
Staff Turnover (12 months)	24.0%	26.0%	45.0%	12.0%
Receivables (in days)	43.5	45.0	55.0	40.0
Payables (in days)	32.1	32.0	34.1	30.0
Current Ratio	0.50	0.56	0.76	0.45
Cash Reserve (in days)	47.6	45.6	32.1	90.0

CEO DATA SHEET

	Current Month	Last Month	Last Year	Budget or Goal
Revenue	144,533	142,456	132,677	144,000
Occupancy (Unit 1)	87.0%	88.0%	90.0%	95.0%
Number of Hours Billable (outpatient)	2,435	2,490	2,680	2,750
Staff Turnover (12 months)	24.0%	26.0%	45.0%	12.0%
Receivables (in days)	43.5	45.0	55.0	40.0
Payables (in days)	32.1	32.0	34.1	30.0
Current Ratio	0.50	0.56	0.76	0.45
Cash Reserve (in days)	47.6	45.6	32.1	90.0

Cash Flow Summary

	Month 1	Month 2	Month 3	Month 4	Month 5	Month 6
Total Receipts:	144,000	144,150	149,400	134,080	120,575	265,625
Ttl. Disbursemnts:	133,271	132,831	134,861	180,541	133,371	216,611
Net Cash Flow:	10,729	11,319	14,539	(46,461)	(12,796)	49,014
Ending Cash Bal.	23,075	34,394	48,933	2,472	(10,324)	38,690

RECAP

In this chapter I have shown you how to get much more out of a resource that is already on hand—your financials. I hope you agree that sharing this information will benefit you, your organization, and the people that you serve.

First we discussed how to use financial reports as a management tool, as well as a board policy tool. People must have the numbers to use them, so let them have the numbers. We went on to review the important things in cash, income and expense, and the balance sheet. There are too many numbers for you to see them all, much less understand them all, and I told you how to tell what's important enough to review.

Third, we looked at non-financial indicators; things that are important, but that don't come from your income and expense sheet, balance sheet, or cash flow projection. I showed you how to put them in context, and to see them quickly and easily. Then we turned to who should see what numbers, and I gave you some *suggestions* on what different staff and board should see. Remember, these are *my* suggestions, and you need to assess their wants individually.

Finally, I showed you an example of one organization's use of its numbers, and how the same numbers can be presented in a number of different formats.

Use your financial information: it is the knowledge that will let you, your staff, and your board all become more financially powerful together. Organizations that are empowered do this consistently, and they consistently train their staff in financial operations, reports, and financial management. You can too.

8. Financing Your Empowerment

OVERVIEW

You now know how to grow your current sources of income and how to develop some new sources of funds. I have also shown you how to estimate the working capital costs of growth and new programs—all of which cost money. Where will it come from? Often as not, if what you are doing or what you plan to do will make money, the source of the funds will be debt.

Remember that one of the characteristics of empowerment is "appropriate leverage". Appropriate is the key term here and in this chapter I'll show you how to determine that. You also need to know what your financing options are.

In the following pages I'll show you where to go for the money you need. First, we'll look at the different options for acquiring money. Then we will look at different kinds of debt and some rules for prudent borrowing. We'll review some important information about equity as well.

Then I'll show you how to work with lenders, how to find a bank, work with a bank, and keep the bank happy.

By the end of the chapter, armed with this information and the information in Chapter 4, you should be able to estimate the amount of money your organization will need and know where and how to go about getting it.

A. WHAT FINANCING OPTIONS DO YOU HAVE?

As you look at your needs over the coming months and years, you will undoubtedly find times when you will need cash. Almost all small businesses do. The challenge is to figure out where to get the money at the least cost for the least risk. There are two main sources of financing for your organization. These are equity and debt. Since it is much less likely that you will ever go after equity dollars, let's deal with them first, and then go on to a more detailed discussion of debt financing.

1. EQUITY

Equity, in simple terms, is the money acquired by selling stock or other ownership shares. You cannot do this in a not-for-profit. Not-for-profits are controlled by the board of directors, not the shareholders, as in a for-profit corporation. So, if you have only a single not-for-profit, or if you have a not-for-profit with an associated not-for-profit foundation or business entity, there is nothing of interest for you in this section. For those of you who have set up, or are considering setting up, a for-profit subsidiary, read on.

For-profit stock corporations sell part of their ownership to outsiders to raise funds. GM, Ford, IBM and thousands of other companies, large and small, sell stock on the exchanges. Thousands of others do it privately to a small number of shareholders as a way of capitalizing (getting money for) their operations. In exchange for their investment, the shareholder expects one (or both) of two things to happen: growth in the value (price) of the shares that they have bought or a dividend paid regularly. Dividends are similar (from the shareholder's point of view) to interest on a loan in that they provide a return on investment. Often, however, dividends are not fixed: they vary with the success of the business. Thus to compensate for the higher risk, they are often, especially in small businesses, fairly high, compared to the going money market rate.

What all this has to do with you and your organization is this: if you plan to have, or already have, a for-profit subsidiary corporation, one of the options you have is to sell stock in it to raise cash. The likelihood of that option being used is very low, however, for a number of reasons. Your corporation's stock is not ever going to be traded on a public exchange, thus there will be no market for an investor to resell the shares you sell. An investor expecting to sell the shares for a gain will not be able to do this. If investors are buying to get a large return, you might just be able to pay less through interest on a loan. Therefore, while the option of selling stock is open to you if you have a for-profit, it is not likely, nor is it particularly desirable for reasons that I will list for you in the section on rules for financing.

2. DEBT

Debt, however, is a good source of financing in many situations for not-for-profits. Remember that one of the characteristics of empowerment is that your organization is "appropriately leveraged". You have many options in borrowing, and I want to go over the basic kinds of loans and their appropriate uses, terms, and normal rate structures. We'll talk more about working with lenders, but here I just want to expose you to what those lenders have to offer.

▶ *Equipment Loans*

As the name implies, these loans are intended to finance equipment (industrial equipment, vehicles, printing presses, commercial laundry, etc.). They are usually for a term shorter than the useful life of the equipment (so that the bank can sell the equipment if you default on the loan). They are collateralized by the equipment itself, but usually are only financed at 80% (you have a 20% down payment) and usually at local prime plus a percentage point or two. Equipment loans come in fixed and variable varieties, and are usually not available for computers, which lose their resale value quickly.

▶ *Working Capital Loans*

These loans are hard to get, and are usually only available if two things are present: you are creating a lot of new jobs as a result of the loan, and you have a government guarantee for the loan. They are loans to essentially give you the cash to grow on. They will be collateralized by your receivables and perhaps other assets, and they can be expensive—often 3 to 4 points over local prime.

▶ *Mortgages*

Most readers are familiar with mortgages, which are long-term financing for buildings. They come in fixed and variable, 10, 15, 20, and 30-year varieties and are very competitive. Because of the large amounts usually borrowed and the long term of most mortgages, I almost always recommend considering the 15-year variety, instead of the traditional 30-year type. Not only do you save enormous amounts of interest, but your equity stake in your property goes up much faster, giving your organization more net worth sooner.

▶ *Lines of Credit*

Lines of credit are pre-approved loans that are then available when you need them. They are intended for organizations that have regular interruptions in cashflow, such as retailers before Christmas (they must spend to build up inventory in the late summer, but don't get the cash back until the late fall). Many not-for-profits have similar glitches in cash flow; it's called the beginning of the local, state, or Federal fiscal year, when contracts are being signed and cash is almost always late.

You need to have a line of credit available, but make sure that you have strict controls in place on its use. Lines are like credit cards, and thus they are potentially very dangerous. Why do you need the line? Because it removes the potential for coming up cash short when a check you need doesn't arrive on time.

A line of credit works like this: you talk with your lender about how much of a line (say $500,000) is appropriate for your organization to have available to meet regular and predictable cash needs. As in any loan application, you will have to fill in forms and be reviewed, but if you are approved, you don't borrow the money until you need it. The day that you do, you simply call the bank and they transfer over as much as you ask for (up to your pre-approved limit) and the interest tab starts running then. The bank will send you an interest bill every month (which you must pay) and you can pay down the line as soon as your cash situation permits. You will probably be asked to "rest" the line (pay it down to zero) at least 30 days a year to show that the loan is not permanent capital in your organization.

Lines of credit usually go for local prime plus 1.5 to 2%. Don't agree to pay any set-up or annual fees. Shop around.

▶ Tax-Exempt Bonds

Ten years ago most organizations that wanted to access funds through tax-exempt bond issues had to get into a large pool, where many not-for-profits joined up to issue a larger set of bonds. The pool spread risk, spread the costs of issuance (which are often high), and, most importantly, made the bonds attractive to buyers who thought not-for-profits were poor risks. The intervening decade has shown that not-for-profits are very good risks, and a larger and larger number of accounting and legal firms now have expertise in issuance, bringing the price for that expertise down as well.

Tax-exempt debt works like this: Your organization has a need for a long-term loan, most likely for a major building project or property acquisition. The commercial rates for a loan from a bank for a 25-year mortgage are, say, 9.0%. At the same time, tax-exempt bonds for 25 years might be sold at 7.825% or even less. Why? Because as a tax-exempt entity you may be able to issue bonds whose interest is tax-exempt to the holder. The holder of a taxable note has to pay tax on the interest. Thus the 9.0% becomes less after taxes (probably about 7.825%). This results in paying a lot less interest over the 25 years.

Are there drawbacks? Sure. First, there is a long lead time to issue bonds, and the costs of issuance (in legal and accounting fees) are high, sometimes up to 5 to 6% of the issuance amount. For example, on a $1,000,000 issue, the fees might be as high as $55,000. This cost reduces your interest savings. Second, nearly all bonds of this type require a fixed rate of interest over the term of the bonds. Thus you are stuck with the rate you start with, even if rates fall nationally. You need to make sure that your bonds are "callable"— i.e., that you can refinance them early if you can save interest.

One very interesting thing about this method of financing is that the bonds themselves can be donated to your organization, and often are.

● **FOR EXAMPLE:** Many churches issue tax-exempt bonds to finance their building programs. This often makes excellent sense, as they can sell the bonds to their parishioners, who then get tax-free interest, while feeling that they are contributing to the church's future. Often, the bonds have a payment schedule based on a 30-year term, but come due in 5, 10, or 15 years. At the end of that time the bonds are either paid off or refinanced. One benefit of selling to your members is that at the call date (the date the bond must be paid), many of these bonds are simply donated back to the church for the amount still outstanding, further reducing the cost of the building program.

☞ **HANDS ON:** If you think you have a long-term financing need that merits a tax-exempt issue, get expert help. This is not a game for beginners. Talk first to your state or national trade association. In many states there are existing bond pools already set up that have regular issuances. Also check with a relatively large CPA or legal firm nearby to ask if they have done single or grouped tax-exempt issues recently. Finally, talk to the various diocese, synods, parishes, and other groups of denominations near you. Many churches and synagogues have issued this type of bond to build their places of worship, and they may be able to point you to the best local help. But do get help.

C. RULES FOR FINANCING

As you have seen above, there a two major sources for financing, debt and equity. Both have some rules that you should stick to if you intend to pursue them. The rules for equity are shorter, so let's look at them first.

1. RULES FOR SELLING EQUITY

If you have or develop a for-profit corporation, as we noted above, you can sell stock to raise capital for the business. This event will rarely occur, since most readers, in setting up a second or third corporation will set it up as a not-for-profit. However, if you are considering selling stock in a for-profit that you have set up or purchased, please refer to the rules below.

a. Don't do it!

By selling stock, you are selling part of the company. You know that. But what you may not have considered is that the stockholder now has a right to look through the company books, to push for more and more profits (which may not be your highest priority) and to generally be a pain. Stockholders, no matter how wonderful they are as human beings, are investors for a reason different than your mission. And worse, they die, and leave their stock to people you may not even know, who may be totally predatory, or a world-class pain to work with.

Try to find another option for financing your need. Don't sell stock. But, if you have no other option—you have to have the money, you can't borrow, and you can't wait—refer to rule b. below.

b. Sell only non-voting shares and have an iron-clad buy-sell agreement.

Non-voting shares are those that don't vote for the board of directors. Thus they have no say in how the company is run. This helps you retain control. A buy-sell agreement is an insurance policy that you buy insuring the life of the stockholder so that, in case of his or her death, the company buys back all the stock and it does not pass on to some unknown person or persons.

As I have said repeatedly, being appropriately leveraged is one of the characteristics of financial empowerment. Even if that is true for your organization, we need to be sure that the leveraging that you have, the borrowing that you do, is in the right amounts for the correct purposes. In the preceding section, you learned about the types of financing options you have. Now I would like to list a number of rules that you should always keep in mind. These are important for both staff and board to remember.

2. RULES FOR BORROWING

It is much more likely that your organization will take on debt, and in this area there are many rules to consider. We've already covered the kinds of debt that are available, but here are some rules to keep in mind when and if you seek debt.

a. Never borrow to make up operating losses.

If you are earning less than you are spending, don't ever borrow to cover the losses, even if you can see the light at the end of the tunnel. The light may be the headlights of the train coming to run you down, and then you are not only squashed, but stuck with a debt to repay. Borrowing to make up losses is like running up a credit card bill you cannot repay. It is a technique used by managers with no stomach for making budget cuts, especially if those cuts include personnel. Don't borrow to cover losses.

b. Always borrow for the correct term—not too long or too short.

Most people make the mistake of borrowing for too long a term. They rationalize that by stretching out the payments they are paying less each month, and thus putting less of a strain on their budget. In truth, of course, the longer you borrow, the more interest costs you have, particularly at the beginning.

● **FOR EXAMPLE:** Let's look at a $100,000 loan for a new building. The lender offers two choices: a 30-year mortgage at 9% (fixed), or a 15-year mortgage at 8.25% (fixed). Note that shorter-term loans are almost always priced lower than longer-term ones, since the lender has a better idea about what will happen to interest rates in the short term.

	30 Year Mortgage 9%	15 Year Mortgage 8.25%
Monthly Payment	$804.62	$970.14
# of Payments	360	180
Total Payments	$289,664	$174,625
Total Interest Costs	$189,664	$74,625

You can see in this example by paying just $165 more per month (or $29,793 over the life of the 15-year loan), the organization saves $115,038 in interest. So buying a shorter-term loan was very beneficial.

Okay, so that makes sense, but what about borrowing for too short a term? You want to avoid this problem because it can strap your organization and reduce your flexibility. Put another way, why borrow at all? You need to have the flexibility of cash on hand as well as some debt to be as flexible as possible. Flexibility has a cost, and it is embodied in the interest expense you incur. In the example above, the organization could just pay the note off in one year and save a lot more interest. But what would the disbursement of $100,000 do to the organization? Probably reduce all its other options for several years. Thus, you want to borrow for the correct term, balancing your interest costs against your cash flexibility.

☞ **HANDS ON:** Even if you have debt, you still need an operating reserve. I know that this sounds counterproductive, since the interest rate you get on your savings will be lower than that you will be paying on your debt (unless rates have recently risen dramatically and you have fixed-rate debt). But this interest differential is the cost of your flexibility and the ability to apply cash where you need it, when you need it, without going in for additional, and often more expensive, debt. Also, when I say that it makes sense to have a cash reserve, I say that in the context of appropriate amounts of debt for appropriate things. If you have long- term debt on buildings and property, that usually is best paid off over the long term unless you come into some windfall.

c. Borrow at a variable rate

I know that this smacks of lunacy to most readers. Why in the world would you borrow at a variable rate when those rates can rise, creating havoc with your cash flow projections? Why not just borrow at a nice safe fixed rate and know what your costs are going to be each month? There are two reasons to borrow at a variable rate. The first is that it is cheaper to start with: a variable rate, one which moves with the prime rate, is less risky for a banker, and therefore can be set lower, sometimes one or two percentage points lower, depending on the term of the loan. Thus your near term interest costs are lower, and it is in the early part of the loan when you pay the most interest as part of your loan payment. Second, the rates can go down as well as up, and if you have a fixed rate, you lose the benefit of that rate change. This can be particularly painful for a long-term mortgage, and, while you can refinance a mortgage (usually at a pretty steep cost), you will have more difficulty refinancing shorter-term debt or loans collateralized by equipment or vehicles which may have lost much of their market value in the first few years of use.

But I agree with your sentiment that you need to know what your costs are, and you can't be staying up nights worrying about interest rate changes. There is a way you can have the benefits of sleep at night, and the interest savings of variable-rate loans: a variable-rate, fixed-payment loan. In this type of lending, the loan rate moves with the market, but your payment stays the same each month. Thus, if the interest rate rises, your loan term lengthens, and if the rate falls, the loan term shortens. For many banks, these are now the only kind of variable-rate (often called floating rate) loan that they sell.

This kind of loan means that you get the benefit of lower initial rates, as well as having predictable cash flow throughout the loan term. The one risk that you have is of paying more money in the long term if rates rise dramatically. Another benefit of the variable-rate, fixed-payment loan is that its initial interest rate is almost always even lower than the traditional variable-rate loan. Why? Because this type of loan lowers the banker's risk. Think about it. When the bank makes you fill out the application form, they want to know how much cash you can afford to pay each month in debt service; the funds that you send to the bank to pay off your loan's principal and interest. Once the bank's calculations are done, they have a pretty good feel for your cash flow and what the likelihood is that you can make your payments. For example, let's pretend that your loan payment is $2,500 per month. If you are approved, the bank is saying that it is fairly sure that you can pay that amount every 30 days. But what if interest rates rise? Can you afford $3,000 per month, or $4,000? The bank is not as sure. But if you have a fixed-payment loan, your regular payment is $2,500 no matter how high rates go. The bank knows you can pay that amount, its risk is less, and therefore your interest rate is lower than for a straight variable rate loan.

The other thing to keep in mind is that almost all variable rates come with limits on the amount that the interest rate can rise or fall each year and over the term of the loan. For example, a loan might say that the initial rate is 8.5% with a cap on rate raises (or reductions) of 1% per year and 4% over the life of the loan. Thus the most you could pay in the second year of the loan, even if interest rates nationally soared, would be 9.5%, and in the third year 10.5%, etc.

☞ **HANDS ON:** When you shop for loans, compare interest rates not just for the starting rate, but over the life of the loan. Let's compare three 10-year $75,000 loans. The *fixed-rate loan* is set at 9.5%. A *variable-rate loan* would be set at 8.75%, while a *variable-rate* *fixed-payment loan* would be set at 8.25%. The interest rate can rise (or fall) no more than 1% per year and no more than 4% over the entire loan. Let's examine what happens to the three loans in the worst case scenario—with rates rising at the fastest pace possible each year.

	FIXED RATE LOAN			VARIABLE RATE LOAN			VARIABLE RATE-FIXED PAYMENT LOAN		
	Rate	Pmt/ month	Total to Date	Rate	Pmt/ month	Total to Date	Rate	Pmt/ month	Total to Date
YEAR 1	9.5%	11,646	11,646	8.75%	11,279	11,279	8.25%	11,304	11,304
YEAR 2	9.5%	11,646	23,292	9.75%	12,083	23,362	9.25%	11,304	22,607
YEAR 3	9.5%	11,646	34,397	10.75%	12,529	35,891	10.25%	11,304	33,911
YEAR 4	9.5%	11,646	45,583	11.75%	12,938	48,829	11.25%	11,304	45,214
YEAR 5	9.5%	11,646	58,229	12.75%	12,308	62,137	12.25%	11,304	56,518
YEAR 6	9.5%	11,646	69,875	12.75%	12,308	75,445	12.25%	11,304	67,821
YEAR 7	9.5%	11,646	81,520	12.75%	12,308	88,754	12.25%	11,304	79,125
YEAR 8	9.5%	11,646	93,166	12.75%	12,308	102,062	12.25%	11,304	90,429
YEAR 9	9.5%	11,646	104,812	12.75%	12,308	115,370	12.25%	11,304	101,732
YEAR 10	9.5%	11,646	116,458	12.75%	12,308	128,678	12.25%	11,304	113,036

Notice that the cost of the variable-rate, fixed-payment loan does not equal that of the fixed rate loan until after year 10, and never comes close to that of the regular variable rate loan. And remember, this is the *worst* case scenario. I do need to say that at the 10th year, the variable rate loan and the fixed rate loan are paid off in full, and there is still considerable principal ($19,512) left to pay on the variable-rate fixed-payment loan. But, once more, you will save serious money over the entire term of the loan.

d. Always retain the ability to prepay at no penalty.

There are still loans and lenders out there that penalize you for paying early. The reason for this is that the lender wants to be able to count on all the income that they can get (in terms of interest), and may want their income at the pace that they expected it when you negotiated the loan. Always ask, and then read the loan document to make sure that there is no penalty for paying early in any form, either a small amount each month or paying off the remainder of the loan in total.

e. Remember that all loans are negotiable.

The essential element that is forgotten in the loan seeking process is that *the bank is selling you money.* You are the customer. Banks are competitive. Thus, look around for the lowest rate, and negotiate ways to lower your costs. Shortening up the loan, changing the collateral needed, increasing payment frequency (from once to twice a month), are all ways to potentially lower your cost. Remember, you have two things that the bank wants: a sound loan risk and a payroll. Many bankers will start the negotiations with a statement such as: "Of course, we'll expect you to transfer you checking account to us from your current bank." Your immediate answer should be: "How much does that lower my cost on this loan?" *Everything*—the term, the rate, the collateral, the payment size, everything—is negotiable. But you have to ask.

D. WORKING WITH LENDERS

Now that you know how and when to borrow, what about lenders? Will they lend you anything? Do you know your options, and how to relate to this key resource? This section will show you how.

First, you have to adopt this attitude: ***Banks are selling you money; you are the customer.***

Second, banks are increasingly competitive and they want a number of things that you have, not the least of which is your payroll. We'll talk more about that in a bit. To win your loyalty in the past, all banks had to do was be willing to cash your checks at no fee. Now however, the rules have changed. Banks are carving out niches: big customers, small businesses, local lending, multi-state or multi-national corporations. You need to find a bank that (1) seeks to work with small businesses and (2) sees you as a business, not as a *non-profit* (money-losing) charity.

Third, you need to understand that most bankers are prejudiced about not-for-profits. You are seen as do-gooders who are nice folks but for the most part lousy business people. You even give stuff away! Bankers know that loans are paid back from profits, not from losses, and you are a "not-for-profit", so how can you pay back debt?

This prejudice of the loan officer may have been exacerbated by a stint on the board of another not-for-profit that was not as businesslike as yours. All of which is to say that you need to overcome the prejudices and convince the banker, even more than your for-profit peers, that your organization is a good risk and should be treated like a valued customer and not someone with an infectious disease.

1. WHAT LENDERS WANT FROM YOU

Let's look at this as a marketing challenge: what do the banks want? Once we identify those wants, we can shape your response to meet them.

Want 1: Banks want money to lend.

We talked above about how banks want your payroll. Why? They want you to use their bank for your checking account so that they can lend your money to someone else during the time (whether it is 48 days or 48 hours) that you have it in the bank. If they pay you 0% for your money in a checking account and can lend it out at 8% they make money. They want your savings, too. Even if they pay you 5.5% and make 7.5%, it's a good deal, because with savings (CDs, money market funds, etc.) there are few, if any, services to provide, unlike checking, where the checks have to be processed.

How do you act? Like someone with an asset, not someone with no shelter for the night begging for a roof over their head. You have your payroll, your budget. They want it deposited at their bank. Fine. What do you get in return?

Want 2: Banks want to lend money.

The way that banks make money is, as outlined in #1, to lend it at a higher interest rate than the money costs them. They want loans, and longer term loans make them more money, as we showed you earlier. They like customers who deposit money with them. They *love* customers who deposit *and* borrow. As long as want #3 is met.

Again, act like someone who is the customer, not someone begging for mercy.

Want 3: Banks want to be paid back, on time.

The worst thing that can happen to a bank is to have to hassle or ultimately foreclose on a loan. It is expensive, time-consuming, and in the case of a not-for-profit, bad publicity. That is why they spend so much time checking you out, looking at your net worth, your other obligations, your cash flow.

How do you act? You share every bit of information that they need, and more. Show them that you know your ratios, that your board has a debt limit, that there are excellent cash controls; in short, that you are businesslike.

Want 4: Banks abhor risk.

Risk translates into higher interest rates. That is why fixed-rate loans are more expensive than variable-rate ones: the risk for the bank is higher. Banks want borrowers to be as low risk as possible, and while some banks are more willing to take on risky clients, others walk away.

You need to find a lender that wants to lend to small businesses and who understands, or at least is willing to try to understand, not-for-profits. But how? That's the subject of our next section.

2. HOW TO FIND AND RETAIN A LENDER

First, let's look at how to find the bank you want, and then we'll examine how to keep that bank constantly impressed with you, your board, and your organization.

a. Finding the Right Bank

To find the bank that you want, start at the top. Find someone (John) who knows the head person at the bank you are interested in (Sally) and ask John to call his friend Sally and do Sally a favor. The conversation goes like this:

"Sally? John. I'm fine thanks. Listen, I just heard that (your not-for-profit) is looking around for a bank. You know, the organization that runs the (program)? They do about $1.5 million a year and have about 60 employees. I know their Executive Director and thought you might want to pursue some new business. Here's the number."

What just happened? John did Sally a favor. He did **not** endorse your organization, or make any claims on your behalf. He offered key information about your budget size, but he offered only that. He has done you *and* Sally a favor, in fact.

Now it is up to Sally. You wait and see what happens. Does Sally call? Does one of her key vice presidents call and invite you down to lunch, and talk about doing business? Or do you get called back by an associate who has been there 15 days and has no lending authority? Or not called back at all?

Try this with three or four banks and you will rapidly find out who wants your business and who does not. Remember, it is crucial that you start with the top person, not just someone in the bank.

b. Building a Relationship

Now that you have found a bank you need to do the following to keep the relationship positive:

1. Find an individual within the bank who is your banker.

Banking is, at its core, a personal relationship, one where a person at the bank works with a person representing the customer: you. Find that person and get to know them well.

2. Send the bank information, lots of information.

Send the bank your monthly statements, cash flow projections, and budgets. Send them the audited statements and the management letters. Send them letters of accreditation, newsletters, notices of grant and contract awards, positive stories in the newspaper. Keep your organization's name on their desk in a positive light. Remember, bankers hate risk, and it is risky not knowing about a borrower. Having all this information lets them know you better.

3. Meet with the banker at least twice a year.

Meet once when you get your audit back, and once six months later. Talk business, not just mission. Discuss your financials, your turnover, your occupancy (or utilization or attendance, etc). Go over new laws, trends, or research that may affect you. Talk business.

4. Get the banker out of the bank.

Invite them to open houses, program start-ups, to board meetings, or just to tour your facilities. Let them see what you do and how well you do with the resources you have.

5. Involve the banker.

Show the banker your capital spending plans, your strategic plans, your business development plans, and ask for their input. Give them some "ownership" in your organization's future. This also alerts them to your borrowing needs and helps them help you plan for those. The banker may also be the source of referrals to your organization; after all, the bank wants you to succeed.

You do all this because you need the banker the day you apply for a loan, and you can't argue your case in front of the loan committee; your banker has to be your advocate. And remember, the other bankers will still have that prejudice against not-for-profits. You need to arm your banker with evidence of how businesslike you are so that he or she can convince the loan committee that you are a good risk.

You need a good banker, one who understands your organization, and who is interested in your organization as a good customer, not one who sees you as a charity case (translation: bad risk). Go shopping, find the right fit and then stay there. Your investment in the relationship will pay off many times over.

RECAP

You need to know how, when, and where to finance your empowerment. Most important, you must understand that you are a customer and not a beggar in any relationship with a lender.

In this chapter, we reviewed the options open to you in terms of financing, including the rapidly-growing option of issuing tax-exempt bonds. We looked at the different sources of loans and investment, and what types of loans are out there for you to investigate.

We went over the key rules for financing anything, ones that you need to keep in mind as you consider borrowing or investing organizational resources into a project, building, or piece of equipment. Finally, we talked about your lenders, how to find them, how to deal with them, and how to keep these oh-so-essential people happy as you grow your organization.

Now that you know where to get the money to finance your growth, the next chapter will show you how to spend it prudently, and even how to spend less!

9. Budgeting From the Bottom Up

OVERVIEW

We've discussed how to get new sources of money for your organization. Now we need to look at the other side of the ledger. How can we spend less while still doing the same mission? Effective budgeting is an important part of both achieving and maintaining your organization's financial empowerment. You need a budget process that reflects your pursuit of the most mission for the money while at the same time spends the least possible money and maintains the maximum accountability.

In this chapter, I'll give you some new ways of thinking about your budgeting, ways that will not only empower you and your staff, but will also cut costs, reduce you and your board's time commitment for budget monitoring, and raise staff morale. All from my budget, you ask? You bet.

First, we'll examine the traditional budget process, how it works in most organizations and why most organizations do it wrong. Then, I'll explain the budget process that I want you to adopt and the four elements of that process that must all be implemented if the process is to be successful. We'll look at examples of organizations that have successfully implemented this and the barriers that they had to overcome. We'll also review the savings that you can expect if you implement all four components of the process.

Finally in this chapter, we'll show you a sample process for budgeting from the bottom up.

A note about the terminology of "bottom-up" budgeting. In *Mission-*

Based Management I espouse a philosophy of the inverted pyramid of management, where the traditional organizational chart is literally turned upside down. In this model the line staff are at the top of the chart, not at the bottom, where they normally reside. If you have adopted this management style, the term "bottom-up" budgeting should be replaced by "top-down". The essence of the idea is that staff nearest to the client can and should have more budgeting involvement than they usually do.

This chapter is one part of this book that you can begin applying tomorrow. You can take the process I describe and decide which part of your organization will be your pilot. You can begin to use the budget monitoring forms at your next staff or board meeting. You can begin rethinking your budget development process now so that you can be ready to implement the next time the cycle comes around. The applications of this chapter are immediate and far-reaching, so let's get started.

A. HOW AND WHY WE DO BUDGETING IN THE WRONG ORDER

Most of us learned to do budgeting the same way we learned to manage: from the top down. We, the managers, because we are managers, know the most. Thus we need to be totally in control of the most important of our commodities: money. Lower mortals (the staff) certainly couldn't do what we do, and they shouldn't have to. Budgeting and budget monitoring is the job for the lofty realms, for those of us who are highly skilled management.

If you detect a note of sarcasm in the paragraph above, your sensors are working correctly. The idea that we managers always know best has some serious flaws and problems, the most important of which is that we *don't* always know best. Sometimes, many times, our staff do. Management should not be dominating, it should be facilitating. Managers exist to get problems out of the way of staff, not to make more problems for them; to help the staff get the most out of themselves rather than to get the most out of them.

However, in the traditional model, what do we do? We decide the budget in the upper reaches of management, we let the board have final say, and then we implement it. We keep the financial statements as a closely guarded secret, distributing them on a need-to-know basis only. We allow staff to request purchases, but then deny them with the blanket and often mysterious statement..."Sorry, it's not in the budget." Well, I'm sorry to be blunt, but this is poor management: it is not letting the staff be their best and, in terms of financial empowerment, it is costing you money! Every year, every month, every day. By limiting the participation in your budgeting process you are cutting people off from information they need and can use. Moreover, you are cutting yourself off from sources of experience and knowledge that you can no longer afford to overlook.

If you think that the description above fits your organization, please, read on. There is a better way.

B. SAVING MONEY THROUGH BOTTOM-UP BUDGETING

So now that we know what we do wrong, let's look at how to do budgeting correctly, and in the process save money and empower our staff. The essence of bottom-up budgeting is to have people who are as close as possible to the provision of service responsible for budget development and implementation. The more line staff are involved in budget development the better. You may already do that. But bottom-up budgeting goes beyond that, giving those same staff authority to spend their budget, and it goes even further by rewarding people who "beat" their budget. Finally, bottom-up budgeting will be the driving force behind a rethinking of the way you utilize the resource of your financial information. You will need to develop more specific and differentiated reporting to do bottom-up budgeting successfully.

There are four main components to bottom-up budgeting and here is the secret: do all four and you will succeed. Do less than four and you will certainly fail. Why? Because the four components of bottom-up budgeting are inextricably linked; they work together as a unit, but cannot survive or even stand on their own. In nature, animals and plants that work this way, as a team, are called symbiotic. You need to do *all four* components to have a positive outcome for bottom-up budgeting. I think as we list the components and discuss them a bit, you will see why they are so important to implement as a group.

THE COMPONENTS OF BOTTOM-UP BUDGETING

1. Train your staff in how to read your financial statements.

It has long been said that "a little information is a dangerous thing". Nowhere is this more true than with financial information. You will be sharing more financial information with staff than ever before. Many staff may never have seen your income and expense statement, may not understand a cash flow, may be totally baffled by a balance sheet. You need to train them in how to read these reports, what they mean, and what they don't mean.

● **FOR EXAMPLE:** Take a look at your most recent balance sheet. If you are like most not-for-profits you will have a part of your balance sheet titled "Current Assets" and in this section is a line item called "Cash" or "Cash on Hand" or "Cash and Securities". Look at the amount in this line item. I have clients who have $500 here and clients who have $500,000. Look again at the number on your balance sheet. Now imagine one of your line staff seeing that item, with no training and out of context, and saying, "They have *THAT MUCH MONEY?*" If your cash on hand is over $10,000 your staff probably would think that you are holding out on them. If it is less than $1,000 they may think you are going broke. What they may not know is that this amount changes over time, that it needs to be taken in the context of the size of your budget (that $100,000 may be too *little* cash on hand for many organizations, not too much), your debt, your payables, and lots of other things.

☞ **HANDS-ON:** In short, the staff need training, and I suggest that your CPA or someone else from outside the organization should come in and give a series of lectures on how to read the organization's numbers. Then, you should have someone internal talk about the financials in terms of where your funding comes from, what makes it increase or decrease, and where the money is spent.

Finally, you are ready to discuss your new budgeting process. But only after the staff is well trained. I also strongly suggest that refresher courses be given once a year. People will need this as they learn more about their budgets by actually doing them. Train, train, train!

2. Give line staff responsibility to develop budgets and the authority to spend that budget.

You may already be using staff close to the provision of service in developing their budget, or you may centralize the budgeting process within senior management to speed it up and keep the information closely held. Bottom-up budgeting requires that you not only use staff in developing the budget but give them the authority to spend the budgets down with very little, if any, second guessing from you.

Why? For a number of very good reasons. First, it makes more sense to do both budgeting and spending locally rather than centrally. People who provide services know what they need to do their job. While they can't, in any organization, have everything that they want, since budgets have limits, they can and should decide how to spend what they can have. Second, staff throughout the not-for-profit sector regularly ask to be more involved and have more impact in their organization. What better response can you have than to give them more control over the budget? Third, if coupled with risk and reward, they will have an incentive to continue doing this additional work. Let's look at an example of what I mean.

● **FOR EXAMPLE:** A residential school had traditionally budgeted based on the groupings of the children in the school: PRIMARY, ELEMENTARY, and MIDDLE schools, as well as ADMINISTRA-TION (Management, Human Services, Support, Fundraising, Finance, Marketing), and OPERATIONS (Food Service, Maintenance, Trans-portation, etc.). Each year at budget time, the directors of these areas developed their budgets (sometimes in meetings with their staffs, sometimes on their own) and presented them to the VP of Finance for assimilation into the school-wide budget that then went to the CEO and the Board for approval.

When they decided to try bottom-up budgeting, they had to think through the size of the unit that they wanted to budget for. They started with two areas where they saw the most likelihood of success, given the interest and enthusiasm of the staff: ELEMENTARY school and OPERATIONS, specifically in Maintenance. Instead of budget-ing for the entire school, or all of Operations, the staff broke down the school into its smallest meaningful unit—the classroom—and involved each teacher or teaching team in the budget process. They negotiated budgets for personnel, substitutes, supplies, field trips, and the like, and then were held accountable for their implementa-tion. The teachers could buy supplies where and when they wanted them, without going through central purchasing. They could "shop the sales" and also didn't have to wait even 48 hours for approval to buy something. They decided where their field trips would be and, in the second year of the transition, even bought transportation cheaper from an outside vendor than from the school's own transportation division!

In MAINTENANCE, the staff had budgets for equipment, sup-plies, repairs, etc., but now had the authority to spend up to their budget line, and were, for the first time, aware monthly of where they were in relation to the budget. The maintenance staff discovered that if they kept a bit of inventory of supplies, they could generate consid-erable savings by also "shopping the sales," instead of their tradi-tional practice of buying things as they needed them. They also shopped more aggressively for equipment, finding used machine tools that worked just as well as new, and having dealers throw in mainte-nance agreements on new purchases.

In short, the system worked, and it worked at the "local" level, because these people were conscientious and thrifty with their money at home, and because they were given a reason to put those habits into play at work.

3. Provide risk and reward based on the successful accomplishment of that budget.

You may have previously trained staff in how to read budgets, and you may have involved them in budget development or even in budget implementation, but for most readers, this area—providing risk and reward in budgeting—will be covering new ground.

First, what do I mean by risk and reward? Simply that staff who spend less than the budget, or bring in more income than the budget, get to keep *half* of the difference. That's the reward. Second, if staff run over budgeted expenses, or under budgeted income, they must explain it and, in most cases, carry forward a "deficit" into future budget years. This deficit bears an interest fee and must be paid back in future savings. That's the risk.

Why is this important? Because without risk and reward, people will, in very short order, stop wanting to put the extra effort in that it takes to save money and bring in new income. Oh, they may be excited about knowing more about your organization's finances, but after the first excitement, this is really a lot of work. Without risk and reward why do the extra work? Look at it this way: when a funder takes back what you don't spend, what is your incentive? To save lots of money? No. Your incentive is to spend it all before the end of the fiscal year or grant period. This is also true for your staff. You must add a significant risk and reward into the equation to make this form of budgeting work, and the magic percentage is 50, no less.

I am well aware that many of your staff have little or no ability to directly affect the income side of the ledger, but some do. Put them at risk. Second, I know that somewhere between 70% and 90% of your expenses are probably personnel, and thus you suspect that the savings from this will be marginal. Think again. You will also save money on people, and we'll talk more about that in the section on *Rewards* in a few pages.

☞ **HANDS ON:** Don't get greedy as a manager about this. If your staff people can save money, or bring in more, great! Don't punish them by taking the savings away, or by cutting next year's budget to take into account the savings from this year. Don't repeat the mistakes of your funders. Remember, if you split the savings (or additional income) 50-50, it will *seem* fair because it *is* fair. Again, *don't get greedy*.

124

Let's go back to our school that was discussed above, the one where the Maintenance staff and Elementary School staff were the first to implement bottom-up budgeting.

● **FOR EXAMPLE:** In the first year of the program, the ELEMEN-TARY SCHOOL teachers saved approximately 9% of their non-personnel items, mostly through buying supplies more cheaply. This kind of savings continues through the time of this writing. In the second year, however, the teachers decided to attack their largest controllable personnel item: substitute teachers. They looked at why they were using the substitutes and found that 25% of the cases were unplanned: illness, a death in the family, etc. But fully 75% of the uses of substitutes were planned in advance; they were for teachers going to conferences and continuing education, allowances for planning times among team members and Individual Educational Plan (IEP) conferences. For the first time, since they had an incentive, the teachers realized that many (but not all) of the continuing education days could be scheduled during vacations. Team meetings could take place after hours, and IEPs were often better for students' families if they were scheduled in the evening. All of these activities were more work (and less time off) for the teachers, but they took them voluntarily because it meant that they could save significant money, and that they would get to use half of that money for things that really mattered to them. That year they saved almost $60,000 in substitute salaries and benefits, returning nearly $30,000 for things that the teachers felt were needed at the school.

The teachers could have purchased supplies, or financed a field trip for the students, or bought some computers, a color printer, software, or even an air conditioner. And it would be their decision, without administrative input. This is key: if they save the money, they get to spend *half*.

Again, the risk and reward portion of this, if it is fair, easily understandable, and (most important) a large enough percentage (50%) will motivate people in ways you did not think possible.

4. Have regular monitoring of the budget by the staff involved and senior management, and share information freely.

By now you have educated your staff, had them help you develop a budget, and promised them that they can spend up to the budget line with minimal interference. You and they have also agreed on the amount of any savings that they can keep. So do you simply cut them loose and say, "Have a nice year!"? No! You need to institute the fourth component of bottom-up budgeting: sharing financial information and regularly giving staff feedback on how they are doing. In a few pages I will show you a budget monitoring template that you can and should adopt throughout your organization. You need to produce these for every budget unit each month, share them with the line staff and have budget review meetings monthly as well, at least for the first year or so. In our example about the school, this would mean that each teacher or each teaching team would get their own statement for their own area, not just a school-wide statement or even one for the Elementary School.

Then you need to sit down with each group and go through their statement, comparing it to their budget. Where there are major deviations from the agreed budget, find out why. Where there are no deviations, keep quiet. Offer support, ask for and answer questions, ask if they are having problems with the system and how it can be improved. These meetings will probably take 15 minutes at most. But they need to be regular, they need to be face-to-face, and they need to be supportive, not re-runs of the Inquisition. Remember, for most staff this will be a completely new experience. They need your support and understanding, they need you to be available and accessible. What they don't need is you hassling them about every purchasing decision. If they make mistakes, fine; they are learning. Praise their successes, and when they fall down, encourage them to get up and try again. Coach, don't dictate.

Again, these four components must be used together. They cannot stand on their own. Please don't just pick the one or two that you like and discard the rest. All you will do is spend a lot of time and money on a process that won't work, and seriously tick off your staff.

One last suggestion: don't try to implement this for your entire organization at once. It is too risky. If you have always kept a tight leash on the budget process, this will be hard on you, too. Start with a single program or area of your organization, the one that you think is most likely to succeed. Initiate it there for a year, while at the same time telling everyone what is going on, and how you hope to expand the program soon. Go through a budget cycle, most of a fiscal year, and then expand the idea. Get the kinks out during the testing or piloting phase and the expansion to the rest of the organization will go much more smoothly.

C. THE BARRIERS

There are a number of barriers to implementing this and also a few easy ways to mess up. Let's take a look at them here.

1. MANAGERS NATURALLY WANT TO CONTROL THE PROCESS AND THE DOLLARS.

It is natural for people who have sought higher and higher levels of authority to want to retain that authority and control. If you have controlled the flow of dollars, signed off on all purchases, negotiated discounts, signed all the checks, it's hard to trust someone else with the money. Additionally, top staff and board members are responsible for the money. If they are responsible, shouldn't they retain control?

Control and oversight, yes. A tight leash with no staff input, no. For a comparison, let's look at that bastion of top-down control, the United States military. Can you imagine a more authoritarian structure? No? Well, look again, and look at an infantry unit as an example: Prior to any combat engagement, there is always a plan for assault or defense. Depending on the commander, lower-level officers will be involved in the development of the plan and will be thoroughly briefed. But then comes the implementation, the combat. The doctrine of the American military is that the local commander, even if it is just a green lieutenant or a senior staff sergeant, can and should make decisions on his or her own as the situation dictates. They will be held responsible for those decisions, as they should be, but the senior commanders realize two things: first that the situation changes rapidly, and second, that they can't be everywhere at once. The officers and NCOs are given latitude to do what needs to be done to accomplish the overall objective. In combat, wrong decisions cost lives, not just dollars. Yet the generals are willing to delegate the authority in order to get the most out of their troops and equipment. I have to reinforce here that the military also invests enormous amounts of money in constant training so that its people can make those decisions under pressure. You should, too.

2. STAFF WILL RESIST BEING HELD ACCOUNTABLE AND WON'T UNDERSTAND THE NUMBERS.

I haven't found this to be too widely prevalent, but it does happen. Most staff, *if properly trained*, will understand the numbers and may even point out some things that you have missed. In addition, if the risk/reward parts of the budgeting process are included, their interest, enthusiasm, and participation are much more likely.

Which is not to suggest that there are not problems: the first being that budgeting looks much easier from the outside than the inside. Nearly all of the staff that you include in budgeting will have at one time or another harbored a thought or a criticism along the lines of "How can they cut that item? Can't they see that it's too important to cut? If *I* could make the decisions, we'd keep that item at full funding." As most readers know, that's easy to say when you don't have to decide whose line item *does* get cut. So be prepared for a little grim reality check for many staff. In good financial times, budgeting is almost (I said, almost) fun. In times of tight money, it can really be unpleasant.

3. THE BOARD/MANAGEMENT/FUNDERS WILL TAKE BACK THE "SAVINGS".

This is a real problem for many not-for-profits, but it isn't just an issue that is forced on the organization by outside funders; often the damage is self-inflicted. Let's start with the most obvious target: the outside funding source. The policy that gets in the way here is "use it or lose it", the out-of-date idea that you must spend all you are allocated or you will get cut the next year. As a manager, I hope that you really dislike this philosophy and are working to get your funders to discard it as their central budgeting policy. However, in the interim, you may be forced to have the staff who save money spend it before the end of the fiscal year. But be consistent with the policy of risk and reward: let them spend their half of the savings.

Now, it's your turn as management. Don't repeat the state's mistake, and reduce a budget line next year just because you saved money this year. Zero base your budgets and build them honestly each year. If you just allow your staff to cut expenses (or to increase income) and then set that new level in next year's budget, you have repeated a key mistake of your funders—reducing incentive. Have the staff build their budget, review it with them, and set reasonable goals for everyone.

Finally, we come to the board of directors. For them I have two cautions. First, read what I said in the paragraph above about management and don't reduce incentives next year by starting the budget at this year's level. Second, support the management as they let the budgeting process, and the risk and the reward, spread throughout the organization. Don't yank the money out from under people who have worked hard to generate it.

D. THE REWARDS

So after all this work, all this training, all this time, what are the rewards of doing bottom-up budgeting? What is the point? Where is the return on the investment? There are a lot of returns, a lot of point, and a lot of benefit. If you train people, if you have risk and reward, and if you don't take savings back in next year's budget, here is what your organization reaps:

1. YOU SAVE MONEY.

People who are at risk spend more efficiently. Period. Now you are probably saying "85% of my expenses are people and this won't save all that much." Well, yes and no. First, let's say that your budget is $500,000 a year and 15% of that is non-personnel. What if this method saved 5% of that 15%? That's $3,750. Would you turn that away if someone donated it to you? Of course not. And next year another 5% comes in and another and another. Lots of return.

And it gets better. My experience is that staff can cut 10 – 15% of non-personnel expenses in the first year and about 7 – 9% per year in the next five years. But the big savings come when staff start figuring out ways to cut personnel costs. They suggest ways to reorganize to use staff better. They cover for each other. They take over for people who leave or retire. For many of my clients who use this plan, savings are realized in the second or third year as staff begin to focus on where the money is, and, for most not-for-profits, it's in the people.

2. YOU IMPROVE STAFF MORALE.

People want to learn, at least most of them do. In fact, in staff surveys that we do for clients, we regularly see two of the top priorities for staff written out as follows: "I want to be more involved and have more effect on the organization", and "I want to learn more while I work here". Involving people in the budgeting, teaching them how your finances work, and giving them a professionally-satisfying experience. It will improve morale, esprit de corps, and teamwork. You also get a good look at staff who are ready to take on other tasks, who learn quickly, and who adapt to the heavier responsibility that this process mandates.

3. YOU USE MORE OF YOUR RESOURCES.

In all of my work, I emphasize that mission-based managers need to get every ounce of value out of every resource. This process of budgeting gets untapped resources out of your staff, and most of them will love it. Some will resist, to be sure, and it will not be a path without potholes, but on balance, the staff you want to keep will really like this and will tackle it enthusiastically, if you let them.

E. A SAMPLE PROCESS

I hope that you are now considering implementing a bottom-up budgeting process, and I want to give you some help as you consider how to do it. Here are some ideas.

1. SELECT A PART OF YOUR ORGANIZATION THAT IS MOST LIKELY TO SUCCEED.

These may be your most energetic and enthusiastic staff, or your most entrepreneurial. They may be the people in a program that can affect its own income, or most easily reduce its own expenditures. The idea is that you cannot make all of this work all at once throughout all of your organization. So pick the area where it is most likely to succeed and try it there.

2. DESIGN THE TRAINING AND THE BUDGET PROCESS WITH THE PEOPLE WHO WILL IMPLEMENT IT.

Have the staff read this chapter, and use the *Discussion Leader's Guide* to walk through the key issues. Get a feel for the training needs, and how to best approach them. Talk about risk, talk about rewards, figure out the schedule on which you will need to implement the program to fit into your annual budgeting process. Look at the reporting templates in the next section of this chapter and adapt them to meet your needs. The essential element here is to have the staff who will be implementing the process have a significant hand in designing it for your organization.

3. TRAIN AND IMPLEMENT FOR THE TARGET GROUP.

Most organizations have found that this is not a one-day seminar. It is ongoing (monthly) training for nearly two years, starting simply and getting more and more complex as time goes on. With the initial training, the budgeting can start, and the additional training reinforces the staff's experiences and gives them more knowledge.

Try things. Adjust those things that don't work, and try again. Talk to the staff. Keep in touch. Your coaching skills will be tested early and often here.

4. BEGIN TRAINING ALL STAFF FOR IMPLEMENTATION OF THE PROGRAM ORGANIZATION-WIDE.

The sooner you start the education, the better, once the initial training has been tested. Let people observe what is going on in the test part of the organization. Look at the results together.

5. IMPLEMENT FOR THE ENTIRE ORGANIZATION.

When the bugs are out (in one or two fiscal cycles) adopt the amended program for the entire organization.

6. REGULARLY REVIEW AND AMEND THE PROGRAM.

Have a staff-based committee regularly review the budgeting process to discuss ways that it can be improved, including planning, training, and execution. Remember: continue to train. Not only do experienced staff need the refresher, but new staff, who have not had the benefit of the initial training, will be coming aboard all the time. Keep training, keep improving, and you will keep benefitting.

F. MONITORING YOUR BUDGETS

All this rethinking of your budgeting process, all the training and coaching necessary to get your line staff involved, all the changes in purchasing and check approval processes will not amount to much if you don't monitor the budgets that you and the staff have developed. You need to monitor your budgets to assure that they are being met. And with so many mini-budgets now being used in your organization this could turn into a major time commitment unless you can figure out a way to be efficient and effective. There is just such a way.

A TEMPLATE THAT WORKS

Here is the key instrument for budget monitoring: a template that you can adopt and adapt to meet your own needs. I have included a shortened version for the purposes of illustration. You can use this for the organization as a whole, as well as for each division, and all the way down to the smallest budget group (such as the teachers or maintenance staff in the example used earlier).

Note that there are eight columns after each line item. (This display is for a monthly report) The columns are: ACTUAL, BUDGET, VARIANCE, % VARIANCE, YTD ACTUAL, YTD BUDGET, YTD VARIANCE, and YTD % VARIANCE. With these columns you can simplify your budget review and monitoring a great deal. Let's examine how.

LINE ITEM	MONTHLY ACTUAL	MONTHLY BUDGET	MONTHLY VARIANCE	% OF BUDGET	YTD ACTUAL	YTD BUDGET	YTD VARIANCE	% OF BUDGET
INCOME								
State Program	55,400	53,000	2,400	4.5%	310,045	321,000	(10,955)	-3.4%
Medicaid	65,443	61,000	4,443	7.3%	422,449	415,000	7,449	1.8%
United Way	5,000	10,000	(5,000)	-50.0%	30,000	60,000	(30,000)	-50.0%
Fees	18,440	19,500	(1,060)	-5.4%	114,598	124,600	(10,002)	-8.0%
Donations	250	500	(250)	-50.0%	10,500	3,000	7,500	250.0
TOTAL INCOME	144,533	144,000	533	0.4%	887,592	(887,592)	(36,008)	4.1%
EXPENSES								
Salaries	105,800	107,900	(2,100)	-1.9%	623,980	602,300	21,680	3.6%
Fringes	9,522	9,711	(189)	-1.9%	56,158	54,207	1,951	3.6%
Occupancy	2,500	2,500	0	0.0%	15,000	15,000	0	0.0%
Insurance	8,000	8,000	0	0.0%	8,000	8,000	0	0.0%
Utilities	1,244	1,200	44	3.7%	7,698	7,400	298	4.0%
Telephone	867	900	(33)	-3.7%	4,680	5,400	(720)	-13.3%
Depreciation	6,588	6,588	0	0.0%	39,528	39,528	0	0.0%
Supplies	2,240	2,500	(260)	-10.4%	12,679	15,000	(2,321)	-15.5%
Travel	1,243	1,500	(257)	-17.1%	11,340	9,000	2,340	26.0%
TOTAL EXPENSE	138,004	140,799	(2,795)	-2.0%	779,063	755,835	23,228	3.1%
NET	6,529	3,201	3,328		108,529	(1,643,427)	(59,236)	

First, you don't need to read every number on the page any longer. Let's look at one of the income items: *Medicaid.* We see that the actual income for the month in question was $65,443. Taken by itself, this number is meaningless, and I still see many financial reports where the month's income and expense are shown without any context. Is this above or below budget, bigger or smaller than last year? So, this template places the context next. It is the column called BUDGET. Here we see that for our Medicaid line, we expected to earn $61,000. Since we now have both numbers, it makes it very easy to do the subtraction and the result of that equation is shown in the VARIANCE column, in this case $4,443. The fourth column turns the variance into a percentage (VARIANCE ÷ BUDGET) to put the numbers into even better perspective. In this case, we see that the organization earned 7.3% more than it budgeted for.

Now, we all know that monthly fluctuations can be deceiving, so we repeat the entire set of columns, ACTUAL, BUDGET, VARIANCE and % VARIANCE, but this time on a Year To Date (YTD) basis. In this case, over the year, we see that the Medicaid line is closer to budget with only a 1.8% variance for the entire year.

To use the template efficiently do this: start by ignoring the ACTUAL and BUDGET columns, and focus on the VARIANCE and % columns. Quickly go down these two columns looking for large variances and large percentages. Mark the ones that are problems, then look across to the year-to-date columns and repeat the exercise.

Go and repeat the same actions for expenses, and, of course, the bottom line. This template allows you to save time and energy at both the board and staff level. If you believe in the budgeting process, let it work. The template allows you to do that quickly and efficiently.

☞ **HANDS ON:** To get the most out of this process, set a limit of both actual dollars and percent of budget under which you will ignore the issue (say $5,000 a month and 5% of budget). Have this as a rule at management meetings and at the board (with the exception of the finance committee, who should be encouraged to ask all the questions they want). Then live by your rule. It will be hard at first. But you need to recognize that small (and sometimes tiny) deviations from budget are normal and are usually not worth your time or your staff's time to run down. Focus on the big items, the ones that break through your percentage or dollar limits.

You have already seen the template in Chapter 7. It will show up in our two chapters on Boards and CEOs (Chapters 12 and 13). This template works, works well, and can work for nearly every not-for-profit. But it cannot work if you don't have the personal discipline to get the benefits from it. If, for example, your board refuses to let the finance committee do the bulk of the financial reviews, and consistently goes through every single line item from personnel to coffee, you'll lose the benefits of this template. And, if your managers don't focus on budget discrepancies, but insist on reviewing every dollar, whether or not they are still within the budget, you will be wasting a lot of time.

Worse, you will be using up the trust and empowerment that you have established by implementing bottom-up budgeting. Remember that a budget is a contract, whether it is between board and staff, or the CEO and a Vice-President, or an area Director and a Maintenance staff. In a contract, if one party holds to their obligations, the other party really doesn't have a lot to gripe about. At least they shouldn't. This template allows for good oversight, good monitoring, and the development of increased trust and delegation at all levels of your organization. Use it!

RECAP

Now you have a handle on better budgeting, and I hope that you will put this information to immediate use throughout your organization. Adapt the budget template for your next board meeting. Talk about what percentage discrepancy from budget will generate questions at your finance committee or board meetings. Start now to adapt your budgeting process so that you are ready for your next full budgeting cycle.

In this chapter, you have seen the ways that most not-for-profits currently develop their budgets and why the order or outcome is often wrong. I have shown you examples of ways that organizations miss a key opportunity for staff involvement and use of staff expertise by limiting staff input in the process.

We next reviewed the four components of bottom-up budgeting which were:

1. *Train your staff.*
2. *Give line staff budget development responsibility and spending authority.*
3. *Provide risk and reward.*
4. *Have regular oversight and information sharing.*

I showed you how and why these parts nccd to all work together and how eliminating any of them will doom the process.

We then went over a budgeting process as an example for discussion, and you saw how important it is for line staff to be involved, but with adequate training.

Finally I reviewed with you an excellent template for budget monitoring, and we reprised the discussion on sharing financial information and using that financial information as a resource to be used to the maximum extent possible.

One more time: Budgeting from the "bottom" of the organization can and will save you money, improve staff empowerment and thus their morale, and save you and the board time and energy in your monitoring responsibilities. But you must train your staff before you ask them to develop and be responsible for their own budgeting. You must put them at risk for not holding to their budgets and reward them if they "beat" their budget, either on the income or the expense side. You also need to closely monitor the budgets that are developed, and do that in the most effective and efficient manner possible. You now have the tools to do all of these things. Pick the area of your organization that you think is most likely to succeed at this and start there. After a year, expand the process to the rest of the organization.

10. Pricing for Empowerment

OVERVIEW

Everything you provide, whether a service or a product, has a cost. It also should have a price, and in nearly every case, the price should be *more* than the cost. You should know all of your costs, and within the confines of the market, charge a fair, but profitable, price.

The problem with pricing is that most not-for-profit managers have been trained to underprice by the people that pay them—the funders. We have been told that we can't recover all the costs associated with a service, that we must match some percentage, or that we must have a set amount of overhead for all programs: all techniques that rip apart the normal fabric of pricing. And, while these techniques are survivable in a monopolistic environment, they are fatal in the competitive era that not-for-profits are entering.

Additionally, if you become financially empowered, you will, at least by my definition, have new kinds of income. You'll be doing new things for new markets. As a result you will have to develop the price on your own, from scratch.

Thus, you need to learn how to price: how to price fairly, accurately, flexibly, and profitably. Easier said than done. But in this chapter, I will show you the basics and some more sophisticated methods of price building. First, we'll examine the components of price, and the ways to identify them. Then we'll look at the pricing training you probably have had in the past, and how it has hurt you.

Next, we'll turn to examples: how to price a service (under grant or contract), how to price a product, and how to estimate cost recovery. We'll examine the market and how to price within it, and then spend some time on the key issue of break-even analysis.

By the time you finish this chapter, you should be able to review your current pricing structure and be able to identify where it needs strengthening. You'll know the components of a pricing strategy and how to position yourself in your markets. You'll also understand the relationship of price and break even and how critical that is if you are to be a successful social entrepreneur.

A. HOW PRICING IS SUPPOSED TO WORK, AND WHY IT OFTEN DOESN'T, FOR NOT-FOR-PROFITS.

There are four components to price: *fixed costs, variable costs, profit,* and *market forces*. It is the sum of these that set your price for a service, a grant, a product, an admission, a tuition, an hour of counseling, a membership, a meal, a week at camp, or whatever product or service it is that your organization sells. When you set a price, you need to pay attention to all four components, or you will set the price in such a way that you will either (a) not be competitive or (b) go broke. For most not-for-profits that I have worked with, the latter is the choice, and here is the first lesson of this chapter: *most not-for-profits underprice*. They do it for a number of reasons: first they don't feel that their services are worth the market rate. They have been told for so long that they are a charity that they no longer feel (or perhaps never have felt) that their services have value. Second, not-for-profit managers are compassionate people who believe that everyone should have their services regardless of ability to pay. That attitude, which I concur with for many social services, has unfortunately evolved into an attitude that no one, not even a funder, should have to pay full cost for a not-for-profit's services. And they don't. They will often ask you to match their payments, which in essence means that you give the funder a 20%, 30%, or even a 50% discount. Third, many not-for-profits have traditionally operated in a monopolistic setting, where they had protection from true competition and only one or two major purchasers—usually the government. Thus the buyer dictated the price, and there was no real reason to argue.

Here is the second lesson of this chapter: *to set prices accurately you need to know your costs.* Most not-for-profits don't really have a good idea about what the real costs are for each service that they provide. You may say, "Of course I know my costs, all I need to do is to look at my expenses and I can see them." True. You can see your costs for the organization as a whole, but not for each service or product that you provide. Do you really know what one unit of service costs? Pick one. It might be a ticket to a performance, an hour of counseling, a week in day care, a membership fee, or a lunch in your cafeteria. Can you find the numbers that tell you how much the fixed and variable costs are for that item? You may think you can, but if I started asking you about your overhead allocation (your fixed cost) for that item, you probably would see how little you really know about the costs of doing that part of your business.

So, that said, let's examine in more detail the different components of pricing.

1. FIXED COSTS

Fixed costs, also known as overhead, are the foundation for any price. Fixed costs are costs that don't change as the volume of sales goes up. For example, if you run a community theater, the cost of the building (either its rent, or its depreciation and maintenance) is fixed, whether you do 50 performances a year or 300. Other fixed costs could be administrative salaries, training for staff, and even utilities. Some types of insurance would go into your fixed costs, but liability insurance probably is sold to you on a performance-by-performance basis, and thus would be a variable cost.

For a 24-hour health clinic, you would have fixed costs for your building, your utilities, and your staff (who have to be there whether or not there are patients). Your inventory-carrying costs (you must have medical supplies on hand, again, irrespective of how many patients you have), your staff training, your marketing expenses, your administrative salaries, your malpractice insurance, your continuing education costs, your communications (telephone and fax) are all examples of fixed costs; they don't change as a result of daily or even monthly fluctuations in the number of patients.

The problem people have with fixed costs is that they are too easy to set and forget. Organizations tend to have a fixed-cost allocation that they apply for all departments, all products, and all services. It is simple, quick, and *always* wrong. Think about it: how could your overhead costs be 18.9% (pick any percentage to fill in here) for all of your different departments? Not only do they take up different space, they each take up a different amount of time for your administrative staff. And, the amount of time they take changes from year to year, or even month to month. One program or service might be able to coast along without your direct supervision this year, but if there is a crisis next year, you'll be putting in a lot of hours. So these costs are not the same from program to program or year to year.

Fixed costs need to reflect your real costs and all of them. The single biggest mistake in pricing is simply refusing to recognize all of your costs.

● **FOR EXAMPLE**: Here are some of the things that I regularly hear as excuses for not including certain costs:

▶ *Costs associated with a building:*
   "We own the building and have paid off the mortgage."
   "We won't charge ourselves 'rent' for the first two years."
   "The rent for our whole building is paid for by our grant."

▶ *Costs associated with personnel:*
   "My time will not be billed to this cost center since I am paid for by our grant."
   "Our financial people will only put in 20% on this project for a year, and then it will trail off. Their salaries are already paid, so we won't include them."

What all of these excuses forget is that these are real costs. Even if your salary is being paid, the time you put in on a service or product is real time, time you cannot spend elsewhere. If your staff are putting in hours on a service or product, those are hours that they cannot use again. Charge them to the project. Buildings, even those that are fully paid for, wear out, fall down, need repairs, require insurance. Charge for the space that the project takes up. Remember, your competition is charging for all their costs: you should too.

☞ **HANDS ON:** When allocating staff time to a fixed cost, remember to add in more than just their salary and fringes divided by the number of hours in your work year. (Note: An annual hours total of 2080 per person is pretty standard, but the real number for you depends on how long your work day is and how many holidays and vacation days you allow.) You need to add to staff cost the costs associated with those hours. This may include rent (or per square foot costs), support staff, computer equipment, etc. These are also real costs, and should not be ignored.

   When figuring building costs, don't forget about utilities. If you rent the building, the cost is pretty straightforward. If you own, use the depreciation plus maintenance, insurance, and utilities to run your numbers. For equipment, use the depreciation, maintenance, and insurance figures.

Be adamant about this: include *all* your costs. In an increasingly competitive environment, you need to know your costs, or you will get killed on your pricing.

2. VARIABLE COSTS

These are the costs that vary with the amount of sales. They are some-times called direct costs. When you have more sales, these rise; less, they go down. If you sell a product, these might be raw materials costs; wages associated with production, shipping, and packaging; or an allowance for waste. If you sell a service, these might include personnel costs, transpor-tation, or supplies.

● **FOR EXAMPLE:** Again, using our health clinic as an example, variable costs would include the cost to process a patient's bill, the medical supplies necessary to examine every patient (such as a tongue depressor, disposable cover for a thermometer, patient information given to every patient, etc).

The difficulty for service organizations in setting variable versus fixed costs lies mostly in personnel. In actual practice, our health clinic won't lay off three nurses for a day if patients don't come in: they need to have the staff there if and when patients show up. But most of the cost of treat-ment is really personnel. So is there a way to factor salaried personnel into variable costs? There is, but for most readers my suggestion is to leave them in fixed costs. As long as your price reflects the recovery of all costs, this method is simpler and the end result is still positive.

That aside, you still need to account for all of your variable costs in setting price. Try to have a number of different people (staff, your accoun-tant, your treasurer) look at the service provision or product manufactur-ing process. Did you get *every* cost? If you deliver meals, did you include the cost of disposable items (utensils, condiments, etc.), of fuel, of any other things such as public health information you might provide in addi-tion to food? Remember, pricing based on only *most* of your costs only recovers *most* of your costs. Get them all. All.

3. PROFIT

Yes, you need a profit. Why? Why can't you just break even? Be-cause you need profits to re-invest in more mission. You need profits to invest in growth, to help you with your working capital needs (see Chapter 4). If you don't add a profit into your price, when you discount your price for large customers or give a low introductory price, you'll be losing money. Profit is okay, and in my view it is essential to successful stewardship of not-for-profits. As you have already seen, making money is one of the essential characteristics of the financially-empowered organization, and the organization cannot make money if its pricing is targeted to just break even.

Add in a profit, market forces permitting. Additionally, as you will see in a few pages, you should add a profit in your initial pricing to allow for negotiating discounts. If your starting price always just covers your costs, you have no room for negotiation. Add in a profit. It's okay. It's good stewardship. It's good mission-based management.

One issue that may vex you is trying to decide how much profit is appropriate. Here, more than anywhere else, the market will dictate. A funder may allow you to recover a certain percentage above costs, but the market is much more flexible. You need to look at what the competition is charging and evaluate your price—and your value—against theirs.

4. MARKET FORCES

The three items above—fixed costs, variable costs, and profit—make the price of a product or service go up. Market forces usually bring it down. That is to say, competitive pressures have a tendency to keep prices down unless there is a shortage. For example, think of what happens to ticket prices the day of a big sporting event such as the Super Bowl, World Series, Olympics, or NCAA basketball championships: there is a fixed supply of seats, a high demand, and scalpers outside the stadium meet the market force by charging what seem to be outrageous fees for tickets. In reality, they are simply asking the market price for an item that will have no value at all in just a few hours.

Such shortages are rare, and most of the time the market keeps your price lower. You need to know what the competition is charging (if it is possible for you to find out) and be sensitive to market pressures. Then you need to decide how much to bend your initial price to meet the market force. Do you drop your price to be the lowest, keep it at your initial mark to be able to continue to give high-quality services, or try to do both?

You probably can't do both, and here is a question I get all the time from clients: "What do I do if we bid $9.50 per unit (to do something), taking into account all of our costs, and someone else bids $5.00? If we are bidding for the government they must take the low bid and we lose every time. My real costs are $9.00 per unit and I don't see how they can do this."

For what it is worth, the low bidder will either do a lousy job and not meet specs, or will be out of business next year. Next year, however, some other low bidder will take his or her place. While it is tempting to bid low and get the work, you will always need to have a minimum price below which you will walk away and not provide a service or product. Otherwise, you will be committing economic suicide.

One other note: since many readers have been operating as a monopoly for years, making the adjustment to a market-based, competitive and, thus, very dynamic environment is going to be difficult. One of the key rules of competition is that prices and incentives are changing constantly, and by this I do not mean annually, which is the usual cycle for you to set budgets (and thus pricing assumptions). You need to review prices much more often than that if you do anything in the open market, if you do anything retail, or if you do anything for which there is advertised competition. Because if you do, you are competing, at least in part, on price. If you assume last week's price is still competitive, you may have lost your edge. You need to be out there asking, looking, keeping in touch with the market. The airlines change between 14,000 and 15,000 fares *a day*. How long since your last price review?

One other basic economic force to keep in mind is the relationship between price, demand, and supply. This is, to say the least, a very dynamic relationship. As the price for an item rises, the demand from consumers drops and the supply rises, since sellers will make more at a higher price. Alternatively, as price drops, demand rises, and since supply also drops because the manufacturer can't make as much money, shortages often appear. Then what happens? In a free economy, the price rises again, *because of the shortage*, and it will continue to rise and fall until it reaches what economists call the "point of equilibrium", that price where demand and supply are equal.

Why is this important to you? Because if you sell something that is in short supply, you can charge more for it. Where there is a glut, you cannot hold your current price firm. Again, as with the airlines, as market conditions change your price may need to change as well.

To review, the four components of price are *fixed costs, variable costs, profit,* and *market forces.* Now we'll look at how you have been mistrained in your pricing, and then get into the actual examples of how to set a price.

B. HOW NOT-FOR-PROFITS ARE TRAINED TO UNDERPRICE

You are trained to underprice. By your funders, mostly, but also by culture. If you are a charity, does your service have value? Will anyone pay for it? "I'd better price it low so that people can come." That's the cultural hook. But the training by funders is more direct and harder to overcome. It goes like this:

"We aren't going to reimburse you for all your costs. We're certainly not going to reimburse you for overhead, only for direct costs associated with this project. You show us a list of your costs, and we'll disagree with some and then only pay you 75% (or 85% or 50%) of what remains. The rest of the cost you have to make up from local sources (this is called matching funds). We'll even be nice and let you use some of your overhead as match."

Such a deal. First, you have to remember that the role model for this in the past has been the Federal government, which has traditionally been extremely punitive to not-for-profits. (Please note that this is the same Federal government that lets large defense or engineering contractors include golf club memberships in their allowable costs, and a fixed profit on top of costs, often 5 to 11%.) Second, the states and counties have followed the Feds' lead, often with even greater zeal.

How can you overcome this training? Remember that you are not a charity, you are a business. I have already exhorted you to include all your costs and to remember that the issue is value, not merely price. For some customers, such as certain governments, you will have to decide whether taking their money at a loss is a good decision. Does the provision of this service do enough mission in your community that it is worth subsidizing? Or should you just say no, as difficult as that may be?

● **FOR EXAMPLE:** When I was the Vice President of the Board of a not-for-profit in our community, we were asked by our state funder to provide housing to persons with disabilities coming out of a state institution. This was excellent mission, from our perspective, but there was a problem: the state wanted us to provide the start-up costs ourselves, and then we could recover them over the first three years of providing the service. They wanted us to open 12 homes at a start-up cost averaging $30,000 *each!* Needless to say, we did not have that kind of working capital, and after a very difficult board meeting, during which our executive director threatened to resign if we did not open the homes, we voted to tell the state, "Thanks, but no thanks." and to tell them why. We had reasoned that if we agreed to do the housing we would effectively put ourselves out of business.

What happened next was exactly what I had suspected would occur: the state blinked, and agreed to give us our start-up money in advance. Why? Because the state was under Federal court order to get the persons with the disabilities out of the institution, and thus it was cheaper to pay our organization the start-up than to lose all state Medicaid funds.

Sometimes you just have to say "No".

C. EXAMPLES OF SERVICE PRICING

Now that you know what you are facing—the components of price, the ways that the market affects you, and the brainwashing you need to overcome—let's set some prices. In this section we'll deal with setting two prices for different services.

1. THE SERVICE: ONE HOUR OF COUNSELING

Fixed Costs Related to Counseling: Overhead, administration, rent of office space, use of clerical for scheduling, advertising: $4,579 per year.

Variable Costs Related to Counseling: Cost of counselor for 45 minutes, cost of billing, cost of reporting and filing: $25.56.

Profit Margin: 3.0%.

As you look at this information, the question is, how quickly do you want to recover your fixed costs; over what number of counseling hours? If the answer is 150, the fixed cost component to be added into the price is $30.48 ($4,579 divided by 150). If the recovery is over 500 counseling hours, then the fixed cost component is $9.15.

Price at a 150-hour recovery:

Fixed Cost:	$30.48
Variable Cost:	$25.56
Profit:	$1.68
PRICE:	$57.72

(This price would be rounded up to $60 per hour.)

Price at a 500-hour recovery:

Fixed Cost:	$9.15
Variable Cost:	$25.56
Profit Margin:	$1.04
PRICE:	$35.73

(This price could be rounded up to $40 per hour, but not rounded down, as the margins would be so small as to preclude any future discounting.)

The decision will rest on what the marketing and business plan say for counseling as well as on past experience of the organization. Is there really a demand for 500 hours of counseling? Can that much be done in a high quality manner? The difference in price is considerable.

2. THE SERVICE: ONE SQUARE FOOT OF CLEANING

Price: $.239 per square foot.

Fixed Costs Related to Cleaning: $98,756 recovered over 500,000 square feet of cleaning per year, resulting in an allocation of $.1975 per square foot.

Variable Costs Related to Cleaning: $.03124.

Profit Margin: 4.5% on top of the fixed cost and variable cost: $.0103.

Market Forces: Other cleaning services that are in the same geographic region. These keep prices down.

NOTE: If the fixed costs were recovered over 600,000 square feet, the price could be reduced to $.206 per foot, since the fixed price contribution could be $.1645 rather than the $.1975 shown above.

D. EXAMPLE OF PRODUCT PRICING

THE PRODUCT: 1 WIDGET.

Fixed Costs: Rent, utilities, depreciation on equipment, administrative overhead, advertising, interest on any loans taken on equipment: $995,870, allocated over 1.5 million units resulting in a $.6639 per widget fixed cost allocation.

Variable Costs: Variable labor, raw materials, waste, shipping, packaging. $2.46.

Profit: 5.5% per unit: $.1718

Resulting Price:
Fixed Cost:	$ .6639
Variable Cost:	$2.46
Profit:	$ .1718
PRICE:	$3.2957

In this example, notice that the decimals area carried out to 4 places. The reason for this is that sales are in the millions of units. A tenth of a cent makes a big difference. Don't round off too fast!

E. THE MARKET AND PRICING

As I mentioned above, one of the four components of pricing is Market Forces. These forces usually work to keep your prices low, but sometimes they can rapidly raise prices, if there is an acute shortage. The market is a constantly changing dynamic among demand, supply, and price; and the graph below shows this well.

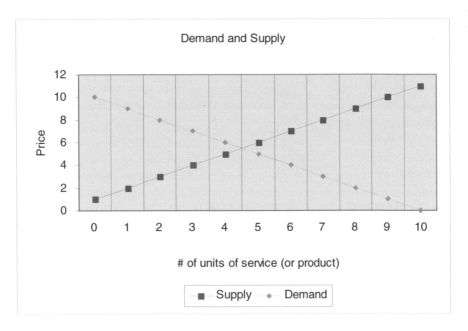

The vertical or y-axis shows price, the horizontal or x-axis shows units of either service or products, and the two lines show demand and supply. Let's examine each line in detail.

First, the demand line. This is the line that is high on the left and low on the right. In this case it shows that at a price of $10, the demand for the product or service is only 1.0, but that, as price falls, the demand rises until, at a price of $2, the demand is 8 units. When you think about this, it's pretty basic; the lower the price the higher the demand. Now let's examine the supply line. Here, when the price is $10 the supply is 9 units. Why? Because at a high price there will be lots of suppliers of the product or service. But as the price drops, so does the supply that people are willing to provide. Again, this is pretty easy to understand. Now, look at the point, just at $5.50 and 4.5 units, where the demand and supply lines cross. This is called the point of equilibrium—the price at which demand and supply are in balance. In a truly unrestricted free market, this point is always reached, although it may change radically over a short period of time. The best examples of this are the financial and commodity markets where communication is instantaneous, suppliers and purchasers are brought together constantly, and the price of a particular item can and does change from second to second.

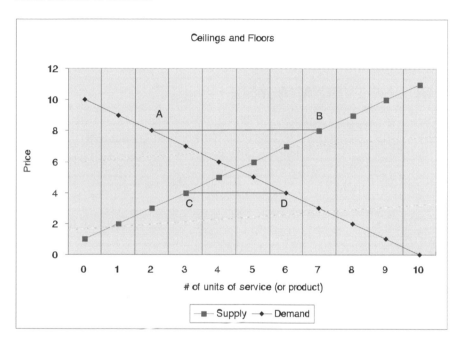

Now let's look at the effect of price ceilings and floors on the market. In this graph, I have added two horizontal lines called *artificial price floor* and *artificial price ceiling*. Examples of these would be price controls (on imports) or crop supports (for farmers) imposed by the government. Look at what happens in the case of price floors, where the price is held higher than the point of equilibrium. The line (from point A to point B) is the floor price. At this price, the demand (point A) is a lot less than the supply (point B), resulting in a surplus. The reverse is true on artificial ceilings, represented by the lower horizontal line from point C to D. Here, at an artificially low price, the demand outstrips the supply, resulting in a shortage.

Additionally, you will find that a market price for certain products or services will change radically with geography. For example, we all know that housing costs more in New York or Los Angeles than in most rural communities, while many retail prices (due to long lines of supply) are higher in rural Alaska or Hawaii than in Seattle. Thus, if you have a service or product that you are selling out of your immediate geographic market, you need to be aware of that locale's market norms and try to accommodate them.

The market works well on its own, but it is also without pity or patience. Cycles of demand, supply, shortage, surplus, and price changes are constantly occurring around us, and to stay aware of what your market and your competition are doing, you need to be constantly looking for information; constantly asking suppliers, purchasers, peers, trade associations, and any others that you can to keep current. Otherwise you will get left behind.

F. BREAK-EVEN ANALYSIS

Break-even is a key analysis in deciding the pricing of your products and services, and it is also an essential skill in developing businesses, one of the characteristics of a financially-empowered organization. First we need to define what break-even is, and then I'll show you how to use it to get a better handle on the long- and short-term impact of your pricing decisions.

Break-even analysis looks at the volume of sales required to recover costs (both fixed and variable) over a certain time period at a certain price. Let me emphasize two things: the analysis is only relevant for one price at a time, and only for the time period represented by the fixed costs. That is, if your analysis is intended to show how many sales you need this month, it will relate to this *month*'s projected fixed costs. For an annual break-even analysis, the fixed costs will be annual, etc.

The benefit of break-even analysis is that it lets you see how long it will take to recover your costs and begin to make money (can you wait that long and do you have deep enough pockets?). You also learn how much sales volume you must do to recover your costs (is it realistic to think that you can do that much volume and remain at high quality levels?), and the relative effects of the fixed and variable costs on your price. Break-even analyses can be done for one product or service on its own, or for a group of products and services combined.

To get a better grip on this, we'll start by looking at the mathematical formula for break-even. Then we'll visually examine break-even by looking at an example in graph form. Finally, we'll see the same analysis in a table form. All three ways work, all three ways will give you the same result, and each method can be used for different ways of explaining your data. For all three methods, we will use the following data for our example:

Fixed Costs Per Month: $9,760
Variable Costs Per Unit of Sale: $3.75
Price Per Unit of Sale: $5.00

First, the formula. Since break-even is the sales volume (or number of units of sales)needed to recover all your costs the formula is as follows:

Sales Volume for Break-Even = Fixed Costs/(price – variable cost)

Using the formula and the sample numbers we see the following:

Sales Volume for Break-Even =   **$9,760/(5.00-3.75)**
= 9,760/1.25
= 7,808 units

Thus, this business needs to sell 7,808 units of service each month to recover its costs and before it begins to make a profit. If it set its price lower, the break-even would be higher. If it can cut fixed costs, or can reduce the variable cost per item, the business can break-even sooner.

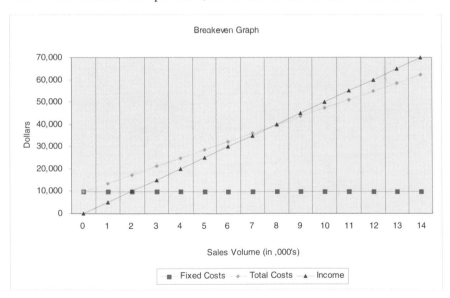

Now let's look at the graphic demonstration of the same data. The vertical or y-axis shows dollars and the horizontal or x-axis shows sales volume. Note that the line labeled "fixed cost" is also horizontal (at $9,760), showing that fixed costs stay the same despite changes in sales volume. The line that ascends from left to right, starting at the fixed cost line, is the total cost line, and it represents the sum of fixed costs and variable costs at any given sales volume. Finally there is the ascending line that starts at 0. This is income. The more sales, the more income. Where the income line crosses the total cost line is the break-even point. Note that this is 7,808— just like in the mathematical calculation. When sales go higher, the gap between the income and total cost lines widens, showing more and more profit. If you were to increase the price per unit, the income line would be steeper, which would move the break-even point to the left, at a lower volume of sales.

This type of graph is easy to do on most popular spreadsheet software, and is an excellent way to explain the impact of pricing decisions to your staff and board.

The final display is a table, shown below:

UNITS SOLD	FIXED COSTS	VARIABLE COSTS	TOTAL COSTS	INCOME	NET INCOME
1,000	9,760	3,750	13,510	5,000	(8,510)
2,000	9,760	7,500	17,260	10,000	(7,260)
3,000	9,760	11,250	21,010	15,000	(6,010)
4,000	9,760	15,000	24,760	20,000	(4,760)
5,000	9,760	18,750	28,510	25,000	(3,510)
6,000	9,760	22,500	32,260	30,000	(2,260)
7,000	9,760	26,250	36,010	35,000	(1,010)
8,000	9,760	30,000	39,760	40,000	240
9,000	9,760	33,750	43,510	45,000	1,490
10,000	9,760	37,500	47,260	50,000	2,740
11,000	9,760	41,250	51,010	55,000	3,990
12,000	9,760	45,000	54,760	60,000	5,240
13,000	9,760	48,750	58,510	65,000	6,490
14,000	9,760	52,500	62,260	70,000	7,740

In this display we see sales volume in hundreds in the left-hand column. The further down the column you go, the higher the sales. Fixed costs, the next column to the right, stay the same in spite of higher and higher sales. Variable costs are shown as the product of the sales volume and the cost per unit ($3.75). Total costs are simply the sum of the fixed cost and variable cost columns. Income is the product of the sales volume number and the price per unit ($5.00). Profit (loss) is simply the result of subtracting total cost from income. In the table, as you move down, losses decrease and eventually turn to profits, at 7,808 units. This kind of a display is also an excellent tool to explain break-even impact to board and staff members.

All three of these methods work, and you need to decide which method is best for you. But whatever method you choose, you need to do a break-even analysis once you decide on a price. Why? Go back to the graph. What if the price that you set results in the income line never crossing the total cost line, or not crossing it until the year 2045? You need to see that now. What effect will an increase in fixed costs have on your cost-recovery cycle? The break-even analysis will show you immediately. How about a rise in the cost of raw materials? Can you absorb it, or do you need to pass it on? Again, the break-even analysis can give you critical information very rapidly.

G. DISCOUNTING

I've shown you how to set prices, account for all your costs, and, in general, make sure that you aren't losing money each time you set a charge, admission, tuition, rate, or fee. Now we need to look at how to set reduced charges for certain customers. The common term for this is discounts, and many markets expect and even demand thcm. This section will look at why you need to have a discount structure and how to set it.

Discounts are based on one of two premises: first, that you have lower costs with certain buying patterns and should pass those lower costs on to the customer or, second, that you want to attract a new customer with a one-time low "introductory price". We'll look at ways to utilize both those approaches, but first a strong admonition: *all discounted prices still need to be at least break-even*. If your initial price is your rock bottom cost recovery level, any reduction from that will cause you to lose money. Your standard price needs to have some reasonably good padding in it, so that if you negotiate it down, you can do so without losing money. This will be clearer when we look at the different kinds of discounts, and how you need to rethink your costs to allow for them.

1. DISCOUNTS THAT ACCOMMODATE BUYING PATTERNS

There are two buying patterns that can qualify for discounts: payment speed and bulk purchases.

a. Payment speed refers to the timeliness of payment. The best of these is payment in advance or immediately upon service, which is un-usual but not unheard of. In this case you don't have the carrying costs that you normally would if your normal carrying time for a receivable is, say, 60 days. The other, more common, example of this is an invoice that you get that says "5% net 10" meaning that you can cut 5% off the bill if you pay in 10 days. (In paying your organization's bills, you should always run the numbers on these offers based on current interest rates. How much do you save by paying early versus the interest you earn keeping the money in the bank? Often these discounts are standard for the seller and do not reflect current interest rates. Sometimes the savings can be significant.)

● **FOR EXAMPLE:** Let's look at an example of such a situation from your perspective as the seller of a service. Your standard price for a unit of service is $200. You normally receive payment in 60 days. At 5% interest (the rate that you would get in interest for those 60 days if you had the money in the bank) your opportunity cost is $2.30, or 1.15%. Thus, if a customer asked for a discount based on cash payment at the time of delivery, could you offer a 5% discount? No, the best you could do would be a 1.15% discount, and that will change as interest rates change.

b. Bulk purchases offer you some other cost advantages. Large customers cost less per unit of sales in administrative time, less in terms of ongoing sales time, and allow you to plan your production (or obligate your service people better). All of these can result in a lower cost to you, one that you can safely and reasonably pass on to the customer.

● **FOR EXAMPLE:** If you sell tickets to a symphony, part of your cost is the cost of processing the tickets themselves, and the carrying costs for the money needed to produce the show before you receive the cash from ticket holders. If you have done a time study on the time it takes a ticket seller to process a ticket order, you may want to offer that amount off for bulk purchases. Let's assume that $2.00 of each advance ticket sale (normally priced at $14.00) is administrative costs for answering the phone, printing the ticket, mailing the tickets out, and processing the payment. For a bulk order, the mailing costs, phone time, and payment processing costs will all be reduced, and, if the numbers work out, you may be able to reduce prices on orders over 10 tickets by $1 each and for over 20 by $1.50 each. Note that I did not take off $2.00 since you still have *some* administrative costs.

Discounts for season ticket holders are based on this concept: one administrative cost for all the concerts in the season, and early payment of the ticket prices.

Additionally, for bulk orders, if you are making a product, you may be able to more efficiently produce the item, by lowering your cost of raw materials, or by negotiating lower (bulk) shipping rates to deliver the product.

2. OTHER DISCOUNTS

There is one other type of discount that you should consider, but only sparingly: the initial discount.

a. In the ***initial discount*** price reduction, you want to lure a customer to your service or product to let them see how good you are, and then, based on the quality of your service, capture them as a customer for the long term. Three admonishments: First, whatever advertising you do on this should clearly state that this is an introductory offer only, and not a long-term rate, fee, or price. Second, don't do this if your services are not truly top quality and competitive. If they are not, you are only building a costly revolving door for customers who buy from you at the reduced rate and then leave. Quality builds the value, and the discount should only get the customer to where they can experience the value of using your organization. Third, the initial discount should still recover *all* of your costs. If not, you are losing money each time.

Finally, be prepared with your numbers when a customer demands a discount. Don't automatically say yes. If they ask for 10% off, run the numbers and tell them the best that you can do, even if it is only 2.5%. And don't say yes to 10% off if you will lose money on it. All you will do is get a lot of orders at the 10%-off price, and lose money on each one!

Remember that discounting is an art *and* a science. Do it sparingly and for your best customers, not as a hook for every customer. Too soon your discounted prices will be the norm from which people start to bargain with you.

RECAP

Pricing is a very, very important skill for you, your staff, and board to learn and practice. Not only is it a way for you to recover your costs, it also sets the stage for the perception people have of your organization. Accurate and flexible pricing is crucial to your success in a more competitive environment.

In this chapter, you have been exposed to the essentials of pricing. We reviewed why and how you should price, the four components of pricing (fixed costs, variable costs, profit, and market forces), and how you have been trained to underprice services. Hopefully you now have started to overcome that training, and will be able to adopt a practice of including all your costs in your pricing.

Next we reviewed the ways to price products and services. We then examined the market and pricing, noting that price is not the key; value is. And, while price is part of the value equation, customer service, and meeting customer wants, are also essential ingredients. Remember, without people buying value, there would be no BMWs, no Rolexes.

We then moved on to the idea of break-even, to get you on the road to understanding the cycle of cost recovery and how it needs to be considered when setting prices. I showed you how to develop break-even analyses in chart and graph form, so that you can not only do the analysis, but explain your work and rationales to other staff and board members. Break-even analyses are key in developing pricing structures, expanded services, or new services and products. You need to be comfortable in using them.

Finally, we looked at some of the rationales for having flexible prices, and how to calculate a discount scale. This is also part of the pricing matrix and is something that the market expects. You need to know how to give discounts while not "giving away the store".

Pricing may not be a skill that you have paid much attention to in the past. Now, however, you have been exposed to the key elements of it, and you and your staff can face bids and price-based contracts with confidence that you are not losing money on each unit of service while trying to make it up in volume!

11. Corporate Structures

OVERVIEW

One problem that arises with many not-for-profits is how to retain their income, or even their hard-earned fundraising dollars in a way that a funder won't come after them. *Sometimes* corporate restructuring is the answer.

Another problem that you may have wrestled with is how to separate business income from your mission income. *Sometimes* corporate restructuring is the answer.

A third problem that may surface is how to appeal to a donor who wants to be sure that your main governmental funder won't use the donation for operations. *Sometimes* corporate restructuring is the answer.

Note that in all three of the examples above, I have emphasized the word *sometimes*. This is because corporate structures are valuable tools to have in your management tool kit, but not ones to apply every day. They are expensive, effective, confusing, and dangerous. For many organizations they prove a real benefit. For just as many they become an albatross.

This chapter will tell you how to sort out the differences. First, we'll take an overview of corporate structuring and examine the most important question: do you really need corporate restructuring? Then, I'll show you the most common and most useful types of corporate restructuring including:

▶ *Additional Not-for-Profit*
▶ *For-Profit Subsidiary*
▶ *Umbrella Corporation*
▶ *Cooperative*

For each of these, we'll review the advantages and disadvantages, and I'll give you some issues to consider.

By the end of the chapter you should be able to do the preliminary diagnosis of whether you should restructure now, or whether you should wait until conditions really merit the time and expense.

One other note: you won't be an expert in corporate structuring just by reading this chapter. Not only are there many subtle and technical issues that can arise, the law in this area changes rapidly as well. Conclusion? Get some help from an expert when and if you think that it is time to restructure.

A. Do You Really Need Corporate Restructuring?

Your organization is a corporation, formed under one of the (501)(c) parts of the IRS code. You may work for a (c)(3), a (c)(6), or a (c)(9), but if you are like 90% of not-for-profit managers, your organization is a stand-alone corporation. That fact provides you with certain opportunities to be involved with, or in control of, other corporations when and if the situation demands it. Thousands of not-for-profits have a second, third, or even fourth corporation associated with the "parent" entity, and many are successful in achieving their organizational goals more efficiently because of the additional corporation(s).

And many aren't. The first rule of corporate structures is: *Keep it simple*. If you can achieve what you want in a simple configuration, or, better yet, without any additional corporations, do it. Why? Because every additional entity is expensive and keeping the finances, governance, accountability, and staffing of more than one corporation straight is a big investment of time and money. Therefore, before you decide to develop a new corporation, ask yourself: is there a *compelling* reason (or, better, a number of reasons) to start this new entity, or can I do what I want within our existing corporation(s)? Usually, the answer is the latter, and many, many organizations that I see have too many corporations. They got there because they wanted to keep up with peers (or competitors) who were forming more corporations, not because they really needed them. Many hospitals have corporate tables of organization that look like engineering algorithms developed for the space shuttle, and they could collapse many of these corporations into one or two and lose no effectiveness, efficiency, or flexibility.

I have seen medium-sized ($8 million annually) organizations with eight corporations, all of which were important, ran smoothly, and had value, and I've seen organizations with two corporations that had one too many. Again, you need to keep it simple whenever you can.

But enough admonitions. Let's examine the various types of corporate structures, their common uses, the advantages and disadvantages, and some examples of how they have been used to create and retain financial empowerment for not-for-profits.

B. ADDITIONAL NOT-FOR-PROFIT

The most common additional corporation is a second not-for-profit entity. These are usually set up as "foundations" to support the fundraising, or as vehicles to hold property or staff.

1. MAIN USES:
- Foundations for fundraising and development.
- Property-holding corporations, designed to maximize rental income from funders, while at the same time achieving the benefits of ownership.
- Corporations required for funding—primarily for Housing and Urban Development (HUD) housing units.

● **FOR EXAMPLE:** A child welfare organization wanted to set up a foundation to harbor its $4.5 million endowment and to be a vehicle from which to attract larger donations. The rationale for a separate entity was that the main funders of the organization were more and more interested in having the organization spend its own money first, before receiving funds for providing services, and the board and staff feared that their hard-earned endowment would be lost. Additionally, more and more large donors were aware of this potential conflict, and wanted to make sure that their donations did not go right back into the general revenue fund of the state. So the organization set up a foundation as a 501(c)(3) and made a donation of its endowment from one entity to another with the restriction that it could only be used to support the original entity.

Why did it need this restriction? Because the foundation was not fully controlled by the child welfare organization, a condition required by its funders' regulations, and not uncommon throughout the nation.

2. ADVANTAGES

If you are going to have a second entity, it will probably be a second not-for-profit. Why? Because you know how to run one, and it is, after all, a not-for-profit and thus much less likely to raise eyebrows. You can also have a tax exemption in a not-for-profit, if you do things that support your second entity's mission statement. In a for-profit you pay tax on profit, no matter what you are doing.

3. DISADVANTAGES

Second (and third and fourth), entities cost money. They have boards which have to meet, records that have to be kept (*very* carefully), and, most expensive of all, an audit every year.

4. ISSUES TO CONSIDER

A number of our clients have not-for-profit corporations as related but uncontrolled organizations to hold property, hold funds, or hold employees, as noted above, but you need to consider whether or not you really benefit from all the extra paperwork and potential political consequences before you form a second entity. Is it necessary? Does it support the mission? Does it enhance your empowerment?

C. FOR-PROFIT SUBSIDIARY

In this configuration, a not-for-profit establishes a separate corporation that is designed to make a profit. Since for-profit corporations are owned by the stockholders, the stock is held in ownership by the not-for-profit (and controlled by the not-for-profit's Board of Directors). The for-profit board is elected by the shareholder (the not-for-profit); the for-profit does its business, has income, subtracts expenses, and pays tax on any profit. After-tax profits can be distributed to the not-for-profit as stock dividends and are not taxed again as unrelated income.

1. MAIN USES
- To attract funds or tax breaks only available to for-profits.
- To allow for unusual compensation for staff.
- To defuse accusations of unfair competition from competitors.

● **FOR EXAMPLE:** A client of ours set up a print shop to provide employment for homeless people in an inner city. After looking at the relative cost of capital to get the business set up, they found that it was much cheaper, even with the taxes that they had to pay, to do it as a for-profit. Why? The 2% ten-year funding to encourage growth in the "enterprise zone" helped, as did the tax abatement on city taxes for five years, the tax credit for each 5 jobs created, and other incentives that the city, the Small Business Administration, and the county helped with, including $150,000 of printing business in the first six months. None of these would have been available in a not-for-profit shell.

2. ADVANTAGES

- A very common format for a business—understandable to a lender.
- A great deal of incentive financing and start-up capital available for new businesses that promise new jobs.
- Flexibility in attracting others to the venture or in compensating certain staff (using the stock).

3. DISADVANTAGES

- *Always* pays tax on profits, even if what the for-profit does is related to the not-for-profit's mission.
- Unusual for a not-for-profit, and this often causes political trouble within the staff, on the board, or with funders or donors.

4. ISSUES TO CONSIDER

- There is often a lot of political fuss over a for-profit subsidiary. Your funders think you have a scam on; your donors assume that since you have a for-profit, you must now be made of money and no longer in need of their donation, etc.
- Don't even think about selling stock to someone else to raise capital. Keep control of your for-profit, and that means owning **all** the stock. Stockholders, even minority ones, have some rights that you might find surprising, such as seeing all your books at any time. Check out these rules carefully before you sell any stock.

D. UMBRELLA CORPORATION

1. MAIN USES

- To provide a central management and policy entity for multiple corporations that support the umbrella.

● **FOR EXAMPLE:** A multiple-service not-for-profit in the South provided a wide variety of services. These included low-income residential sites (through HUD), traditional mental health services, a for-profit subsidiary to employ people with chronic mental illness, and consulting to other providers throughout the state. To allow the organization to maximize its income through all of its funders, and to acquiesce to the various organizational regulations its funders imposed, this not-for-profit decided to form an umbrella corporation encompassing the following organizations: a controlled subsidiary 501(c)(3) to provide services, another for each HUD project (there were four corporations here), a for-profit subsidiary for the employment agency, and a final 501(c)(3) that housed all the employees. Employee time was then sold at cost to most of the other organizations. The umbrella corporation had the policy board, signed most of the contracts, and purchased employee services as needed. This admittedly complex arrangement worked very well *because there was a specific need for each corporation, and the need was great enough that the cost of running the separate entity was justified by either the savings or the additional income.* In the case of the HUD corporations, HUD reimbursed the additional costs of running separate entities.

2. ADVANTAGES

- There is a lot of flexibility if these are set up correctly. You can place property, people, and profits in separate entities, and if established well, there is the ability to adapt in the future.

3. DISADVANTAGES

- These set-ups are complex, costly, and look weird to a wide variety of board, staff, and funders. The accountability requirement is very high, and the paperwork, contracts, invoices, and accounting must be of the highest caliber. People will ask questions and you need to be prepared to answer them in a "squeaky clean" manner.

4. ISSUES TO CONSIDER

- If you think you are going to be adding corporations at some point to your current configuration, try to plan out the entire configuration now, and fit the pieces in as they are needed. If you talk with an advisor about how to establish the various entities now, you can save yourself time and money later on. But only do this if there is a *compelling* reason for each and every entity you establish.

E. COOPERATIVE

Cooperatives are funny animals, but surprisingly common. You see them all the time, but don't realize it. A grain elevator, a purchasing coop for raw materials, a fruit growers cooperative: all of these have the same basic components. A cooperative is a for-profit venture that has shareholders. Unlike a standard corporation, however, the cooperative board is elected by the shareholders without regard to how many shares they hold: small or large, each shareholder has the same number of votes. But, when profits are distributed, they are proportional to ownership.

1. MAIN USES
• Bringing groups of people or organizations together to do business more efficiently and to purchase expertise, goods, or services that they could not do individually.

● **FOR EXAMPLE:** A group of social service providers on the West Coast needed to reduce the cost of transporting all of their varied clientele each day. A committee analyzed where costs could be cut and decided that scheduling, maintenance, and purchasing of vehicles, fuel, and parts, were things that were costing too much on an agency-by-agency basis. A cooperative was established, and each agency invested its vehicles and some cash. Scheduling, maintenance, and purchasing were all centralized. A full-time mechanic was hired, as was a manager. A building that had housed an old tire dealership was purchased and used for maintenance. Costs were reduced. The quality of maintenance, done in-house for the first time, went up. All of the organizations, whether they had 150 vehicles or 5, had an equal say in policy decisions. When profits were distributed after three years, the dividends were not distributed evenly, but based on participation in the vehicle pool.

2. ADVANTAGES
• There is one essential advantage for a cooperative. Organizations that invest in it all have the same representation on the Board. Thus it is a very appealing set-up for collaboration and partnership between organizations of different sizes.
• Most funding incentives (low-interest loans, tax breaks) that are available to for-profit corporations are available to cooperatives.
• There is even a specialized bank set up to help cooperatives (The National Cooperative Bank in Washington, D.C.).

3. DISADVANTAGES
• Mostly the reverse of the advantages: if you have the biggest investment, you don't have the most control. At a larger organization, this may be a tough sell to a board of directors.
• As with a for-profit corporation, you always pay taxes on any profit.

4. ISSUES TO CONSIDER
• If you have a number of organizations that want to get together but the size difference between the smallest and largest is getting in your way, you may want to consider using a cooperative. While not a household word, cooperatives are very common, with some

of the Fortune 500 being organizations of this type (Sunkist, Land O' Lakes).

Another consideration in corporate structures is to make sure that you get some outside help, and outside help that is knowledgeable in the issues that are important to you. These issues include the state and Federal corporate and tax laws *and* your funders' regulations. Remember, one of the key reasons you will have multiple corporations is to help your empowerment. Get good help and keep focused on the outcomes you want.

The secret to successfully using corporate structures to achieve empowerment and remain there is to remember that structures like this are very specialized tools, to be used to achieve very specialized ends. As in any job, using the right tool is essential. Those of you who have worked with wood know what happens if you use a hammer to drive in a screw. The screw will usually go into the wood, but it will come loose very quickly, because its threads don't have anything to grip. Using the wrong tool has not had the desired result. To use the analogy a bit further, sometimes it's best not to use a tool at all. "If it ain't broke, don't fix it." Keep that in mind as you consider corporate structures. Keep it simple for as long as you can, and then use the correct tool for the job.

RECAP

Now you know the main corporate options that are open to you as you consider your path toward empowerment. In this chapter, we reviewed the major choices that not-for-profits use. These are:

► *Additional Not-for-Profit*
► *For-Profit Subsidiary*
► *Umbrella Corporation*
► *Cooperative*

We went through the most common uses of each type of restructuring, looking at the advantages, disadvantages, and issues to consider that revolve around each type.

I also cautioned you that corporate structuring is not, in and of itself, a panacea for keeping what you earn, or avoiding irrational funding policies imposed by funders. But restructuring is one tool you need to know about, and to use if the special situation that merits its use arises.

And that is the real message I want to reinforce with you: knowledge is power. Knowledge helps you to be flexible and to use the best tool at the best time to get the most mission out of your decisions.

Corporate structuring is one of those tools. Specialized, expensive, but, in the correct circumstances, incredibly effective. Use it sparingly.

12. Financial Empowerment for the CEO

OVERVIEW

If you are the CEO of a not-for-profit, you most likely came to your job from the program side rather than from the business side. That is, your initial training in college, at graduate school, or on the job was in the direct service that your organization provides. Thus you may think of yourself first as a teacher, a preacher, a social worker, a nurse, an artist, or a musician, and not as the chief staff person for your not-for-profit.

There is nothing wrong with that perspective, and it is shared by thousands of your peers as executive directors, directors, senior vice presidents, or what I will refer to you as throughout this chapter: chief executive officers (CEOs). While you may have come to your current job through an interesting and unexpected career path, you are now the person who has the ultimate day-to-day responsibility to ensure that your organization continues to provide services in a high quality and fiscally sound manner.

And for most CEOs, that is the rub: fiscally sound. You know how to assure quality in service; it's what you know best. But the money side? That's different. How can you keep your finger on the service pulse of the organization when you have to spend all your time trying to read and understand all the financial statements that your VP of Finance and your CPA keep sending you? How can you do strategic planning if you are worried that someone is misspending funds, or spending too much on things, or that the bills won't get paid on time? How can you interact in the community if no one but you can sign checks?

Answers to all three: you can't. That is why this chapter is included. I have prepared these pages specifically for CEOs who are not financial whizzes, who are not genetically predisposed to understand the difference between a quick ratio and a current ratio, who don't eagerly anticipate the arrival of each month's financial statement, and who do not consider curling up in front of the fire with their balance sheet recreation. Does this sound like you? As I said above, you have a lot of company, and hopefully a lot to benefit from reading this chapter.

First, we'll look at what your financial responsibilities are as CEO. We'll go through not only what you need to do, but why and how you can delegate certain things without losing sleep. Next, we'll go over the things that you can do to strengthen your organization financially and, not coincidentally, make your own job easier. Third, we'll take a look at the information you need to see to do your job correctly, more efficiently, and more effectively. It will be fewer numbers than you ever thought possible. Finally, we'll look at practical financial controls that can let you sleep at night while not shackling your staff.

A. THE ROLES OF A CHIEF EXECUTIVE OFFICER IN A FINANCIALLY-EMPOWERED ORGANIZATION

I want to start the discussion about what the financially related roles of a CEO should be by emphasizing the two words *should be*. Financial empowerment is an opportunity for senior staff, particularly the CEO, to finally get to the things that they should be doing rather than all the things that they are currently doing, focusing on daily finances and operations. Remember I said earlier that financial empowerment frees you to manage rather than administer, and it does. If you let it. If you can't let go of some of your current financially-related administrative tasks and make the move to manager, then the financial empowerment of your organization will not realize its full benefit.

Let's look at what I feel are the roles of a mission-based CEO of a financially-empowered organization. Then we'll have a little test for you! Remember, these are the roles that relate to financial issues.

1. OVERSIGHT—CHECK AND BALANCE

Just as the board is a check and balance on the staff, so you are within the staff. You need to oversee budget development, but not do it; read the financial reports, but not prepare them; assure that taxes are paid, but not cut the checks; read and sign the tax and filings that your organization must do, but not prepare them. Checks and balances are there to prevent problems, to reduce temptation by letting everyone know that someone is watching.

2. PLANNING

Planning, at all its different levels, is a key role of senior managers, and particularly of the CEO. You alone can get the truly "big" picture of the organization, and get a good handle on where you are and where you are going. Spending time checking out the future and your organization's role in it is important for programs and for finances. *What* you will be doing has a direct impact on *how much* money you will need and *when*. Knowing this in advance is a critical advantage for your organization. Planning starts with knowing your current status, and this means having good information. We will get to that in a few pages.

3. MARKETING

While marketing is the ultimate team sport, the CEO is both captain and coach. You need to lead the constant assessment of your markets and their changing wants, particularly in relation to key funders. Good marketing—meeting customer wants—means more money from happier customers. No marketing means sure organizational decline. There are a lot of places where the CEO needs to lead by example: marketing is one of them.

4. REPORTING TO THE BOARD AND FINANCE COMMITTEE

You need to ensure that the Board, Officers, and Finance Committee have the information that they want and need when they want and need it. This does not mean that you need to prepare it, or even that you need to be at the Finance Committee meetings—CEOs often delegate that work to their VP of Finance. But it is ultimately your responsibility to ensure that the information is accurate, timely, and focused. Boards have an oversight role that is even more important than yours, and they cannot do it well without having the numbers; make sure that they get them. For more information on sharing your numbers, see Chapter 7. For more information on the kinds of things Boards should be doing in relation to financial empowerment, see Chapter 13.

5. BUDGETING

As with reporting, the day-to-day task in this area is that of the Financial Manager, VP of Finance, or whatever you call your top financial person. Additionally, if you agreed with my discussion about bottom-up budgeting, your role in the budget process will be much less, and you will focus much more on oversight and support than on creation of every budget spreadsheet.

That does not diminish the importance of the CEO's involvement with budgeting. You are the link between the plans of the organization and the cash flow. You are the steward of the mission: is the budget reflecting your desires to implement that mission? You need to know your budget and monitor it closely. But let your staff lead here as well.

6. FUNDRAISING

Fundraising is a necessity for nearly all not-for-profits. You have the ability to ask for donations, and this is a resource you dare not ignore. Is it competitive? You bet. Can it be very technical and sophisticated? Yes. Should you get help, either on staff or from outsiders? Absolutely. But that doesn't mean that you delegate it totally. Rather, as you move from chili suppers to more sophisticated and larger donors, you, as the CEO, will need to be present and a highly visible part of the fundraising team. Let your development person set up the meetings, but you are the one who needs to go and either make the pitch or be there in support.

7. COMMUNITY RELATIONS

This area is a close relative of marketing, but it is not the same. Community relations involves being out of your office, connecting to the community in a number of ways: belonging to (and attending some meetings of) the local Chamber of Commerce, joining and attending a service club, participating in a council of not-for-profits, being a part of a community development organization. In whatever way possible, you must be visible so that people learn more about your organization, more about your services, and more about you. This connection will translate into money at some point—service dollars, donations, referrals, admissions. Spend the time to be out and about. Let your staff know that it is part of your job.

With these seven roles in mind, let's look at where you spend your time now and where you should be spending it. In the chart below you will see each of your seven roles that relate to finance. Take a look at them, and record the amount of time you now spend on each, then set some goals for yourself to increase the time you spend in some or all of these areas. Next, look at my examples of non-desired behavior and see if you can set some goals to reduce or even eliminate these time wasters. Add other behaviors you now know you shouldn't spend time on.

The desired roles are the key roles that you need to focus your time on in relation to financial empowerment. I am sure that you do all of these things now, but the critical question you have to ask yourself is: am I doing my job correctly, in the proper role? As I said earlier, you cannot

	DESIRED ROLES	% of time I Spend Now	% of time I want to Spend
1	Oversight		
2	Planning		
3	Reporting to Board		
4	Marketing		
5	Budgeting Oversight		
6	Fundraising		
7	Community Relations		
	UNDESIRED ROLE		
1	Developing a Budget		
2	Micromanaging a Budget		
3	Approving all Expenditures		
4	Signing all checks		
5	Hoarding financial information		
6			

do budgeting the way you always have—you will probably have to learn how to delegate more through bottom-up budgeting. You cannot just report to the board—you need to use your reporting mechanisms to make your financial information more effective. All of these things will come with time.

√√√√Four Hints to make your job easier

√ 1. Let someone else sign checks too. If you currently must sign all checks, you not only slow things down, but it takes up too much of your time. As your role changes to one of oversight, planning, budgeting, and outside duties, you need to pull away from the detail. Have one or even two other people authorized to sign checks, perhaps up to a certain amount. And, if you really need to see every check, see them *after* they are mailed. Have your financial person give you a file folder with copies of the checks that went out stapled to the purchase order or receipt. Then you can feel assured that the checks are all right, but you don't have to hold up the process of getting the cash out the door.

√ 2. Go to financial training—or set up tutoring with your CPA. If you are not fluent in financial issues, go to one of the many courses available on finances for non-financial CEOs. These are usually just a day, and relatively cheap. Or, talk to your CPA about courses they may teach, or about setting up tutoring for you at the CPA's office. You need to be fluent in terminology and understand cash flow, balance sheets, ratios, and know how to monitor the key numbers of your organization.

√ 3. Get numbers you need to see in a format that is understandable. You and your CPA can talk through what numbers you need most (see section C), set some goals, and then have your financial staff develop a report that works for you. Remember: numbers, words, and pictures are all fine, but put them in context.

√ 4. Subscribe to a business magazine and start to read it. Whether it is *Business Week, INC., Forbes,* or *Fortune,* start reading something that discusses business and finance regularly. This will move your mindset toward businesslike management. You will be amazed at how much in the business press is relevant to what you do, and how many good ideas you will pick up.

B. ACTIONS THE CEO CAN AND SHOULD TAKE TO STRENGTHEN A FINANCIALLY-EMPOWERED ORGANIZATION

Throughout this book, you have read about the characteristics of the financially-empowered organization; you have learned about reporting systems, estimating capital needs, bottom-up budgeting. But what do you, the CEO, do to implement all of this? What specific actions can you take to assist in the process of becoming and remaining financially empowered? From a different point of view, what are things that only you, because of your position, can do to get the process started? Here is a list to consider:

1. TRAINING

You need to train all of your staff (including yourself) in how to understand your numbers, what affects your income and your expenses, how much cash it takes to grow, etc., etc., etc. This training is long, repeated, and takes the shape of both formal sessions and constant coaching. Remember, the more your people know and understand about your numbers, the better. First you must train. And you, as CEO, need to push this, to participate in the training, and to be the coach afterwards.

2. WIDE REPORTING OF NUMBERS

Once your training is underway, share the numbers. And, as we said in Chapter 7, share them in ways that are understandable, meaningful, and useful. *Knowledge is power. If you share it, everyone gets powerful together.* Share your numbers with the staff. Talk about them. For example, post the productivity numbers on the bulletin board, or budgeted income versus actual, or occupancy versus target. Make people realize that numbers are important in a not-for-profit and that they can contribute to the mission.

3. BOTTOM-UP BUDGETING

When the training is ongoing and the people have seen the numbers, use the line staff to create the budgets. You as CEO have to lead here, coach, and assure. For much, much more on bottom-up budgeting, see Chapter 9.

4. HELPING STAFF LEARN TO PUT MONEY ASIDE

One of the most common barriers not-for-profits confront as they travel down the path to empowerment is that of the tendency to spend what cash they have now. And why not? The needs are great, the needs are now, and who are we to save for later? The problem is, of course, that if you spend it all now you will always be living hand-to-mouth. CEOs need to lead here by example, but most of all, by explanation and showing the mission value of setting some money aside today to allow the organization to be there to help people tomorrow. Talk to your staff, your board, and your funders all the time about this. Involve line staff in the goal setting that budgets how much gets set aside each month and under what conditions.

These four things are ones that you, and you alone can initiate and follow through on. They can't be delegated, can't be avoided. They are essential to your development as a mission-based manager and to your organization's movement toward financial empowerment.

C. THE INFORMATION YOU SHOULD HAVE

It goes without saying that you need information to run your organization: how many people you serve, what your funders want, how your staff are doing. Much of this information is best expressed in numbers, and often it is financially based, such as your income, your budget, your cash balance. There are other numbers, ones that you need to be seeing as well, ones that have weird sounding names like "current ratio" or "capacity" rates or "return on investment." To be completely frank, there are enough numbers to bury a CPA. Of course, a CPA might be happy buried in numbers. I suspect that you have better things to do, and you certainly cannot afford to spend all your time trying to make sense of numbers, figures, ratios, and balances.

So which numbers are important and which are not? Where should you spend your time? How do you separate the meaningful wheat from the trivial chaff? Once you decide *what* you need to see, how *often* do you need to see it? Daily, weekly, monthly?

Making those choices is difficult, but essential if you are going to fulfill your oversight role while reserving any time at all for marketing, community relations, fundraising, planning, and the other roles we discussed earlier. I can't tell you what you need to see. That is a function of your organization, your education level, and the status of your finances. For example, if you are in a severe financial crisis, you may need to see a cash balance every day. Alternately, expenditure versus budget analyses probably won't have much meaning more often than on a monthly basis. What I *can* tell you is the general categories of information that are essential for you to see, and then give you some guidelines by which to choose.

Let's make a start by going over the categories, then we'll focus on the guidelines. Remember, you need to see *something* from each of these areas.

1. CASH FLOW

Cash, as I said earlier, is blood, air, food, and water to your organization: without it, the organization dies, and immediately. Thus monitoring cash should be part of your regular routine. Remember, cash is different from accrual, and thus you can be running out of cash while your income and expense statements say you are making money each month. You need to have a regular update not only on what your current cash status is (how much actual cash is in your checking account, savings account, CDs or other securities that can be turned into cash quickly), but more importantly, you need to have an idea of what your cash situation will be, over the coming six months.

What you should see: 1. A cash flow projection for the coming six months, updated at least monthly. 2. An interpretation of your cash situation translated into "number of days cash on hand" at the end of each month along with your statements and balance sheet. (For examples see Chapter 7.)

2. STATEMENTS BY AREA VERSUS BUDGET

When we talked about sharing financial information in Chapter 7, we talked at length about having information that was useful, meaningful, and understandable. You need to apply that here, by having your financial staff develop statements that show your actual income and expenses for each line item, and then compare the actual to budgeted amounts on a monthly and fiscal year-to-date basis. And then you need to further see these by program area, so you can tell which area of responsibility is meeting budget, exceeding budget, or lagging behind. This is an important piece of information that allows you to perform both your oversight function this year and your budgeting function next year.

What you should see: Statements monthly for the organization and each key area within it. If there are areas that are having real trouble, you may want more detailed numbers for them. (For examples of these formats see Chapter 7.)

3. RATIOS

Ratios are ways to decipher the often confusing information that is provided on a balance sheet, and they make it much easier to track certain parts of your financial status. For example, if your organization has Current Assets of $1,347,844 and Current Liabilities of $874,576, you have more cash and things that you can turn into cash than you have immediate things to pay off, and that is good. But is it good enough? How can you track it over time? With a simple ratio called the Current Ratio which divides Current Assets by Current Liabilities. In the example above the current ratio would be 1.54, which for most organizations is pretty good. The smaller numbers that the ratios provide are much more manageable for most people.

There are dozens of ratios, but you only need a few to really get a monthly handle on your financial status. Talk with your CPA about which ratios are right for you, and then to your trade association about industry norms, if there are any. If not, you and your CPA, and perhaps your finance committee, will have to come up with goals and benchmarks for your organization. Get an understanding of ratios and use those that mean something for your organization.

What you should see: Three to five ratios each month along with your balance sheet—compared to previous month and previous year—and your organizational goals for that ratio.

4. BALANCE SHEET DATA

There are some other things on the balance sheet that I think you should see broken out and, again, put into some context. These are items like Total Debt, Receivables, Payables, and any Unearned Income your organization may post. These items are important to keep a handle on. If debt gets out of hand, you can sink in a sea of interest expenses; if receivables get too big, people are not paying you on time and you can run out of cash; if payables are too big, your vendors will be mad at you and you may in fact, be running out of cash already! In all of these cases, you need figures that show your status in terms of now, last month, last year, and your goal. In the case of the payables and receivables, you should have your financial person put them into the form of "days" of receivables or payables, indicating how old (and perhaps overdue) they are. For example, a payable of 30 days is probably fine, and most people let them go that long, but if the number jumps to 45 days one month and 60 the next, it's worth asking a lot of questions in a hurry. Note that the debt number can be actual dollars, or put into a ratio.

What you should see: Along with your monthly statement, you need an extra sheet with ratios and balance sheet information put into context. (For examples, see Chapter 7.)

5. NON-FINANCIAL INDICATORS

There are other numerical indicators that are important to you as a mission-based manager, and they don't all have to do with finances. For example; employee turnover, occupancy, days of attendance, number of patient encounters, job applicants placed, new parishioners who have joined, number of bus runs per day, number of paying members, and average class size are all non-financial indicators that could help you monitor events at your organization.

What you should see: A set of numbers that are important to you. Many of these numbers may be available weekly or even daily, but don't overload your staff or yourself. Again, put the information in context against last week, last month, last year, and your goals.

6. PRODUCTIVITY INDICATORS

Are you seeing more clients, serving more parishioners, housing more people, educating more students? Great! But are you doing it more efficiently? Are you even getting too efficient? (I know that sounds like an oxymoron, but it can happen.) The only way that you know is by developing and monitoring some productivity indicators. For example, let's say your mental health center had 4,500 visits last year and 3,670 the year before. That's good growth. But if last year you had 12 counselors, they each saw an average of 375 patrons, or 1.7 patrons per counselor per day, (for a 220 working day year). If, the year before, you had only 9 counselors, and they each saw 407 patrons, or 1.85 patrons per counselor per day, a big difference. The organization had more encounters, but lower efficiency. This number is a productivity indicator, and you can find others like it to monitor.

How could there be too much productivity? What about a classroom with 45 kids? For some schools, the desired number of kids per teacher (class size) is between 21 and 34, and you wouldn't want more. For many private schools the outside limit is 18 or 20 per room. By monitoring these numbers you will get a handle about your efficiency and any overcrowding you may be experiencing in a format that you can easily understand at a glance.

What you should see: Develop productivity indicators that are meaningful to you and see them monthly. Again, see them in context versus previous months or years and against goals.

7. GUIDELINES

As I said before there are a lot of numbers, ratios, and trends that you can monitor, so many that you may be buried by them. So how do you tell which to see and which not to? Try this decision tree:

1. Is this number a life and death issue for the organization, the staff, or the people we serve? (In the case of cash flow the answer is yes.) See these numbers.

2. For the rest of the possible numbers you could monitor, ask this question: If I look at this number, and the trend is bad, or even a crisis, what would I do? And, whatever I would do, is that appropriate for me to do, or should someone else be monitoring the number and acting on a crisis? If solving a problem pointed out by a number is your job, then monitor it. If not, have someone else do it.

3. Do I need to have this number at the tip of my tongue for marketing, managing, or fundraising. If so, monitor it; if not, don't!

Which numbers are important to you will depend on you, but successful managers can keep the *total* number of numbers that they see (beyond their statements and cash flow projections) to 10 to 15. That's right, *ten to fifteen.* That includes ratios, balance sheet indicators, non-financial information, and productivity data. Limit yourself for two reasons: you have a management life beyond the numbers, and it forces you to give your staff a break. If you have two people running around getting these numbers every morning, you will make their life miserable and see too much data. You'll be unable to manage, plan, market, and do all the other fun stuff you get paid for! Control yourself.

E. FINANCIAL CONTROLS

There are a number of financial controls that you should be aware of as a CEO. Many readers will already have a number of these in place, but it never hurts to review the need for and application of these kinds of controls, and for newer CEOs there will undoubtedly be some fresh thoughts to consider.

1. AUDITS

I assume that your organization gets an annual audit performed by a Certified Public Accountant. You should, even if your funders do not require it. An audit not only will catch almost any bookkeeping mistake that is made, so that your financial assumptions and projections will be based on accurate numbers, but it also provides a check and balance on anyone thinking about "playing footsie" with the idea of embezzlement. Audits are really your first line of defense against both error and fraud. Get one every year, and have a *management letter* attached to it. This will inform you of anything that you and your staff can do to improve the financial management of the organization. Don't fret that there will be things found wrong, because there will be, but these are things you *want* to know. By pointing them out, your CPA is allowing you to keep a small error from becoming a big one.

2. CASH

By cash I mean coins, bills, and checks, or such things as food stamps (if you handle them) that can be turned into cash easily. You want to have excellent checks and balances on cash, because it is so tempting. First, get everyone bonded who touches cash, as well as the people who sign purchase orders, sign for receivables, or sign your checks. This is cheap insurance against their fraud. Second, depending on how big your staff is, have different people do the various tasks that touch cash. For instance, have one person sign purchase orders and another sign checks, one deposit checks in the bank and another reconcile the checking statement. For help in this area, turn first to your CPA and then ask your peer executive directors what cash controls they have. Make these controls good, and stick to them. Ninety percent of fraud comes in the cash area, and the key is to reduce temptation. Let everyone on staff know that controls are in place so that they won't be tempted!

3. CHECKS

Who can sign checks, how many signatures should be required, and at what dollar level multiple signatures should be mandatory is one of the most common questions I hear. The answers, of course, are that it depends. It depends on your culture, your staff, your board, the financial condition of your organization, and how recently someone in your organization (or sadly, even in another not-for-profit in your town) stole. We all tend to tighten up after the horse leaves the barn, to mix metaphors. Basically, I believe that 97% of people are really quite trustworthy, and for most organizations, multiple signatures for the daily or monthly predictable expenditures are a waste of everyone's time. Certainly for payroll they are, because payroll is so standardized and one of the first places an auditor looks. If you feel that your board would be happier if they had to co-sign on checks over $5,000 or even $10,000, then do it. And, as I said earlier, don't be the only person who can sign checks on a regular basis. Let your deputy director, or some other staff person who is around more than you be able to sign the checks. We work for one national organization (with about 300 staff) whose Executive Director personally signs all non-payroll checks. He is often on the road 10-15 days at a time, and while he is gone, the checks do not move, which is more than a little frustrating as a vendor!

4. RECONCILIATION

One of the duties that your financial person should have is to reconcile the bank statement each month, balancing your check ledger against the bank's. Once this is done, you should see the results, as well as be handed the checks, in numerical order. Every couple of months, go through the checks, picking 10 or 15 out at random, making sure that the payee is someone you recognize, that the signature is appropriate, etc. Do this in the presence of the person who reconciled the statement so that they know you are doing it (and thus know that if they play fast and loose with some checks they are likely to get caught.) Also ask about any missing checks that you notice. Just one more control.

5. POLICIES

You also need financial policies covering the kinds of controls discussed above, as well as conflict of interest, bidding, reimbursement, and any other area that fits. Make sure that all affected staff have copies of these policies so that they can be aware of the controls and are never tempted to test them.

Finally, use your CPA and your network of peers to constantly improve your controls. These kinds of policies and controls are not the "set it and forget it" kind. Keep at them and peace of mind will be your reward. Your CPA is paid to help you, and your peers will be glad to help if you share your ideas and innovations in turn.

RECAP

I hope that as a result of reading this chapter, you have a better handle on how to do the financial side of your job as CEO without it becoming an all-consuming monster. While it is true that money is necessary for you to continue to provide high quality services, the services and the future of the organization deserve your time as well, and thus you cannot be spending every minute on the numbers.

In this chapter, I showed you how nearly all of your responsibilities as CEO have a financial side to them, and what the limitations of those responsibilities are. Remember, if you trust your financial staff, delegate to them. If you don't, fire them. We then looked at actions you as the CEO can take to strengthen the organization, especially sharing your financials internally with all staff, training everyone in the financials, and practicing bottoms-up budgeting. If you still doubt that this works, don't. It does. Remember, knowledge is power and if we share the knowledge we all get powerful together.

Next, we reviewed at some length the financial information that you should see daily, weekly, and monthly to be able to run you organization. I suspect that you were surprised at how few numbers there can be, which is not to say that you can't overdo it and add every number your organization develops every month. But a few critical numbers can help you manage, let you plan, and give you assurance that you know what is going on, even when you are not there.

Finally, we went over some practical financial controls for cash, checks, audits, etc. These are designed to work for smaller organizations as well as huge ones, and have the emphasis is on "practical".

Being an executive director, CEO, senior vice president, or whatever title you have, is a serious responsibility. The staff, board, community, and most importantly, the people you serve are counting on you to be the steward of your organization's resources, and to get the most possible mission for the money. To do that you have to understand, but not be consumed by, the financial side of your job. I hope that this chapter has helped you on the path to that status, and that the next chapter, which focuses on the roles of the board of directors in a financially-empowered organization, will complement the things that you have learned here.

13. Financial Empowerment for Boards

OVERVIEW

Boards of directors are fiduciaries: that is, they are responsible for the fiscal and programmatic outcomes of the organization that they oversee. As a board member, you have responsibilities and liabilities that you may not have considered, ones that you may have been misled about, and ones that you may have had no idea were even an issue.

This chapter is designed to help board members better understand and execute their financial responsibilities. Some of the tenets of financial empowerment may require a change in the way that your board does business, reviews financial information, sets organizational policy, takes risks, and relates to the organizational mission.

Before reading this chapter, board members should have read Chapters 1 and 2, which review the characteristics of success for not-for-profits and also discuss the key elements of a financially-empowered organization. You need that information before you move into this chapter.

In the following pages, we'll look at the responsibilities of board members in a financially-empowered organization. And, I'll point out your risks and how to reduce them. I'll show you how boards can act to implement and support the activities that create and maintain a financially-empowered organization. We'll cover the kinds of financial information that you should be seeing, and warning signs you should watch for. I'll describe the kinds of financial controls that should be in place, and how you should monitor their updating.

177

By the end of the chapter you should have a much clearer idea of your role as a board member, and how your actions can serve to make the organization even more financially empowered.

A. THE ROLES OF A BOARD MEMBER IN A FINANCIALLY-EMPOWERED ORGANIZATION

To clearly understand the responsibilities that board members have in relation to financial empowerment, we first need to look at the overall responsibilities of boards. The list below is broken into two sections: "Non-Financial Responsibilities" and "Financial Responsibilities". Note that many of the "non-financial" responsibilities have financial spinoffs—if you don't do a good job with the personnel policies, your organization may well be sued; if you hire the wrong executive director, he or she won't be able to pull off financial empowerment.

1. NON-FINANCIAL BOARD RESPONSIBILITIES

- ▶ *Hire executive director.*
- ▶ *Evaluate the executive director's performance in writing at least annually.*
- ▶ *Review and amend bylaws every two years.*
- ▶ *Establish personnel policies and monitor compliance.*
- ▶ *Nominate and elect officers.*
- ▶ *Represent the organization in public.*
- ▶ *Help recruit new board members.*
- ▶ *Perform volunteer program work.*

2. FINANCIAL BOARD RESPONSIBILITIES

- ▶ *Act in an oversight and check-and-balance capacity.*
- ▶ *Fulfill all of the IRS and state not-for-profit reporting require-ments.*
- ▶ *Set policy and establish organizational goals.*
- ▶ *Assure that fiscal policies are in place and followed.*
- ▶ *Help develop and adopt budgets.*
- ▶ *Assure compliance with funding stream's policies and regulations.*
- ▶ *Oversee fundraising and raise funds.*

I am not going to go into the non-financial list in any detail except to say that these issues are covered in much more detail in *Mission-Based Management.* I do want to go through the list of Financial Responsibilities at some length, to make sure that board members understand better what they are responsible for doing or having done.

▶ *Act in an oversight and check and balance capacity.* This is the broadest and most encompassing role, but one that touches on reporting, appropriate roles, controls and policies. Oversight does not mean looking over the shoulder of the CEO or Vice-President of Finance. It does mean actively asking questions to ensure the appropriate use of hard-earned funds in ways that support the organization's mission.

▶ *Fulfill all of the IRS and state not-for-profit reporting requirements.* Always keep your nose clean with the state and Internal Revenue Service. Make sure that taxes are paid and forms are filed.

▶ *Set policy and establish organizational goals.* Boards are responsible for broad policy and must do long-range planning to set those policies in place. The policies that relate to financial empowerment are detailed later on in this chapter.

▶ *Ensure that fiscal policies are in place and followed.* We'll talk more about controls at the end of this chapter. Boards should be very concerned about financial oversight and that means good cash, receivables, payables, and budgeting policies. For financially-empowered agencies it also mean adopting some new policies, and we will cover those later in this chapter.

▶ *Help develop and adopt budgets.* Even in an organization that is doing bottom-up budgeting, the board must have final say about how the resources of the organization are allocated.

▶ *Ensure compliance with funding streams' policies and regulations.* Every funding source, even donations, has a different set of requirements of how to monitor expenses and audit past work. The board needs to ensure that these requirements are met, met completely, and met on time.

▶ *Oversee fundraising and/or raise funds.* Not all boards take active roles in fundraising. That may be left to a committee, or it may not now be a significant source of income. If you do decide to build an endowment it certainly will be essential.

These roles are important to understand as you look at the rest of this chapter. Knowing about them will give you some framework for the remainder of the discussion.

3. STATE LAWS PROTECTING NOT-FOR-PROFIT BOARDS

Nearly all states now have a statute that protects members of charitable not-for-profit boards of directors from *certain kinds* of liability. I applaud these laws, as they remove an impediment which keeps people from giving of their time to make our nation's not-for-profits stronger. However, this should not make board members complacent about their responsibilities as fiduciaries, because the law does not protect board members from liabilities incurred as a result of any or all of the following:

Mismanagement: If your board acts in conflict with normal, common sense management and oversight—if it ignores accurate and appropriate information provided by the staff or funders or if it votes to do things in conflict with statute, regulation, or its legal contractual obligation—the members of the board may be liable for action as a group and as individuals.

● **FOR EXAMPLE:** A board of a disaster relief organization had been advised that there was trouble on the staff between a male supervisor and a female employee. This trouble came to a head with the supervisor advising the Executive Director to fire the employee for insubordination and refusal to perform her job duties. The problem became evident when the employee filed a grievance citing gender-based discrimination and harassment. The board's Personnel Committee followed their policies, had a hearing, and recommended that the employee be retained and that the supervisor be disciplined. The corporate attorney agreed.

Then the board went against both its own committee's recommendation and the recommendation of its own counsel and voted to uphold the termination. The employee sued. Who was liable? The board members—as a group and individually.

Non-Management: There are two common types of non-management: inadequate oversight of staff and not attending meetings. In the first case, the board members don't check to ensure that all of the governmental and funder requirements have been met (see the list above). In the second, the board members simply don't come to meetings and wrongly assume that they are immune to actions taken by the board in their absence. They are not.

● **FOR EXAMPLE:** A close friend of mine was on the board of a small private elementary school which, after a long period of financial decline, closed. The board and executive director put in long hours over many months to try to save the school, but to no avail. After the school's final day the assets were sold, and my friend thought that this chapter of his life was over. Until the IRS showed up. It seemed that during the financial crisis, the executive director had felt it was more important to pay rent and salary than to pay those bothersome social security taxes! The bottom line? The directors were each personally liable for nearly $10,000. Why? Because as the fiduciaries it was ultimately their responsibility to ensure that the taxes were paid.

Conflict of Interest: Board members are not allowed to profit or benefit unduly from their service on a 501(c)(3) board. This means that they cannot be paid salaries, or use the inside information gathered at board meetings to benefit themselves or their families. Board members can be reimbursed for travel costs associated with attending board meetings, committee meetings, and meetings with funders or staff, but they cannot benefit in other ways. Your organization needs a conflict of interest policy for its board members and, once there is one, it needs to be enforced.

● **FOR EXAMPLE:** An arts organization called me after being cut off from their primary funder. They wanted me to consult with them on reinstating their funding, and asked us to advocate with their funder. The organization had had repeated warnings from the funder that its board of directors had a conflict of interest in the way that it was contracting, and that it was not following its own bylaws. Both of these accusations were true. The board had voted to contract for insurance services with a firm whose primary owner was a board member, and this was in violation of their own conflict of interest policies. Additionally, it violated the state funder's requirements of bidding for services (which was not done). The board members told me that the reason that they contracted with the insurer was that he was "the best in our small town". I told them that I was sorry but that there was nothing I could do except advise them to live by their own policies and to abide by the regulations of the funder.

You need to set rules that you enforce. Here, the fact that the organization had conflict of interest policies *but ignored them* probably made them look worse than if they had had none to start with.

B. HOW TO REDUCE YOUR (AND YOUR ORGANIZATION'S) FINANCIAL LIABILITIES

There are a number of ways that a board and staff can work to reduce the liability of the organization and, thus, of the board of directors. The list below will get your board on the right track.

1. READ THE FINANCIALS.

This sounds basic, but so often board members don't look at much beyond the bottom line, or worse, they just listen to a finance committee report and accept it without any critical thinking. For a format that transmits all the important information that boards need, but lets them get through the finance committee report without having to turn a board meeting into a sleep-over, see Chapter 7. The successful implementation of this suggestion requires that the staff gets the board its information well in advance (3 to 4 days) of the board meeting, not 3 to 4 minutes in advance.

2. COME TO MEETINGS.

This is the antidote for the "non-management" that I described earlier. Board members need to be at meetings, having done their homework before they arrive. They need to ask questions, listen to the discussions, and make their best judgement on each issue, not just be a warm body that voted "aye" on everything. If people dissent on a key issue, record the dissenters by name—this protects everybody. There is no safe harbor in not attending meetings. If you are on the board, you need to be there.

3. HAVE A CONFLICT OF INTEREST POLICY AND STICK TO IT.

Your organization should have a conflict of interest policy for the board and, in this day of two-income households, for the staff as well. The policy should outline your way of ensuring that members of the board and their families do not unduly benefit from their service on the board. Some organizations preclude board members or their firms from contracting with the organization, some do not. Some agencies don't even allow board members in the room when an issue is on the table with which a member has a conflict. Some let the member be an active part of the discussion, but not vote. Whatever your policies are, you need to state them clearly, train your board in what they mean, and enforce them rigorously. A board that has the reputation in the community of lining its own pockets is a disaster in community relations, fundraising, and marketing. Nothing wrong needs to have occurred: the *appearance* of impropriety is enough to sink you. Be "squeaky clean".

4. HAVE AN AUDIT EACH YEAR WITH A MANAGEMENT LETTER.

One of the best forms of protection boards have against either error or fraud is an audit. Many, but not all, funders require an audited statement. My advice to you is simple: get one, get one every year, and get one with a management letter. An audit may seem expensive, but it is one of the best expenditures you make each year. It will assure the board that funds are being appropriately spent and convince funders and donors that you are managing the organization in a businesslike and appropriate manner. The management letter is designed to point out areas of fiscal management, such as cash controls, that can be improved. This also is critical information for boards to see, and gives them the assurance that an objective outsider is keeping watch over the technical issues that they are probably not expert in. Get an audit every year.

5. HAVE DIRECTORS AND OFFICERS INSURANCE.

Called D&O for short, this kind of insurance protects board members and officers from liabilities that ensue as part of their role as fiduciaries, but not because of mismanagement, non-management, or self dealing. For example, if someone slips on the organization front steps and gets hurt, board members would be protected from personal liability claims by this insurance. If, however, the board had ignored a recommendation from staff and their insurer to fix the loose step that caused the fall, then the insurance wouldn't be worth much.

Remember that earlier in this chapter I noted that many states now have laws that do much the same thing as D&O—protect board members from liabilities that are not caused by the three actions listed above. This may mean that buying D&O is superfluous and an unnecessary expense for your organization. Check your state statutes and see if there are important differences between the statutes and the insurance, and then decide whether or not any differences are worth the premium expense.

C. BOARD ACTIONS TO STRENGTHEN A FINANCIALLY-EMPOWERED ORGANIZATION

There are a number of things that only board members can do to make the organization more financially empowered, or to facilitate that empowerment. Staff are hired to do the day-to-day work of the organization; providing services and managing operations, finance, marketing, and planning. The board has an important set of functions which we went over at the beginning of the chapter.

But what specific actions can boards take to get the organization going and keep it on its way? Here's a list.

1. STREAMLINE YOUR REPORTING.

Having information that is unintelligible prevents the board from being able to act in an oversight role. Having too much information, or too detailed information, or information that isn't put into context, not only prevents effective oversight, but also gets in the way of allowing board members to do the other things on the list of responsibilities that we reviewed at the beginning of the chapter. The first thing boards should do is streamline their reporting. This means getting the information that is needed to the people that need it in an understandable format when they need it.

Part of this streamlining includes delegating rigorous oversight to the Finance Committee and Treasurer, and having the general board comfortable with not seeing every single number every single month. This can be a major stretch for some boards who are used to having what I consider undue oversight, but such habits often spring from stress related to the organization never having enough cash. Through financial empowerment the organization will have not only sufficient cash, but a reasonable surplus, which should reduce board tension and allow them to back off a bit.

In Chapter 7 we had an extensive discussion of making better use of financial reporting and in the next section of this chapter you will find a discussion about who on the board should see which information. But the action the board needs to take is to streamline and make more sensible the financial information that it sees.

2. TRAIN THE BOARD IN HOW TO READ THE INFORMATION THAT IT GETS.

Now you have a great set of financials, ones that make some sense out of all your bizarre funding streams, rates, donations, and earned income. The board gets what it really needs, and the Finance Committee and

Treasurer see a lot more. You're not done yet, not until you take the time to train people to understand these reports.

What do I mean by train? I mean taking the time to talk through each report, how it is generated, what each line item is, what it means, and how to make the most appropriate use of the report as a board member. Where there are comparisons (expenses versus budget, occupancy versus goals) explain how the benchmark was developed and why it is important. Try to have all the board members do this session together so that they all start at the same place. You may be very surprised at who "gets it" and who doesn't. But train, and have a refresher course once a year. If the Board Treasurer is a good teacher, have that person give the training. If not, perhaps your CPA or Vice President of Finance can do the job.

Whoever leads the training, they need to do the *what, why*, and *how*: what the line item is, why it is important, and how to use it.

3. DEVELOP AND MAINTAIN POLICIES.

It is the board's responsibility to set policies, including those on financial issues. In the area of financial empowerment you need the following discussions and policies or guidelines. These should be studied first by the Finance Committee and then adopted by the board.

▶ A policy on debt, including who can authorize borrowing, establishing a line of credit, as well as debt-to-net-worth goals.

▶ Establishment of an endowment (either in a restricted fund or separate corporation).

▶ Establishment of a mission reserve, including policies and procedures for the reserve's size, funding, use, and distribution.

▶ Establishment of a policy on budgeting goals and profits.

▶ Establishment of a financial empowerment plan (see Chapter 14 for an example).

▶ Establishment of guidelines and goals for receivables, payables, cash reserve, and appropriate ratios.

These actions will bring the board into the financial empowerment loop. They will require an awareness of the financial situation of the organization that may have been lacking in the past, and will force the board members to think beyond today's cash shortfall to tomorrow's empowerment.

D. THE FINANCIAL INFORMATION YOU SHOULD SEE

Now that I have scared you with a long discussion about board responsibilities, and told you how to reduce risk both for the organization and the board, let's look at the financial information board members must see to be good fiduciaries.

Not all board members need to see the same information each month or at each meeting. The board Treasurer, for example, will need to review information in much more detail than most other members of the board. The members of the financial committee will see more displays and spend more time on numbers than other members of the board. This differentiation based on job description makes sense and is consistent with my discussion in Chapter 7 about staff members and board members receiving differentiated information based on their needs and wants.

That having been said, I do not want to leave the impression that there is *any* financial information that a board member should not have access to. Let me state it a different way: ***Any board member should be provided any financial information any time they want to see it.***

This broad statement is intentional, and I know that some information, such as salaries, may have to be provided only with a strict control for confidentiality (and having signed statements to that effect is a good idea). The point is that staff cannot and should not tell board members that any financial information is off limits. If they do, the board should be up in arms in a nano-second.

The board should be *very* concerned if financial information either is slowed down significantly in its delivery or, worse, stops coming altogether. In every one of the 25 or so not-for-profit organizational collapses that I have studied, the board members stated that they got financial information late or not at all. I tell board members that when the numbers stop coming, demand to know why. Call the Board Treasurer, and don't wait until the next board meeting. Call *now*. Have the Treasurer *demand* the financial reports. If that doesn't work, call the banker and ask about checking and savings balances and unusual activity. Ask, demand, and find out what is going on. Remember, the board is ultimately responsible for the financial integrity of the organization. When numbers stop coming, it's almost never because the computers were down or the printer broke. Check it out and soon.

With those admonitions hopefully etched in your mind, let's look at the more regular condition of financial reporting on a monthly basis, and examine some samples of who should see what. I will start at the most general level and work up to the Treasurer, who will be seeing financial information in the most detail.

1. THE BOARD OF DIRECTORS

Boards should see everything whenever they want to, but that does not mean that they should see everything all the time. If the Board has prudent controls in place, and if the Finance Committee and Treasurer are doing their respective jobs, there is no reason for detailed review of all financial information by the board either in writing or at the board meetings. The exceptions to this are in a financial crisis, or at budget time.

In most cases the board should see just summary information. But in all cases the members should get their information 4-5 days before the board meeting in order to study it and note any questions that they may have:

What you should see:
> ▶ A display of the status of income and expenses versus the budget.
> ▶ A balance sheet for the end of the most recent reporting period.
> ▶ A display of cash status and a projection of cash balance for the end of each of the next six months.
> ▶ At budget time, the board should see the entire budget along with all budget assumptions.

(For examples of board financial displays see Chapter 7.)

2. THE FINANCE COMMITTEE

The next level of oversight is that of the Finance Committee. This small group of board members should see more detail about the same items as the board, and should also set policies and goals for the board to consider. The Finance Committee should meet separately from the board, and if your board only meets once a quarter, the Committee should meet monthly.

What you should see:
> ▶ A more detailed display of income and expenses compared to budget. For example, the Finance Committee should see the reports for each program in the organization, not just the summary for the organization as a whole.
> ▶ A more detailed cash flow, showing all anticipated receipts, disbursements, and assumptions under which the projections were developed.
> ▶ A balance sheet and ratios every reporting period.
> ▶ A listing of debt, maturities, interest rates, and remaining term each month.
> ▶ A list of investments (CDs, money market funds) each month with interest rates and maturities.

▶ An update on funding changes, and any political or other issues that may affect income or expense.

▶ The annual budget in draft form, and like the income and expense statements, these budgets should be for all areas of operations.

▶ The business plans for any new areas of operations or markets.

▶ The long-term capital plan for the organization.

3. THE TREASURER

The job of Treasurer is a critical one. The Treasurer is the most critical link between the staff and the board in regard to financial information, policy, and status. If the board trusts that the Treasurer is competent and doing his or her job, the organization will be able to operate as it should. If the board does not have that trust, it will inevitably immerse itself in financial detail to a level that is unhealthy.

The Treasurer must also truly understand the finances of the organization and this includes the often arcane funding streams, rates, and regulations that come from government. Thus the Treasurer must spend the time to become fluent in the financial operations of the organization. This is asking a lot in terms of time and, as a result, I often recommend that the Finance Committee, which is chaired by the Treasurer, be vice chaired by someone who is, in effect, Treasurer-elect. This gives a person more time to become familiar with the numbers and their relations to services.

What you should see: The Treasurer should see everything needed to do their job. Some suggestions of things that other organizations have found prudent for the Treasurer to see:

▶ Bank reconciliation form each month

▶ Letters of funding award

▶ Preliminary budget figures

▶ Cash balances weekly

▶ Methods of rate calculation for organizations that receive funding based on a calculated rate.

The Treasurer should talk weekly with the Vice-President of Finance and get even more information if there are financial problems. He or she should accompany the CEO and the Vice President of Finance to the bank once a year to both show board commitment and to hear what the banker says. Being Treasurer is a tough, demanding, and time-consuming job, but an essential one for any financial empowerment to occur.

E. FINANCIAL CONTROLS

You should have financial policies in place that deal with cash control, reimbursement policies, check signature requirements, who is authorized to obligate debt, etc. Most of these controls are fairly standard and I urge board members to consult with two sources regularly to assure that their policies are up-to-date and as all-encompassing as possible: the organization's CPA and peer groups. As I said in my discussion of the need for audits above, your CPA has both a professional and a legal obligation to help you reduce and eliminate potential opportunities for fraud or inadvertent error. The CPA is also an excellent person to bring into your biannual review of financial policies. He or she can help you design the best policies possible for an organization your size. Other organizations may have excellent ideas that *their* CPAs developed for them—at their expense and not yours. So ask, and be willing to share your policies in return.

While most of these procedures are standard, I want to spend some time on two issues that seem to vex many boards: check-signing authority and authority to obligate debt for the organization. Both come up over and over in my work with clients, and so I want to spend a few moments here to answer some of the questions that may be on your board's mind.

1. CHECK SIGNATURE AUTHORITY

The issues are: how many signatures should be on each check, whose signatures and, if you allow single signature checks, is there a limit over which there has to be more than one signer? The answer, which you probably can predict is: it depends. You don't want to slow down the organization so much that bills or, worse, payroll goes out late. But at the same time, you want some control on cash flow out. My advice is that you entrust single signature check signing to more than one staff person (usually the CEO and VP of Finance) and have a financial limit that requires two signatures if there are checks written over that amount. For some organizations that limit will be $1,000. For some it may be $20,000, or even higher.

Some board members have said to me that they want to see every check as it goes out to ensure that funds are not being misspent. I think that is a waste of time and an insult to staff unless the organization is on the brink of bankruptcy. If the board is seeing the appropriate information, if they are seeing cash flows, income and expense statements versus budget, then they should have a month-to-month handle on things. The board's Finance Committee and its Treasurer should have even a closer eye on things. If, with all this oversight, you still don't feel that you can trust either or both of your top staff people to sign checks, don't insult them with undue oversight. Fire them and get some people that you *can* trust. Many boards just get in the habit of treating their staff like three-year-olds and it's not fair to the staff or a good use of board time and energy.

One other reality check: your funder's or state's regulations, or any accrediting body that you work with may have rules or restrictions on check signing. Make sure that you follow any of those that are applicable to you.

2. THE AUTHORITY TO OBLIGATE DEBT

I am sure that some readers feel that I am too liberal on the issue of check signatures. On this subject of debt, however, I take the other extreme. Have a tight, tight leash on debt. Some organizations let their CEOs borrow in the name of the organization, sign for debt, etc. I think this is a big mistake. Even the authorization for a line of credit withdrawal, something that is designed to be quick and easy, should be approved by the Board President or Treasurer. Your banker can be told that he or she has to call one of the officers to get approval when the staff asks for funds from the line. This is a key check and balance. Keep control of your debt. If staff have too much leeway, the temptation to borrow to cover short-term cash flow ("we'll pay it back before the end of the month and the board won't even have to know") may be too strong.

Finally, in the area of financial controls, I need to urge you to make sure that your controls are up-to-date and meeting your organization's needs. At the outside, your policies and procedures should be formally reviewed and approved by the Finance Committee and then the Board every 24 months. In most cases, there will be just minor adjustments, but the importance of reviewing the documents cannot be overemphasized. It refreshes everyone's mind as to what the policies are, and assures that any changes in tax law, personnel law, regulation, or simply standard control practices are included in your controls documents. Have your CPA help you in this review. His or her fee is well worth it.

Having good financial controls is an important part of your board's role. It will help fulfill the board members' oversight responsibilities and give them some peace of mind so that they don't have to be in the office counting petty cash each day.

RECAP

I have tried to craft this chapter to allow it to be used primarily by members of the Board of Directors as they seek to fulfill their roles on the road to financial empowerment. Board members are policy setters, planners, and financial fiduciaries, and thus it is ultimately they who must decide whether or not the organization will develop the policies, discipline, and culture to become and remain financially empowered. Staff may develop budgets, but board members adopt them. Board members are the only ones who can authorize the establishment of a restricted fund or an endowment. They are the ultimate authority on cash reserves; and on the development of policies on mission reserves, borrowing, and risk-taking.

In this chapter we've covered a number of things that I hope will make that job easier. We started with a thorough review of board roles with a focus on the roles related to finance. I showed you how connected nearly all board roles are to financial well-being, and how thinking about policy and the big picture are the appropriate things to do rather than going over the checkbook every day.

We moved next to ways to reduce your board's and your organization's liability, including such simple and inexpensive things as reading financial statements and attending board meetings, and more complex and expensive things such as having audits performed annually.

We then touched on ways that the board can strengthen an organization and make it more financially empowered. These actions are things that the board can do best, including the setting of policies, training itself, and streamlining the reports it sees so that they make sense. It is important here to remember that these are all functions that the board can and should initiate with the staff as part of the empowerment plan. If the board does not do these things, the foundation for empowerment is not in place, and as new board members come on, some of the momentum for empowerment may be lost. Having the policies and reporting in place will help keep the momentum.

In order for board members to be board members and not financial advisors, it is important for them to be seeing enough reports to perform their oversight functions but not so many that all they discuss is finances. We then reviewed the different levels of information needs that the Treasurer, the Finance Committee, and the Board members in general have.

Finally, we talked about what financial controls should be in place and how to ensure that they are current. We focused in on two areas—check writing authority and authority to obligate debt—that seem to consistently perplex boards.

After going though this chapter and absorbing the ideas and cautions, you should be able to act in a way that helps the organization towards empowerment rather than impeding its progress. Changing an organization from financially unstable to financially stable to financially empowered is a lot of work, over a lot of time. Staff, board, community, and funders all have to play their parts. But deciding to seek empowerment, making the policy decision to set off down the road; that is a board action and an action of the board alone. As you retain more and more assets, there are more assets to oversee, and oversight is ultimately a board function. And, ensuring that the assets are used for more mission, yes, that is a board responsibility as well.

Board members can be full partners in the empowerment quest. With the ideas and cautions found in this chapter, that partnership should be much easier.

14. Mobilizing for Empowerment

OVERVIEW

I hope that by now you want your organization to become an empowered one. You are willing to take the long road, make the sacrifice if it results in more mission capability, more flexibility, more responsiveness. I've told you that you will have some resistance, and you've read my ideas on how to overcome that hesitance or outright opposition from board, staff, or funders.

But I assume that you still are asking: "OK, so I know all that, but what do I do? How do I get started? What actions do I take? There is so much to do, where do I begin?" Fair questions all, and like any of us, it helps to have specific suggestions to get started, to take the single step that initiates the proverbial long journey.

In this chapter, I'll try to show you those initial steps, and the ones that come after them. We'll start at the beginning, with the organizational action steps that will get you, your staff, and your board started.

Throughout the book, I've shown you the characteristics of empowerment and covered them subject by subject. In the next section you'll see dozens of ideas and activities to help move your organization ahead.

After all those specifics, you still may be unsure of exactly what to do. So, I'll also show you an actual sample empowerment plan, complete with assumptions, goals, and timeline.

With all these pieces of information in hand, you will be ready to move to the final chapter, where I'll show you how to join your mission to your empowerment. But first, let's get to the specifics.

A. ACTION STEPS TO TAKE

The steps outlined here are ones to get you organized and doing things in the correct order. I offer ideas and parameters for action, but you will need to interpret them to meet your organization's own unique needs. This may mean a different kind of empowerment committee, or a different sequence of training. But whatever your decisions, try to include as many of the items listed here as possible, and keep them in the order provided. Your likelihood of success will be much higher.

1. GET A COMMITTEE.

Establish an Empowerment Committee, one that will both develop your empowerment plan, and also be responsible for its implementation. Try to keep the Committee small, seven to nine people at most. Include the CEO, your head financial person, and the Board Treasurer. If there is a Chief Operating Officer (often called Deputy Director), that person may be included, as might any development staff person you have. I am also in favor of including a middle manager, and a line staff person on all such committees. If you have enough slots, add another member of the Finance Committee, perhaps the vice chair that I discussed in Chapter 13. Additionally, your banker and CPA may be added to the group for certain meetings.

This committee should meet regularly, and its initial task will be to develop an empowerment plan, as described in 3 below.[1]

Once you have established your Empowerment Committee, you should go directly to the next step.

2. TRAIN THE COMMITTEE.

Not only should the Committee members all read this book, but there should be a session scheduled with your CPA and banker to discuss the financial realities of your organization. You need this to assure that everyone on the Committee starts from the same level of understanding about income, expenses, debt, ratios, reserves, your funders' restrictions on earnings, etc. This training may take one meeting or five before you feel that you are ready with enough information to move ahead.

---

[1] I recommend that the members of the Committee all read this book. The *Discussion Leader's Guide* will help take you through the planning process. It uses the assessment tool found in the appendix, and then helps you set goals for each area of your organization. The *Guide* will really help you keep on track.

3. PLAN.

The act of planning is essential to becoming empowered. As I have said over and over, the empowering of your organization will take time, and it will be easy to get distracted and forget where you are going. The way to avoid that is to put down on paper where you want to go, and the measurable steps you will take to get from here to there. That's called a plan and, in this case, developing one is easier than you might think.

The development of the plan should not take more than 60 days, as the sequence of planning is really to (1) assess where you are, (2) set the goals, and (3) figure out how long it will take you to get there. I've included a sample plan at the end of the chapter to help you in your planning efforts.

4. EXPLAIN THE PLAN TO STAFF.

Once you have developed the plan, show it to the staff and, in a separate meeting, to the Board of Directors. Taking the time to do this now is essential. You will be initiating training, asking staff to take part in bottom-up budgeting, perhaps establishing a foundation, or revving up your fundraising activities. Soon, the staff will see more financial information, hear more about productivity and outcomes. They will know something is going on, so keep them informed from the start.

Staff need to hear about the plan early and, most importantly, about the outcomes and their relation to the mission. Spend time on the mission reserve, and how that will directly benefit the people that you serve.

But don't paint too rosy a picture. Talk about the length of time involved (years), about the sacrifices (real), and about the barriers (many). Let them ask questions, and make sure that you hand out either the entire plan or a summary that they can look through and think about.

5. START TRAINING STAFF AND BOARD.

I've only mentioned training about 40 times so far in this book, and here is when you start it: soon. Training staff and board in how to read financials, how to understand your income and expense streams, how to read a balance sheet, and how to help in the budgeting process is a long-term (in fact, never-ending) job. Find a trainer, get a curriculum established, reserve some dates, and get started now. Go "slow but steady", with a lot of review and a little new information each time. And, most importantly, managers need to be available to help staff with questions. Teaching and coaching are both very important here.

Now that you have gotten your organization started, what kind of things do you need to include in your actions to implement your plan? That's next!

B. PRACTICAL STEPS TO ACHIEVE THE CHARACTERISTICS OF EMPOWERMENT

In Chapter 2, I introduced you to the eight characteristics of a financially-empowered organization. In the pages that followed we reviewed a great deal of information: ideas on borrowing and budgeting, cash projections and cash flow reporting, pricing, and working with funders.

Now it's time to put it all together, within the context of the eight characteristics. The list below includes the practical things that you can do to implement the ideas in this book and achieve the characteristics and the accompanying benefits. You will see that some suggestions show up in more than one place. That's because some actions have more than one positive result.

What I don't want you to feel is that all the items within this book are theory, or just for someone else's organization. These are things that you *can* do with your organization. They are finite. They are measurable. They are achievable. You should start now. You will also see that the format of these pages allows you to assign each task and includes a deadline and space to mark completed.

1. THE ORGANIZATION HAS MORE REVENUE THAN EXPENSES IN AT LEAST 7 OUT OF 10 YEARS.

1-a. Develop and adopt a board policy that requires a positive net revenue in the budget for each fiscal year.

Deadline: _____
Assigned to: _____
Completed: _____

1-b. Review all funders' policies to identify those funders who claim any unexpended income or do not allow any net revenue for services.

Deadline: _____
Assigned to: _____
Completed: _____

1-c. Review all policies of funders who require the spending of unrestricted income prior to grant awards.

Deadline: _____
Assigned to: _____
Completed: _____

1-d. Develop a written strategy to retain what your organization earns through restricted accounts, separate corporations, or other mechanisms.

Deadline: _____
Assigned to: _____
Completed: _____

1-e. Write your state and Federal legislators discussing the need for not-for-profits to be able to retain their net income, and how this will benefit the state and Federal government and the taxpayers by having a stronger network of contractors with whom to "privatize".

Deadline: _____
Assigned to: _____
Completed: _____

1-f. Train all staff in marketing, emphasizing the fact that team effort and excellent customer service are essential in an increasingly competitive world.

Deadline: _____
Assigned to: _____
Completed: _____

1-g. Review your fundraising (development) plan. Do you need additional internal or external expertise in fundraising?

Deadline: _____
Assigned to: _____
Completed: _____

1-h. Develop a strategic plan that calls for profitable operations, assesses new markets, and includes the establishment of an endowment, mission reserve, and more staff training.

Deadline: _____
Assigned to: _____
Completed:

2. THE ORGANIZATION HAS A CASH OPERATING RESERVE OF AT LEAST 90 DAYS

2-a. Decide what number of days of cash reserve is best for your organization, as a base and at the end of each quarter.

Deadline: _____
Assigned to: _____
Completed: _____

2-b. Calculate the number of days of cash on hand at the end of the most recent reporting period. Do this by taking your most recent balance sheet, looking at the assets, and dividing the cash on hand by your annual budgeted expenditures. Divide the result by 365. The result is the number of days of cash you have for average operations.

Deadline: _____
Assigned to: _____
Completed: _____

2-c. Develop a board policy on cash operating reserve. Include the appropriate uses of the reserve, and who should authorize its depletion beyond a set minimum.

Deadline: _____
Assigned to: _____
Completed: _____

2-d. Check funders' regulations to ensure that your operating reserve falls within their guidelines. For example, many United Ways allow no more than 30 days reserve.

Deadline: _____
Assigned to: _____
Completed: _____

3. THE ORGANIZATION GETS AT LEAST 5% OF ITS TOTAL INCOME FROM EARNINGS ON ENDOWMENT.

3-a. Establish a restricted account to hold initial funds.

Deadline: _____
Assigned to: _____
Completed: _____

3-b. Consider establishing a separate corporation to act as a foundation.

Deadline: _____
Assigned to: _____
Completed: _____

3-c. Review your fundraising activities and revise your development plan. Do you have the skills on staff and board to achieve this plan?

Deadline: _____
Assigned to: _____
Completed: _____

3-d. Establish a funding mechanism for the foundation. (All donations, 70% of donations, 20% of net, 2% of all income?) Make this board policy.

Deadline: _____
Assigned to: _____
Completed: _____

3-e. Set a goal for the size of your endowment at the end of each of the next 5 years.

Deadline: _____
Assigned to: _____
Completed: _____

3-f. Develop policies on the use of the restricted fund/endowment. What uses will it be put to? I suggest that only the earnings of the endowment be used for operations, that principal be retained except in *very* unusual circumstances, and that policies for loaning funds from the foundation to your organization be established.

Deadline: _____
Assigned to: _____
Completed: _____

3-g. Review your funders' rules and regulations about restricted funds and second corporations. Make sure that any fund or corporation that you establish is within their rules and accomplishes your goals.

Deadline: _____
Assigned to: _____
Completed: _____

3-h. Find an outside development consultant to conduct an assessment of your community, your visibility, and staff/board skills. The assessment should tell you what you need to do to make your endowment plan a reality.

Deadline: _____
Assigned to: _____
Completed: _____

4. THE ORGANIZATION SHARES ITS FINANCIAL INFORMA-TION WIDELY, AND PRACTICES BOTTOM-UP BUDGETING.

4-a. Plan and establish an ongoing training program for staff and board members in how to read and understand your financials. Include segments on where your income comes from, what affects it, how expenses are budgeted, and how they may be budgeted in the future.

Deadline: _____
Assigned to: _____
Completed: _____

4-b. Talk with board, finance committee, staff, your CPA, and your banker about what financial displays would be of most use to them. Do they want numbers, text, charts, or a combination?

Deadline: _____
Assigned to: _____
Completed: _____

4-c. Talk with peer organizations and ask for samples of their internal reports as well as external ones.

Deadline: _____
Assigned to: _____
Completed: _____

4-d. Review the capabilities of your current software to prepare the reports you want. Can you link it with spreadsheet, database, or other commercial report-writing software to prepare the numbers you want in the format your staff asks for easily, quickly, and flexibly? (Unless you have very old accounting software, the answer should be yes.)

Deadline: _____
Assigned to: _____
Completed: _____

4-e. Have the senior management team develop a chart of reports; which report goes to which person or group, and how often.

Deadline: _____
Assigned to: _____
Completed: _____

4-f. Begin to distribute the information. Remember, share your numbers and everyone benefits!

Deadline: _____
Assigned to: _____
Completed: _____

4-g. Develop a schedule to initiate bottom-up budgeting. Start with the department or departments most likely to succeed. Work closely with them, making sure that all their staff are attending all the financial training.

Deadline: _____
Assigned to: _____
Completed: _____

5. THE ORGANIZATION SUPPORTS ITS MISSION DIRECTLY BY ESTABLISHING AND USING A RAPID-RESPONSE MISSION RESERVE.

5-a. Establish a restricted account, or a separate account in your foundation.

Deadline: _____
Assigned to: _____
Completed: _____

5-b. Decide on the funding mechanism for this account. (1% of income, 30% of net, 25% of donations?) This will discipline your savings. Make this board policy.

Deadline: _____
Assigned to: _____
Completed: _____

5-c. Establish the rules by which the funds will be distributed, by whom, for what, and on what schedule.

Deadline: _____
Assigned to: _____
Completed: _____

5-d. Establish goals for the fund's size for each of the next five years, and how much you plan to distribute.

Deadline: _____
Assigned to: _____
Completed: _____

5-e. Decide on what projects will be funded first, and how soon.

Deadline: _____
Assigned to: _____
Completed: _____

5-f. Discuss the mission reserve frequently with staff, board, and funders. Include its establishment in any newsletter or circular and, when projects are funded down the road, always publicize it.

Deadline: _____
Assigned to: _____
Completed: _____

6. THE ORGANIZATION IS APPROPRIATELY LEVERAGED.

6-a. Review the current status of all debt. Are interest rates at a point where a consolidation of your loans, or renegotiation would benefit you? (Repeat this exercise every 18 months or when interest rates change significantly.)

Deadline: _____
Assigned to: _____
Completed: _____

6-b. Talk with your CPA about appropriate debt-to-net-worth benchmarks for your organization. Review this with your finance committee and establish a policy to that affect.

Deadline: _____
Assigned to: _____
Completed: _____

6-c. If you own property with no debt, can you borrow against the property to finance growth, or to take advantage of market opportunities?

Deadline: _____
Assigned to: _____
Completed: _____

6-d. Review your relationship with your bank. Is it time to shop for others? Establish a long-term relationship with your individual banker. Visit him or her every 6 months to discuss your business, your plans, and your credit needs.

Deadline: _____
Assigned to: _____
Completed: _____

6-e. If you do not already have one, establish a line of credit with your bank.

Deadline: _____
Assigned to: _____
Completed: _____

6-f. Establish a five-year capital expenditure plan. Update this plan annually.

Deadline: _____
Assigned to: _____
Completed: _____

6-g. Talk with your banker about your capital expenditure plan, and discuss how to best fund the capital needs. Review this with the finance committee, and include it in your cash flow projections.

Deadline: _____
Assigned to: _____
Completed: _____

6-h. Set clear guidelines on who can authorize debt. Establish them as board policy (see Chapter 13).

Deadline: _____
Assigned to: _____
Completed: _____

7. THE ORGANIZATION HAS REVENUE FROM NON-TRADITIONAL NON-GOVERNMENTAL SOURCES: IT HAS BUSINESS INCOME.

7-a. Review with your board your willingness to take risk, and set some initial limits on risk-taking.

Deadline: _____
Assigned to: _____
Completed: _____

7-b. Review your current service array. Are there things that you do now that you could do for a different population, a different geographic market, or are there ways to use your skills and resources in a lucrative way?

Deadline: _____
Assigned to: _____
Completed: _____

7-c. Develop feasibility studies and business plans as appropriate (see Chapter 6).

Deadline: _____
Assigned to: _____
Completed: _____

7-d. Train all staff in marketing skills to ensure that you retain your current customers.

Deadline: _____
Assigned to: _____
Completed: _____

7-e. Begin reading one or more business publications (*INC., Wall Street Journal, Forbes,* etc.).

Deadline: _____
Assigned to: _____
Completed: _____

7-f. Join the Chamber of Commerce. Attend their meetings. Take training in business development.

Deadline: _____
Assigned to: _____
Completed: _____

7-g. Set goals for business development: how much of your income do you want from new sources of revenue in 5 years? In 10? Include these goals in your strategic plan.

Deadline: _____
Assigned to: _____
Completed: _____

8. THE ORGANIZATION IS FINANCIALLY FLEXIBLE ENOUGH TO ACCOMMODATE CHANGES IN SERVICE DELIVERY.

8-a. Review your assets and liabilities every 12 months. Are your current and quick ratios at the levels that provide flexibility?

Deadline: _____
Assigned to: _____
Completed: _____

8-b. Set levels of cash (and credit) reserves that allow you to invest in new services or the expansion of current ones.

Deadline: _____
Assigned to: _____
Completed: _____

8-c. Make sure that purchases of property do not unduly restrict your ability to alter service provision patterns as funders change their wants.

Deadline: _____
Assigned to: _____
Completed: _____

8-d. If you own property, evaluate the benefit of selling the building, leasing the property, and using the net cash to fund expansion and growth. (Repeat this every 18 to 24 months.)

Deadline: _____
Assigned to: _____
Completed: _____

8-e. If you own property with no debt, can you borrow against the property to finance growth or to take advantage of market opportunities?

Deadline: _____

Assigned to: _____

Completed:

As I said earlier, these are practical hands-on ideas for you to use. Make a list, noting the ones that are already in use, and then look at the ones you still need to work on. Split them into those that the CEO must do, those that other staff can do, and those that the board must address. Then, put the lists in priority order and get started!

C. ONE ORGANIZATION'S EMPOWERMENT PLAN

I'm sure that even with the list of ideas that you have just reviewed, putting the entire financial empowerment plan together may still seem both overwhelming and a bit inhibiting. In the hope of overcoming both of those understandable feelings, I've included an empowerment plan for a human services organization to let you get a view of the big picture.

There are a number of things that I want you to look for as you read through the plan. The first is that there are assumptions. All plans are based on assumptions. These are "best guesses" based on the information at hand when the plan is written. The second thing to note is the goals. This organization has clearly stated where it wants to go and how to get there. Third, note how long all of this takes. You are looking at a five-year plan. Even with a "fast track" development plan, the goals take a while to reach and some are not achieved in five years.

1. DESCRIPTION OF THE ORGANIZATION

The organization, which we'll call the NFP, provides a variety of human services to a multi-county area. The organization is broken down into four major service components: Residential, Community-Based, Employment Development, and Community Education. Residential and Community-Based services make up more than 80% of the total organizational income.

The staff and board have decided to develop a plan that not only empowers the organization but also reduces its dependency on government funds.

2. FINANCIAL STATUS

The total income of the organization in the last fiscal year was

$1,545,000. It ended the year with a net revenue of $22,855; cash of $96,570; and a mortgage on its building of $312,000 (at 9.5% with 6 years to go on a 20-year mortgage). The current assessed value of the building was $1,670,000.

The NFP receives state, Federal, local, user fee, and donated income. It no longer participates in the United Way. Overall, the organization gets 85% of its total income from government sources. Part of its 5-year plan is to reduce this income stream to under 70%.

In two of their programs, the NFP has a "use-it-or-lose-it" situation. In the others it can keep any earnings, which historically have been little or none.

The NFP does very little fundraising, and has little (if any) net worth beyond the value of its building. Its cash reserves were 23 days at the end of last fiscal year. In the past five years, the NFP has posted one year of a financial break-even, two of small losses, and two of net revenue (1% and 1.5% of income), respectively.

3. FIVE-YEAR FINANCIAL EMPOWERMENT PLAN

Assumptions
- Government funding will grow at 2.5% overall the next five years.
- Inflation of expenses (including salaries) will be at 2.0% per year.
- The prime rate will stay within one point of 7.5%.
- Interest on savings and reserves will be 5.5%.

Goals
1. Establishment of a 100-day cash reserve at the end of each fiscal year within three years.
2. Establishment of an endowment whose interest and dividend income will contribute 7% of the organization's total income within 8 years.
3. Establishment of a mission reserve that funds its first project within 18 months.
4. Use of bottom-up budgeting throughout the organization within 2 fiscal years.
5. Establishment and annual updating of a five-year capital expenditure budget.
6. Attain an overall 6% net revenue over expenditures for the five-year period.
7. Reduce the percent of total revenue from government sources from the current 85% to under 70% within five fiscal years.

Discussion

The decision to establish these goals was long and hard. It was decided that the cash reserves were a high priority as growth was to be funded through this reserve. The mission reserve establishment was also fast-tracked to improve staff and funder morale.

Year 1 Goals

Net Income: Break-even
Cash Reserve: 20 days
Fundraising: $50,000
Mission Reserve: $10,000
Business Income: $50,000
Endowment: $20,000

Note: In this year, the organization hoped to not only break even, but start to save. It would increase its fundraising slowly, make its first deposit into mission reserve, and start a small business. At the same time, it was laying the groundwork for other activities: developing feasibility studies for new businesses, examining its corporate structure, and marketing more to its key funders.

Year 2 Goals

Net Income: $75,000
Cash Reserve: 50 days
Fundraising: $100,000
Mission Reserve: $20,000
Business Income: $250,000
Endowment: $55,000

During this year the organization hoped to more than double its endowment, add to its mission reserve and really begin to see a return on its fundraising investment. It would need to spin off its endowment, and to also potentially spin off its business into a separate corporation.

Year 3 Goals

Net Income: $200,000
Cash Reserve: 100 days
Fundraising: $100,000
Mission Reserve: $30,000
Business Income: $400,000
Endowment: $150,000

In this year the marketing begins to really pay off with a net income of almost $200,000, a business income of $400,000 and a cash reserve hitting the 100-day goal. Remember, as the organization grows it will need to continually add more cash to its 100-day reserve to keep it at that number of days.

Year 4 Goals
    Net Income: $250,000
    Cash Reserve: 110 days
    Fundraising: $200,000
    Mission Reserve: $100,000
    Business Income: $600,000
    Endowment: $300,000

Year 5 Goals
    Net Income: $550,000
    Cash Reserve: 150 days
    Fundraising: $250,000
    Mission Reserve: $100,000
    Business Income: $500,000
    Endowment: $450,000

In the final two years of the planning cycle most of the goals set forth will be achieved, *if* these numbers can be reached. Let's examine how this might translate into a spreadsheet for further study by the organization.

Discussion
The organization set its goals and then developed the spreadsheet below, based on its assumptions. As it turned out, some of the goals will be achieved, while some look like they need to be reset.

As you can also see, the projections result in a lot of cash being accumulated in the last two years, a situation that is unlikely to occur, even with 95% of growth being eaten up in new expenses. Other new programs will undoubtedly be started.

But this plan provides for nearly all of the goals to be met. Note that endowment allocations are for all fundraising, plus endowment earnings, minus all development expense. Mission reserves are simply allocations voted by the board. Ninety percent of the year-end mission reserves are allocated for use the next year.

	LAST FY	YEAR 1	YEAR 2	YEAR 3	YEAR 4	YEAR 5
INCOME						
Federal	978,543	998,114	1,018,076	1,038,438	1,059,206	1,080,391
State	243,067	267,374	294,111	323,522	355,874	391,462
County	55,440	77,616	108,662	152,127	212,978	298,170
User	253,400	345,410	414,492	497,390	596,868	716,242
Development	15,500	45,000	95,000	140,000	200,000	250,000
Endowment Income	0	0	600	3,711	9,052	17,494
Other Interest	550	5,795	3,378	8,217	21,366	46,521
Business	0	45,983	410,000	435,000	524,000	575,000
TOTAL INCOME	**1,546,500**	**1,785,291**	**2,344,320**	**2,598,406**	**2,979,346**	**3,375,279**
% of Govt Funding	82.6%	75.2%	60.6%	58.3%	54.6%	52.4%
% from Endowment Income	0.0%	0.0%	0.0%	0.1%	0.3%	0.5%
EXPENSES						
Existing Expenses	1,546,500	1,608,360	1,672,694	1,739,602	1,809,186	1,881,554
Expenses from Growth	0	110,794	101,493	140,197	183,047	228,145
Development Expenses	0	35,000	43,750	54,688	68,359	85,449
Mission Reserve Allocations	0	0	9,000	18,900	28,890	47,889
Business Expenses	0	50,581	405,900	391,500	471,600	517,500
TOTAL EXPENSES	1,523,645	1,804,735	2,232,837	2,344,887	2,561,083	2,760,537
NET REVENUE	22,855	(19,444)	111,483	253,519	418,263	614,742
Return on Income	1.48%	-1.09%	4.76%	9.76%	14.04%	18.21%
CASH FLOW						
Cash from Net Revenue	22,855	(19,444)	111,483	253,519	418,263	614,742
Depreciation	36,667	36,667	36,667	36,667	36,667	36,667
Debt Received	0	0	0	0	0	0
Debt repaid	(45,459)	(47,500)	(48,500)	(52,140)	(56,789)	(61,390)
Net Cash Flow	14,062	(30,278)	99,649	238,046	398,141	590,019
ALLOCATIONS:						
Mission Reserve:	0	10,000	20,000	30,000	50,000	100,000
Endowment:	0	10,000	51,850	89,024	140,693	182,045
FUNDS STATUS						
Cash Reserve	96,578	46,300	115,950	323,995	722,136	1,312,155
days operating reserve	23.1	9.4	19.0	50.4	102.9	173.5
Mission Reserve	0	10,000	21,000	32,100	53,210	105,321
Endowment	0	10,000	61,850	150,874	291,567	473,611

RECAP

In this chapter, we've tried to put all the elements of financial empowerment together in a format that allows you to develop all the characteristics of the empowered organization.

First, we went over the things you need to do to get going, including the establishment of a committee of people from throughout the organization, the training of those people, and then planning how to achieve your empowerment. After the planning is done, you should go into the "explaining" stage, where you talk with staff, board, funders, and the community about your plans. And then, you start the long and continuing process of training staff in your financials and your empowerment plans. These steps will get you organized, but what specifically can you do?

We showed you that in the next section where we reviewed the eight characteristics of empowerment and made dozens of practical hands-on suggestions on how to achieve each.

Then, I showed you a sample empowerment plan, complete with assumptions, goals, and financial projections. This sample plan is one that I encourage you to use as a model as you move ahead.

Now you have the theory, the applications, and the rationales for moving toward financial empowerment. What's left? Only the most important thing—putting it all together. And that's the subject of our final chapter.

15. PUTTING IT ALL TOGETHER

OVERVIEW

You have nearly come to the end of this book, but before I leave you I want to help you tie all the pieces together and cover one overarching subject: keeping what you earn.

In this chapter I'll first give you some suggestions on how to not let all your hard work go to waste in the event that one of your funders tries to take back money that you have legitimately earned. There are a number of techniques that have worked for organizations like yours, and they are important to know about, so that if such a situation arises for you, you will be ready.

Then, we'll go over the characteristics of empowerment one last time, to reinforce their value and importance for you. Following that, I'll take you through some strategies for working with staff and board to assure that you don't spend every dime as soon as you have it.

Finally, I'll refer you to some of the information in the appendices, so that you know what you are missing if you don't keep turning pages after the end of this chapter.

By the end of this final chapter, you should have ideas on how to keep what you earn, have a fresh sense of where you need to go to become empowered, and you will know what additional resources this book holds for you.

A. KEEPING WHAT YOU EARN

You have read a lot in this book about how to spend less, account better, and become financially empowered as an organization. While that is important, many readers have undoubtedly been working their way through these pages with one concern hanging over them: that their funders will take back whatever they don't spend. Funders tend to do that. Too many, I'm sad to say.

Right off the top let me assure you that I do not have the magic bullet to convince your funders instantly and easily that letting you keep what you earn is smart policy. But what is contained in this section will help you convince *some* funders that taking away your earnings is both bad policy and a short-term financial gain that results in long-term financial loss to them.

The strategies in the following list are designed to let you legally keep what you earn from being taken back by funders, using their rules and regulations. They are suggestions and ideas that have worked for many other not-for-profits, and one or more may work for you if they fit with your funders' regulations. Check first. Don't just do any or all of these because I said so; make sure that the effort will have a commensurate benefit.

1. HAVE RESTRICTED ACCOUNTS.

One of the best and simplest ways to keep earnings is to put them in a restricted account: an account that is designated, restricted, for a specific purpose, such as a capital account or an endowment (see next section). For the funders who want you to spend your money first (the United Way being the most notorious example), restricted accounts are often considered off limits. In other cases a business account is set up solely for a new venture and the "profits" are left in the restricted account, only to be used for business-related expenses. If the business has a mission benefit, this can be very smart.

All restricted accounts must be set up by Board action and audited as such. They are restricted: you cannot just transfer money in and out at will. Here is yet another excellent example of why it is essential to know the regulations, rules, and policies of your funders. Will this simple and inexpensive action help you? Find out.

2. FORM AN ENDOWMENT.

One of the characteristics of a financially-empowered organization is that it gets at least 5% of its annual income from earnings on its endowment. When you do the arithmetic, that adds up to a lot of money sitting around earning interest and dividends. Won't your funders come after it saying that you should spend it? Won't your employees ask why they can't have that pile of cash? The answer is: "Probably". So what can you do to protect your nest egg? The simplest thing is to put the money in a restricted account within your current corporation. The restrictions on the account limit access to the funds in the account to a severe financial crises (perhaps as defined by 3/4 of the board) and to its earnings.

The other solution is to establish a second not-for-profit that is designed to hold funds for your main organization. If you want the second organization to be more flexible, and potentially hold property and lease it to the main not-for-profit, you probably will need to form the second corporation as a related but *uncontrolled* organization to meet the regulations of your funders in relation to contracting between your different corporations. In that case you would be giving your money away to an organization you don't technically control. How do you ensure that some future endowment board is not going to start giving your money to some other not-for-profit? You make your "donation" to the second corporation, the one housing your endowment, a restricted donation, requiring the funds and their earnings be used for your organization by name.

One other reason that a lot of our clients have endowment corporations (usually called foundations) is that they are a competitive advantage in fundraising. Larger and more sophisticated donors know all about funders wanting your net revenues, your profits. They want some assurance that their donations will not go that way, and a second corporation provides that assurance.

3. KNOW ALL YOUR COSTS.

How does this preserve your profits? How can knowing your costs help you keep what you earn? Knowing all your costs assures that you only declare the profits that you really have. Most readers have annual audits and so the profits of the entire corporation are going to be easily seen. But where a lot of organizations fail is in the area of assigning those costs properly to a particular grant or contract, and the resulting *appearance* of a net revenue causes the funder to ask for money back, money that is not legitimately the funders'. Usually these end of grant or contract accountings are not done by an auditor, but by internal staff. If a fixed amount for overhead is used, as we discussed in pricing, you know the costs are wrong. If depreciation, or the rent on a building that is owned and paid for, or the time of the Executive Director, are not accounted for and included, the resulting payback to the funder is an unnecessary loss.

● **FOR EXAMPLE:** An organization bids for and is awarded a $140,000 contract to run a midnight basketball league. The funder pays only for documentable costs associated with the league, or up to 15% overhead. Any unspent funds have to be returned. The organization uses a fixed percentage of 12% internally for its administrative contribution, but in this case the overhead for the new program is more in the area of 19%. In addition, in its bid, the organization does not include the costs of transportation to and from the courts for staff and some players who would be bussed, since the buses are funded by another program and are "not busy" at night.

At the end of the contract year the organization has to return $9,300 because of two things: not documenting the cost of the mileage for transportation (gas, maintenance, insurance, and depreciation are legitimate expenses) and not doing timesheets for administrative staff so that the full cost of overhead could be recovered.

Know the regulations of your funders and know all your costs. Use your improved internal financial reporting systems to keep better track of costs, budgets, and contract-by-contract expenses.

4. SEPARATE CORPORATIONS.

In some situations, such as the endowment/foundation discussed above, you will want to separate a second corporation. Another reason for this is to house a profitable business or to hold property and lease it at fair market value to the main not-for-profit and retain the profits for later mission use.

Understand that putting such activities in a separate entity will not "hide" the activity from a savvy funder. In your main not-for-profit's audit, your auditor will have a statement about "related organizations". Thus a funder who knows how to read an audit will figure out what's going on. But, the fact that the funds are separate may meet the restrictions of the funder's regulations, and if you can rationalize your actions in a mission-based fashion, this action may solve some of your profit retention problems. For more on corporate structures, see the discussion in Chapter 11.

5. MOVE TO CONTRACTS RATHER THAN GRANTS.

This action may not be totally in your control, but it is more likely that a contract will allow you to keep your net revenue than will a grant. Try to get your funders to move to true contracting for services. Work with your state and national trade associations toward this goal. If all of your funders let you keep your earnings, you could ignore items 1 to 4 here. What a great situation that would be!

6. LOBBY WITH LEGISLATORS AND CONGRESS ABOUT "USE IT OR LOSE IT".

This is longer term action than any other item, but we all have to make the case with legislators that you earn your money and, if you truly bid your work, you ought to be able to keep what you don't spend. Use my line if you like: "Why should not-for-profits be denied the benefits of capitalism? Let us be social entrepreneurs, take risks, and reap the potential rewards." Talk to funders, legislators, and the press about the lunacy of "use it or lose it" and how it encourages poor spending decisions and results in your organization remaining permanently financially disabled.

Talk to everyone who will listen. Start now. We have 30 years of prejudice and misperceptions to overcome.

B. THE CHARACTERISTICS OF FINANCIAL EMPOWERMENT (REPRISE)

You first were exposed to these characteristics in Chapter 2. After reading the rest of the book, they should make more sense, and seem more achievable. Let's revisit them again, remembering that I broke them down into Measurable, Management, and Mission categories.

▶ **MEASURABLE:**

1. The organization has more revenue than expenses in <u>at least</u> 7 out of 10 years.
   ■ If you don't meet this test, most of the rest of the goals will be unattainable.

2. The organization has a cash operating reserve of <u>at least</u> 90 days.
   ■ How many days are best for you? It depends on your situation, but you want to have enough not to be constantly worrying.

3. The organization gets <u>at least</u> 5% of its total income from earnings on its endowment.
   ■ An endowment is for large organizations and small ones, and is a resource that cannot be overlooked.

4. The organization has sources of revenue from non-traditional non-governmental sources: it has business income.
   ■ More and more not-for-profits are involved in business ventures: it is the definition of "unrestricted income."

► **MANAGEMENT:**

5. *The organization shares its financial information widely, and practices bottom-up budgeting.*

■ Share your numbers and share the responsibility of doing budgets. You, your staff, and your organization will all benefit.

6. *The organization is appropriately leveraged.*

■ Prudent debt in organizations that are making money can provide important services now rather than later. Just remember, debt, in organizations that consistently lose money, is a surefire path to bankruptcy.

► **MISSION:**

7. *The organization supports its mission directly by establishing and using a rapid-response mission reserve.*

■ This is what it is all about—if you are going to become financially empowered, you should have a funded and active mission reserve.

8. *The organization is financially flexible enough to accommodate changes in service delivery.*

■ Times change, service patterns evolve, and, in a competitive environment, you need to be able to respond quickly and efficiently. Can you?

So there they are. Measurable outcomes. Ones that can be implemented by management, and ones that will improve your mission capability. Taken together they will strengthen your organization, increase its control over its own destiny, and very likely provide leadership for other not-for-profits in your community.

Remember that financial empowerment is not the end, but the means. Doing more mission should always be your ultimate goal. If you keep your course set on that beacon, the work will be worth it.

C. LEARNING NOT TO SPEND IT NOW

You now have the tools to plan, save, and spend wisely. You can bring in new income, budget better, and know how much cash you will need. But can you save? That's a tough discipline for many not-for-profits.

A client of mine and I were talking recently about how hard it is to put money aside when there are mission needs staring you in the face. She put the dilemma very succinctly when she said, "Serving is a whole lot more fun than saving." And she's right. When people who need service confront you and ask for help, it is very difficult to rationalize a plan to defer providing service in order to put $5,000 aside each month.

If you come from an organization that is relatively new, or one that has never had much (if any) excess cash, you will face this issue head on, and not only from within yourself. You will have board, staff, and funders who will argue along the lines that, "We've never put much cash aside before and we've gotten along OK," or "It's immoral to hoard cash when there are so many needs out there" or "If we have extra cash, why don't we give it to the staff? We don't pay them enough now."

I understand, and I disagree with all of these positions, at least until the point in time where your organization achieves its empowerment. Let's look at each argument in turn. The first person states that you have "gotten along OK." If you haven't been empowered, you have been cash strapped, either on occasion or all the time, and organizations who are living hand-to-mouth spend most of their time looking for the next handful, and not focusing on the long-term issues. You may have *survived*, but mere survival does not meet my definition of "getting along OK," and doesn't even come close to maximizing your mission capabilities.

The second argument is also false and, in addition, doesn't hold up to rigorous review. Is it better to spend all your money for needed services today and then not be in business at all next year, or should you focus on what you do best and retain the empowerment to help more people later? This brings us again to the skill that I maintain is essential to successful not-for-profit managers and boards: saying "no" to a good idea, saying "sorry" to a real need. There are simply more needs in your community than you could ever meet, so you must pick and choose what your organization does, who you serve, and when you serve them. Trying to be all things for all people is a sure recipe for poor services and financial ruin, after which you will be of no value to anybody!

All of which is not to contend that it is easy to say "no", particularly since most readers were probably trained in one of the "helping" professions. It is never easy, but it is increasingly necessary, and on the road to empowerment it is a first step that all must take.

The third argument has merit if you have not given your staff a raise since the end of the last crusade, and it is essential to try to compensate staff fairly. But it is also important to have reserves on hand so that when cash is tight you can pay the salaries that they *do* have. Certainly staff should be rewarded for good work and paid fairly, but don't just assume that "leftover" cash should always go to them. Also think of how the staff feel about just getting the "leftovers." Doesn't that devalue them? I think it does.

☞ **HANDS ON:** As I noted at length in *Mission-Based Management*, don't automatically assume that staff want more money. They may want ownership in how the organization is run, or more time with their outside interests (like their families). Ask before you compensate. You may be surprised at what you are told, and it does not make sense to give someone something they don't want.

All of which brings me to the issue of how to learn not to spend it today. There are three parts to this: *marketing, policies,* and *pain control.* Let's go through each individually.

Marketing the need for savings is straightforward, and we've already talked about what to do: tie the mission to the savings in as many visible, identifiable ways as possible. Remember, marketing is finding out what people want and giving it to them. What do your staff and board want? If they are like most of my clients, they want a mission to justify their sacrifice. Give them one and tell them about it all the time. Use the mission reserve, which is the most visible embodiment of the point of financial empowerment. Tell people over and over what the point is. And then tell them again. Doing this will prevent and diffuse a lot of hostility toward your cash reserves.

Policies: Set policies in motion right away that state the need for net revenue, that give a target for cash reserves, a five-year goal for an endowment (and what the endowment can and cannot be used for), and how the mission reserve will be used. Stating these early, and involving staff and board in their development, will get most if not all of the issues on the table and allow more understanding of everyone's perspective, which is essential. All of the policies are then in writing and people know where things stand. Thus, they don't have unrealizable expectations about the money, and get frustrated later.

Pain avoidance is pretty commonplace in savings, and the psychology is valid: what you don't see you won't spend. This is why 401(k)s—payroll deductions for savings, retirement, or investment—are so popular. The money is deducted automatically, *before* you can get your hands on it. Try setting up such a discipline for your organization. With board backing (in the form of policy) put half of all donations in a restricted account that will be the start of your endowment. Also, try putting 2, 3, or even 5% of all funds that come through the organization into a money market account. Have your financial person do this first, before they pay all the bills, and learn to budget for it. If you have a windfall, put 50% of it away, and use the other 50% on current critical needs. Slowly but surely the funds will build up.

Your bank may even help by deducting $1,000 or $2,000 per month from your checking account to go directly into a money market fund. Talk to your banker about ways to make savings a less painful event for you, your staff and board.

RECAP

In this last chapter, I have taken one last opportunity to reinforce the eight characteristics of financially empowered not-for-profits. You need these characteristics for your organization to be capable of providing a quality mission to the people that you serve.

We next reviewed ways to keep what you earn, and not have to return it to funders. These included:

▶ Forming an Endowment
▶ Corporate Restructuring
▶ Restricted Accounts
▶ Working with Elected Officials
▶ Knowing all your costs.

All of these can contribute to a long-term strategy of increasing your retention of earnings.

Next we reviewed some strategies for working with staff and board to learn the discipline of saving despite the tugs to spend all of it now. Saving is a critical component of empowerment, and you need to start doing it now.

Your organization and the people you serve will benefit from the ideas and techniques that I have shared with you. I have one last request. Go to the next pages and read my final words to you.

THE APPENDICES OF THIS BOOK

I have included appendices that immediately follow this chapter. These include some important information that I want to preview for you here, so that you will be more likely to use the material.

ORGANIZATIONAL SELF-ASSESSMENT

I hope you used this tool when you were reading Chapter 2. If you didn't, now is a good time. Assess yourself now, in a year, and in 24 months. Is there improvement? I hope so!

BIBLIOGRAPHY AND COMMONLY-USED FINANCIAL RATIOS

I've included suggestions for further reading, organized by subjects such as marketing, finance, business development, and the like. I have also included a section on resources from the Internet. This section also lists common financial ratios, the formula to calculate them, and a description of what each ratio measures.

FINAL WORDS OF ENCOURAGEMENT

Your organization has a mission. It may be to educate, to heal, to entertain, or to discover. You and your staff may help the financially destitute or minister to those in need of spiritual healing. Whatever your mission is, you need to use all the resources at your command—your staff, board, community, buildings, equipment, volunteers, and your money—to do the most mission possible every year. But using all your resources and using *up* all your resources are two different things. If you work your staff or board (or yourself) to exhaustion this year, none of you will have the energy to face next year's challenges. Similarly, if you use up all your money this year, you won't have the resources to address the unforeseen demands that your mission, your community, and, most importantly, the people that you serve will place on you in the coming year.

If your organization is financially strapped, it may well be mission-driven, but it will not be fully mission-capable. The attainment and maintenance of financial empowerment brings a whole new set of mission capabilities as well as responsibilities for using your new empowerment.

I have told managers and board members for over 15 years that you are stewards of the public trust, keepers of the promise of your mission statement. While financial empowerment is tough to achieve, and tougher still to maintain, it is a critical element of any organization's capacity to survive, thrive, and be mission-based. Good stewards, ones who believe in their mission and who take their responsibilities seriously, will find ways to overcome the barriers, develop the disciplines of planning and saving, and change the culture of the organization so that empowerment and mission are inextricably linked. *More money, more mission.*

I have given you the tools. I have shown you the how and the why. I cannot, however, do the job; only you can do that. You must couple the knowledge gained by reading this book with the desire and commitment to help your organization achieve financial empowerment.

Don't wait. Don't say, "We'll talk about empowerment after we get over this crisis." There will be another crisis tomorrow. Start today. The world will not wait for you, and the people your organization serves need you to be there for them, not just after "this crisis" but long into the 21st century.

Good luck!

Financial Empowerment Self-Assessment

This self-assessment is designed to allow you to take a look at your current financial empowerment status. There is no score, no scale on which you can rate yourself. This is intentional, because I don't want you to feel that you are in the "low", "medium", or even "high" range for answers. You are where you are, and you need to know how much further you need to go. Start by answering each of the questions completely and honestly.

1. Has your organization had more revenue than expenses in at least 7 out of the last 10 years?

☐ Do you have a board policy that requires a positive net revenue in the budget for each fiscal year?

☐ Do you know which funders' policies require them to claim any unexpended income or do not allow any net revenue for services?

☐ Do you know which funders' policies require you to spend unrestricted income prior to grant awards?

☐ Do you have a written strategy to retain what your organization earns through restricted accounts, separate corporations, or other mechanisms?

☐ Have you trained all staff in marketing, emphasizing team effort and the need for excellent customer service in an increasingly competitive world?

☐ Do you have a fundraising (development) plan? Do you need additional internal or external expertise in fundraising?

☐ Do you have a strategic plan that calls for profitable operations, assesses new markets, and includes the establishment of an endowment, mission reserve, and more staff training?

2. *Does your organization have a cash operating reserve of at least 90 days?*

☐ Do you have a policy on what number of days of cash reserves is best for your organization?

☐ Do you regularly report the number of days of cash on hand at the end of each reporting period?

☐ Do you have a board policy on cash operating reserve, including the appropriate uses of the reserve, and who should authorize its depletion beyond a set minimum?

3. *Does your organization get at least 5% of its total income from earnings on its endowment?*

☐ Do you have a restricted account or a separate corporation to hold your endowment?

☐ Do you have a funding mechanism for the endowment; a way to put money aside?

☐ Do you have a goal for the end of each of the next 5 years for the size of your endowment?

☐ Do you have policies on the use of the restricted fund/endowment?

4. *Does your organization share its financial information widely, and practice bottom-up budgeting?*

☐ Do you have an ongoing training program for staff and board members in how to read and understand your financials?

☐ Do you regularly ask the board, finance committee, staff, your CPA, and your banker about what financial displays would be of most use to them? Do you then provide them with those numbers?

☐ Do you regularly meet with staff to discuss both financial and non-financial information?

5. *Does you organization support its mission directly by establishing and using a rapid-response mission reserve?*

☐ Do you have a Mission Reserve as a restricted account or a separate account in your Foundation?

☐ Do you have a policy on the funding mechanism for this account?

☐ Have you established the rules by which the funds will be distributed, by whom, for what, and on what schedule?

☐ Have you established goals for the fund's size for each of the next five years, as well as goals for how much of the fund you plan to distribute?

☐ Have you decided what projects will be funded next? Have you shared that information with staff and board?

6. *Is your organization appropriately leveraged?*

☐ Do you review the status of all debt every 18 months, and consider refinancing?

☐ Have you established appropriate debt-to-net-worth benchmarks for your organization?

☐ Are you happy with your bank? Do they provide you with a wide array of services?

☐ Do you have a pre-approved line of credit with your bank?

☐ Do you have an annually-updated five-year capital expenditure plan?

☐ Do you have written guidelines on who can authorize debt?

7. *Does your organization have revenue from non-traditional non-governmental sources: business income?*

☐ Do you have an outside business? Is it generating adequate net revenues?

☐ Do you have goals for business development? How much of your income do you want from new sources of revenue in 5 years, in 10?

8. *Is your organization financially flexible enough to accommodate changes in service delivery?*

☐ Do you review your assets and liabilities every 12 months? Do you have enough liquidity?

☐ Do you have established levels of cash (and credit) reserves that allow you to invest in new services or the expansion of current ones?

☐ Do you consider the impact on flexibility when purchasing property?

(Self-Assessment Worksheets are included in the *Financial Empowerment Discussion Leader's Guide*.)

Bibliography and Reading List

There are nearly endless resources for further study. If you are interested in finding out more about any of the following topics, I have included excellent and fairly recent resources.

ACCOUNTING AND FINANCE

Droms, William G. <u>Finance and Accounting for Non-Financial Managers</u>. Reading, Massachusetts: Addison-Wesley Publishing Co., 1979.

Dudick, Thomas S. <u>Profile for Profitability: Using Cost Control and Profitability Analysis</u>. New York: John Wiley & Sons, 1972.

Follett, Robert. <u>How to Keep Score in Business: Accounting and Financial Analysis for the Non-Accountant.</u> Dillon, Colorado: Alpine Guild, Inc., 1978.

BUSINESS PLANNING

Albert, Kenneth J. <u>How to Pick the Right Small Business Opportunity</u>. New York: McGraw-Hill Book Company, 1977.

Brinckerhoff, Peter C. "The 10 Biggest Mistakes People Make on Their Financial Projections." <u>Nonprofit World</u> March/April 1994: 17-19

<u>Business Planning Guide</u>. Dover, New Hampshire: Upstart Publishing Company, Inc., 1985.

Corporate Alternatives, inc. <u>A Business Planning Guide for Not-for-Profit Organizations</u>. Springfield: Corporate Alternatives, inc., 1992.

Dible, Donald M. Business Startup Basics. Fairfield, California: The Entrepreneur Press, 1978.

Greene, Gardiner G. How to Start and Manage Your Own Business. New York: McGraw-Hill Book Company, 1975.

Hogsett, Robert N. Profit Planning for Small Business. New York: Van Nostrand Reinhold Company, 1981.

James, Robert W. Decision Points In Developing New Products. Washington: Small Business Administration, 1976.

Mancuso, Joseph R. How to Start, Finance, and Manage Your Own Small Business. Englewood Cliffs, New Jersey: Prentice-Hall, Inc., 1984.

Meyers, Herbert S. Minding Your Own Business — A Contemporary Guide to Small Business Success. Homewood, Illinois: Dow Jones-Irwin, 1984.

Pryde, Paul. Small Business Incubator: A How-To-Guide. Washington: Community Information Exchange, 1984.

Schabacker, Joseph C. Small Business Information Sources. Milwaukee, Wisconsin: National Council for Small Business Management Development, 1976.

Starting Your Business — A New Planning Guide. Partners In Marketing. Indianapolis: Indiana Small Business Development Centers, 1991.

Texas Instruments Incorporated. Business Analyst Guidebook. Dallas: Texas Instruments, Inc., 1982.

The Small Business Directory. Washington: U. S. Small Business Administration, 1991.

The States and Small Business: Programs and Activities. Washington: U. S. Small Business Administration, 1991.

Whole, Joseph S. Evaluation: Promise and Performance. Washington: The Urban Institute, 1979.

Wiewel, William et al. Business Spin-Offs: Planning the Organizational Structure of Business Activities. Chicago: University of Illinois at Chicago Circle Center for Urban Economic Development, 1982.

ENTERPRISE FOR NOT-FOR-PROFITS

Cagnon, Charles. Business Ventures on Citizen Groups. Helena, Montana: Northern Rockies Action Group, 1982.

Crimmins, James C. and Mary Keil. <u>Enterprise in the Nonprofit Sector</u>. New York: Rockefeller Brothers Fund, 1983.

<u>Enterprise For Not-for-Profits</u>. (Videotape and workbook). Springfield: Corporate Alternatives, inc., 1986.

<u>Nonprofit Piggy Goes to Market</u>. Denver, Colorado: The Children's Museum of Denver.

<u>Profit Making By Non-Profits</u>. Los Angeles, California: The Grantsmanship Center, 1982.

JOURNALS

<u>American Journal of Small Business</u>. Baltimore, Maryland: University of Baltimore, 847 North Howard Street.

<u>Journal of Small Business Management</u>. Milwaukee, Wisconsin: National Council for Small Management Development, 600 West Kilbourn Avenue.

MANAGEMENT AND ORGANIZATION

Brinckerhoff, Peter C. <u>Mission-Based Management</u>. Dillon, CO: Alpine Guild, 1994.

Corporate Alternatives, inc. <u>Incentive Systems for Not-for-Profit Employees</u>. Springfield: Corporate Alternatives, inc., 1986.

Corporate Alternatives, inc. <u>Organizational Planning in the Not-for-Profit Sector</u>. Springfield: Corporate Alternatives, inc., 1988.

Dickson, Franklyn J. <u>Successful Management of the Small and Medium-Sized Business</u>. Englewood Cliffs, New Jersey: Prentice-Hall, Inc., 1976.

Petrof, John V. et al. <u>Small Business Management Concepts and Techniques for Improving Decisions</u>. New York: McGraw-Hill Book Company.

Rose, Linda A. <u>Personal Management for the Small Company: A Hands-On Manual</u>. New York: American Management Association, 1979.

MARKETING

Baunback, Clifford H. et al. <u>How to Organize and Operate a Small Business</u>. Englewood Cliffs, New Jersey: Prentice-Hall, Inc., 1973.

Brinckerhoff, Peter C. "Pricing Your Product or Service." Nonprofit World May/June 1992: 8-11.

Brinckerhoff, Peter C. "Return on Investment — How Much Do Nonprofits Need?" Nonprofit World September/October 1989: 10-11.

Brinckerhoff, Peter C. "Watershed or Waterloo? Two Key Steps in Business Development." Nonprofit World July/August 1990: 9-10.

Buskirk, Richard H. and P. J. Vaugh, Jr. Managing New Enterprises. St. Paul, Minnesota: West Publishing Company, 1976.

Corporate Alternatives, inc. A Step-by-Step Marketing Guide for Not-for-Profits. Springfield: Corporate Alternatives, inc., 1989.

Mondello, Michael. "Naming Your Price." Inc. July 1992: 80-83.

Steinhoff, Dan. Small Business Management Fundamentals. New York: McGraw-Hill Book Company, 1974.

Tate, Curtis E. et al. Successful Small Business Management Fundamentals. New York: McGraw-Hill Book Company, 1974.

RAISING CAPITAL

Alarid, William. Money Sources for Small Businesses: How You Can Find Private, State, Federal and Corporate Financing. PUMA, 1991.

Corporate Alternatives, inc. Capital Estimation and Budgeting for Not-for-Profit Organizations. Springfield: Corporate Alternatives, inc., 1987.

Gladstone, David J. The Venture Capital Handbook. Reston, Virginia: Reston Publishing, 1983.

Raising Venture Capital — An Entrepreneur's Guidebook. New York: Deloitte, Haskins, & Sells, 1114 Avenue of the Americas, 1982.

TAX IMPLICATIONS OF NOT-FOR-PROFIT BUSINESS OPERATION

Employers Tax Guide (IRS Publication Number 15). Washington: Internal Revenue Service, Department of Treasury.

1992 Federal Tax Handbook. New York: Thomson Professional Publishing, Inc., 1991.

Galloway, Joseph M. The Unrelated Businesss Income Tax. New York: John Wiley & Sons, 1982.

Tax Guide for Small Business (IRS Publication Number 335). Washington: Internal Revenue Service, Department of Treasury. United States. General Accounting Office. Statistical Data on Tax-Exempt

Organizations Earning Unrelated Business Income. Rostenkowski, Daniel. Document 85-43. Washington: GAO, 1985.

CURRENT PERIODICALS

Association Management. Washington, D.C.: American Society of Association Executives

Boardroom Reports. New York: Boardroom Reports, Inc.

Business Strategies. Chicago: Commerce Clearing House, Inc.

Contributions. Newton Centre, MA: Cambridge Fund Raising Associates

Harvard Business Review. Boston, Massachusetts.

Journal of Nonprofit and Voluntary Sector Marketing. London, England: Henry Stewart Publications

Marketing UPDATE. Vienna, VA: NISH

The Nonprofit Counsel. Washington: Charitable Productions Company, Inc.

Nonprofit World. Madison, Wisconsin: The Society for Nonprofit Organizations.

Sales & Marketing Management. New York: Bill Communications, Inc.

INTERNET RESOURCES

There are hundreds of resources for not-for-profits on the Internet, and they are growing every day. If you have access to the Net and a good interactive web browser, take a look at these pages:

Corporate Alternatives, inc.: *http://www.fgi.net/~corpalt/*

Meta Index of NonProfit Sites: *http://www.ai.mit.edu/people/ellens/non-meta.html*

Nonprofit Fund Raising and JobNet: *http://www.nando.net/philant/*

Nonprofit Information Center: *http://www.silcom.com/~paladin/ nonprofits.html*

soc.org.nonprofit: a newsgroup for not-for-profit managers, *news:soc.org.nonprofit*

Also, search through the Net with a search engine such as YaHoo or Excite and use the key words "nonprofit," "not-for-profit," and NFP.

Commonly-Used Financial Ratios

As I noted in the body of the book, there are a number of ways that ratios can help both staff and board members monitor your financial status over time. The ratios noted below are just the most common of hundreds of ratios used by managers throughout the world. Ratios help simplify large numbers and make the information useful rather than confusing.

It is important to understand that ratios are best used in two ways: first as a way of comparing data over time, and second as a way of comparing your organization against some benchmark. For example, the current ratio measures liquidity. It is calculated by the formula:

CURRENT ASSETS ÷ CURRENT LIABILITIES = CURRENT RATIO.

This calculation produces a number such as 1.27 or 2.14. Without a benchmark, and without a history against which to compare this number, it is meaningless. If, however, you know that the trend is for the ratio to go up (or down), and if it is over your benchmark, then it has value to you as a manager.

There are literally dozens of ratios used but I will only show you four of the most important. I urge you to sit down with your banker and your auditor, look at your current balance sheet and income and expense statements, and decide which ratios make sense to monitor, how often you should look at them, and what benchmarks you should use.

COMMON FINANCIAL RATIOS

RATIO NAME	CALCULATION	What the Ratio Measures
Current Ratio	*Current Asset ÷ Current Liabilities*	Your ability to pay your current obligations with cash and items that can easily be turned into cash. A higher number is better, to a point.
Quick Ratio (also called the Acid Test Ratio)	*(Cash + Receivables) ÷ Current Liabilities*	Again, a liquidity measure, but this one measures your ability to pay your obligations in a more conservative way. More is better here as well.
Debt to Fund Balance	*Total Debt ÷ Fund Balance*	This measure is one of how highly-leveraged your organization is. Lower is better, again, to a point.
Fixed Assets to Fund Balance	*Fixed Assets ÷ Fund Balance*	This is a measure of how much of your capital is invested in buildings and equipment, and thus not available to pay current obligations.

Index